MINDFUL EATING

THIS COOKBOOK IS DEDICATED TO THE GUESTS OF MIRAVAL WHO HAVE MADE THIS BODY OF WORK POSSIBLE. THANKS TO THEIR ENTHUSIASTIC EMBRACE OF MINDFUL EATING AND THE POSSIBILITY OF MAKING EACH MEAL A BEAUTIFUL MOMENT.

MINDFUL EATING

M*I*RAVAL

HAY HOUSE, INC.
CARLSBAD, CALIFORNIA • NEW YORK CITY
LONDON • SYDNEY • JOHANNESBURG
VANCOUVER • HONG KONG • NEW DELHI

Copyright ©2012 Miraval Resorts, LLC

Published and distributed in the United States by: Hay House, Inc.: www.hayhouse.com® • Published and distributed in Australia
by: Hay House Australia Pty. Ltd.: www.hayhouse.com.au • Published and distributed in the United Kingdom by: Hay House UK, Ltd.:
www.hayhouse.co.uk • Published and distributed in the Republic of South Africa by: Hay House SA (Pty), Ltd.: www.hayhouse.co.za •
Distributed in Canada by: Raincoast: www.raincoast.com • Published in India by: Hay House Publishers India: www.hayhouse.co.in

produced by: Stonesong
design by: Vertigo Design NYC
photography by: Dana Gallagher
photos on pages viii, ix, x, 13, 212, 214, 287: Courtesy of Robin Stancliff for Miraval Resort

LIBRARY OF CONGRESS CONTROL NUMBER: 2011938940

Hardcover ISBN: 978-1-4019-3823-9
Digital ISBN: 978-1-4019-3875-8
15 14 13 12   4 3 2 1
1st edition, May 2012

PRINTED IN CHINA

CONTENTS

A NOTE FROM THE OWNERS

When we first visited Miraval, we came for a relaxing reprieve from our busy lives. We soon realized that Miraval was more than a retreat; it offered us a glimpse of a healthy lifestyle that we chose to embrace more fully in our everyday lives.

One significant discovery for us was the incredible, award-winning cuisine that was healthful *and* flavorful. We wanted to take some of the lessons learned—and nutritious, delicious recipes—home with us. It quickly became apparent that we weren't alone, as Miraval's cooking classes have soared in popularity, and the resort has been inundated with requests for recipes and tips.

This cookbook is the culmination of Miraval's dedication to passing its wisdom and insights on to a wider audience. We are proud of *Mindful Eating* and hope it will help you and your loved ones lead healthier, happier lives.

— STEVE AND JEAN CASE

THE MIRAVAL EXPERIENCE

There are spas…and then there is Miraval.

Miraval means "View of the Valley," a poignant name for this exclusive desert retreat nestled in the foothills of the Santa Catalina Mountains just north of Tucson, Arizona. And although some trips take you to places you've never been before, even to destinations that few others have ever seen, Miraval Arizona Resort & Spa offers the most inspiring getaway one can imagine—a journey unique to everyone who visits.

Consistently rated among the world's top spas and resorts by TripAdvisor and SpaFinder and publications such as *Travel+Leisure, Spa* magazine, and *Condé Nast Traveler,* Miraval has earned its trendsetting reputation as America's destination for life betterment, where guests feel, are, and can be more.

Since its beginning in 1995, Miraval has upheld a powerfully simple vision: *Life is more meaningful and enjoyable when your physical, emotional, spiritual, social, and intellectual components are in balance.* To that end, Miraval offers more than 100 unique, life-enhancing programs and activities. Guests plan their stay filled with an abundance of choices, including innovative Chill-Out spa treatments, self-discovery activities led by insightful well-being specialists, dynamic growth and development Clue-In programs, outdoor challenges, yoga and Pilates, stress-management techniques, and nutritional counseling. All aim to help people better manage our fast-paced world and life's daily demands.

Clearly, a stay at Miraval is fulfilling—and the cuisine is certainly a highlight. Fresh, healthy, nutritious fare is rewarding and beautifully created, complementing the overall experience with a flavorful flourish.

Guests from around the world relish the resort not only for its luxury, but also for the deep comfort they can find nowhere else—speaking to Miraval's authentic wish for every guest: *You won't find you anywhere else.*

www.MiravalResorts.com

MINDFULNESS

MINDFULNESS is a term heard and seen often at Miraval, and it is the core concept that shapes Miraval's programs and environment.

Mindfulness is a conscious approach to being in the present moment—an elevated awareness of one's surroundings and also of oneself. It is a vivid perception of one's choices, strengths, and potential.

Mindfulness is empowering yourself and optimizing your energy in order to live a balanced, healthier, and better life, each and every day.

And just as Miraval guests are empowered by their experiences here and become able to make positive directional changes when they are at home, we hope that you, too, will be inspired by this book and what you learn from these pages.

DELICIOUS FOOD MEETS MINDFUL EATING

"Mindful Eating" is the art of reacquainting yourself with hunger and letting it cue you to eat, rather than feeding your emotions. Miraval employs the same values to the meals we serve as with everything else the resort offers—that is, choice remains the guiding principle of its approach.

Within these pages are more than 200 beautifully crafted recipes and simple techniques to use at home so that you can choose from an array of healthful, flavorful options. We also provide you with the tools to make smarter choices by giving you a better understanding of correct portion size and the importance of using fresh local ingredients over processed foods.

Thoughtfully prepared, this cookbook combines precisely calibrated flavors and nutrition to award-winning, gratifying effect. These gorgeous dishes represent an invitation to continue eating the Miraval way—by expanding and mixing and learning more about your needs while bringing diet into balance.

THE MIRAVAL CULINARY & NUTRITIONAL STAFF

CHAD LUETHJE

With culinary sensibilities uncannily attuned to the philosophy of mindful eating, Executive Chef Chad Luethje has led the culinary operations at Miraval since 2008. He has honed his skills over more than two decades, creating delicious, nourishing food in the kitchens of luxury resorts and spas across the country. Growing up in the rolling hills of Northern Virginia's farmland and also the Southern Arizona desert has given him a unique perspective. He loves using local and regional ingredients to create beautiful, fresh, healthy cuisine with unexpected flavor and texture combinations. Chef Chad has also appeared twice as a member of two hand-selected teams to present at the prestigious James Beard House in New York City. When he's not in the kitchen, Chef Chad enjoys spending time with his family as well as pursuing his outdoor passions of mountain biking, hiking, and photography.

JUSTIN CLINE MACY

Executive Sous Chef Justin Cline Macy is a true artist, and his connection to Miraval was a natural one. Growing up on the other side of the sprawling Catalina Mountains in the small town of San Manuel, Justin learned the ways of Miraval from his mother, who worked at the resort for many years. Building on Miraval's innovative philosophy, he is known for creating dishes inspired by pictures and memories. By giving his creations a deeper meaning, and allowing guests the opportunity to do the same, Justin passes along an appreciation for beautiful food that can be enjoyed more mindfully, no matter where you are.

KIM MACY

A graduate of a Le Cordon Bleu cooking school, Pastry Chef Kim Macy has mastered the elusive art of desserts—the mindful balance of decadence and indulgence. All the while creative in concept and presentation, Kim crafts a gorgeous array of desserts that vary in portion size, color, and texture. Incorporating vibrant fruits and trading in sugars for sweet nectars, Kim's techniques continue to evolve organically, constantly being inspired by her deep love of food and sharing that passion, one bite at a time.

MICHAEL TOMPKINS

As President and General Manager of Miraval, Michael Tompkins's role is one of stewardship and to ensure consistency and the full integration of mindfulness throughout the resort's guest programs. "All the components of Miraval work together to reinforce the entire experience. The integration of spa, wellness, and food, when combined with experiential learning, allows our guests to receive the benefits of the entire mindful lifestyle and take it home with them."

JUNELLE LUPIANI

Raised in a home where meals were always the centerpiece, Staff Nutritionist Junelle Lupiani understands the importance of developing a healthy relationship with food. Leading the daily seminars at Miraval on "Mindful Eating," Junelle emphasizes wholesomeness and helps guests arrive at healthful behaviors, gently and without judgment. More than anything else, though, she helps guests take the wealth of nutritional information available to them and apply it to their choices in their everyday lives.

COOKING HEALTHY: GETTING STARTED

It seems like every day brings new affirmation and proof of the benefits of a healthy, balanced lifestyle. Here at Miraval, we have dedicated ourselves to providing a place where you can nourish your mind, body, and soul.

The thought of making a major lifestyle change by learning to make healthy food can be pretty intimidating. With this book, we share the secrets of our kitchen and take the mystery out of creating delicious, beautiful, nutritious meals. You will learn how to re-create Miraval favorites in the comfort of your own kitchen, as well as how to create healthy classics of your own.

As you journey through the recipes, please take a few minutes to ensure that you have a safe, clutter-free work environment. Are your knives sharp? Do you have the right kitchen equipment and essential ingredients? In this section, we provide you with suggestions for a properly equipped kitchen and well-stocked pantry, as well as knife safety tips. In "The Basics" chapter, you will find many recipes that provide the base that supports the delicious, healthy recipes throughout the book: from our special cooking-oil blend, vegetable stock, grain and bean recipes, to Miraval mayonnaise, spice rubs, and reductions…it's all at your fingertips.

One of the most important things to keep in mind is that cooking (in most cases) isn't rocket science. The beauty of healthy cuisine is that if you already know how to cook, then you are well on your way to creating healthy, delicious meals. The techniques of sautéing, steaming, poaching, grilling, braising, marinating, and so on are universal. Part of the fun of creating healthy food is how much you learn when you bring the concept of mindfulness into the equation—from the ingredients you're adding to the way in which you prepare each dish. We will teach you the basics of texture and flavor, as well as the techniques of our award-winning kitchen.

Our goal in creating every Miraval dish is for your first thought to be how great it looks and tastes, with its health benefits popping into your mind as more of an afterthought. We want you to think, *Wow! This meal is delicious, and it's good for me, too!* instead of, *It's not bad…for health food.* When it comes to food, we believe that flavor and health are paramount, and there is no reason why they can't coexist in each and every dish. So, let's get started. Please join us in our kitchen….

CHEF CHAD'S HELPFUL COOKING HINTS

ADD CITRUS ZEST AND JUICE, or a dash of vinegar, to brighten food flavors and reduce the amount of salt a dish needs.

FILL YOUR SALTSHAKER WITH KOSHER SALT instead of iodized salt. Kosher salt's larger granules come out of the shaker more slowly, which will help cut down on your sodium intake.

USE KOSHER SALT IN YOUR COOKING. It tastes better than iodized salt and the larger granules dissolve more slowly, so you can see how much salt you've actually added to a dish. Kosher salt is also better for you: it contains approximately 30 percent less sodium to an equal measure of iodized salt.

USE A SPRAY BOTTLE TO ADD OIL to your recipes instead of free pouring from the bottle. In this way, you can better control the amount being used, as a spray bottle dispenses on average between ⅛ and ¼ teaspoon of oil at a time.

SUBSTITUTE a mixture of plain nonfat yogurt and reduced-fat mayonnaise whenever a recipe calls for regular mayonnaise. (Use a 3:1 ration of yogurt to mayonnaise.) The mixture is flavorful, the consistency is very similar, and it contains far less fat and calories.

THE FLAVOR OF VEGETABLES AND SOME FRUITS dramatically deepen with roasting or grilling. If you don't want to use a grill, you can oven roast them or char them over an open stove-top flame. At Miraval we roast pineapple and mango, as well as beets, bell peppers, chili peppers, onions, tomatoes, eggplant, garlic, onions, and shallots to include in our sauces, soups, and salads.

ADD A COMBINATION OF FRESH AND DRIED HERBS to your preparations for stronger aromas and more pronounced flavors. Dried herbs have more concentrated flavors than fresh ones, so add them to a recipe first. Add fresh herbs at the end of the recipe, as their flavors are more delicate and their aromas fade quickly.

BE AWARE OF HEALTHIER INGREDIENT SUBSTITUTIONS and use them whenever you can to lessen the fat and calorie measures of a recipe. Substitute low-sodium vegetable stock for chicken stock, for example. Use pureed potatoes mixed with soy, skim, rice, coconut, or almond milk in place of heavy cream.

REPLACE BUTTER with Miraval Oil Blend (see page 19), extra-virgin olive oil, or canola oil in baking and sautéing. And olive oil makes a great replacement for butter in mashed potatoes.

AGAVE SYRUP is a favorite ingredient in the Miraval kitchen. This natural sweetener has 1.5 times more sweetening power per calorie than sugar and a very low glycemic index. Agave syrup makes a great substitute for refined sugar or corn syrup.

SUBSTITUTE applesauce, pureed fruit, tofu, or flaxseed meal to replace egg in most recipes.

EGG-WHITE OMELETS tend to stick to the pan during cooking. To eliminate the need for using extra oil or butter in their cooking, precook the egg whites in a bowl in the microwave until they rise and start to become fluffy (about 45 seconds). The whites then can be combined with steamed vegetables and cooked in a small sauté pan for a perfect omelet.

USE A QUARTER- OR HALF-CUP measuring cup to control portion size when plating food.

SERVE FOOD ON SMALLER PLATES so that portion sizes look bigger. Eat only what's on the plate; don't go back for seconds!

TO COOK A MIXTURE OF VEGETABLES, add the firmer varieties to the pan or steamer first in order to ensure even cooking and retain the greatest nutritive values. For instance, carrots take longer to cook than squash or asparagus and should be added to the pan first. Toss the cooked vegetables in a bowl with one or two squirts of olive oil or Miraval Oil Blend, a dash of kosher salt, and finely chopped fresh herbs for a satisfying and easy side dish or pasta topping.

APPEARANCE goes a long way toward making food more appealing. Dress up your plates by piping mashed potatoes from a pastry bag with a star tip into the center of the plate; garnish with fresh herbs; and drizzle with reduced vinegars, herb oils, small diced vegetables, and so forth.

PACK COOKED GRAINS into a small cup and then invert the cup onto the plate. Gently lift away the cup and arrange vegetables around the pile. Add fresh herb sprigs as a garnish. Be sure to keep height in mind while arranging everything on the plate.

WHEN SHOPPING FOR PRODUCE, look for vibrant colors and fruits and vegetables that are firm to the touch and not wrinkled. Make sure that the stem ends of vine-ripened fruits and vegetables (melons, zucchini, and so forth) are green and not moldy.

FRESH HERBS should look full, bright, and vibrant—never wilted. If you see something in the produce section that you're not familiar with, ask for a sample or a suggested use to get your imagination going.

ESSENTIAL KITCHEN EQUIPMENT

One of life's mindful lessons is learning that using the right tools can turn any task into a successful experience. In this same light, the right kitchen tools and equipment can make cooking easier and more enjoyable, surely inspiring you to spend more creative time in the kitchen. Here, our team shares their list of essential equipment found in both the Miraval kitchen and in their kitchens at home.

SHARP KNIVES

The most important knives to have are a quality 8- or 10-inch chef's knife; an Asian-style (thin) cleaver or Nakiri; a long serrated knife (preferably with a slight heel, like a chef's knife) for slicing bread, cutting citrus, and peeling melons; a 3-inch paring knife; and a carving knife.

And while you can purchase a 9- or 12-knife block (and spend a great deal of money doing so), in our experience, you'll only need this many knives when the first three are already dirty!

POTS AND PANS

Every kitchen should be stocked with quality pots and pans. We recommend at least one each in small, medium, and large sizes of sauté pan and saucepan. In addition, it's useful to own a large heavy pot for cooking pasta, a large heavy stockpot for stocks and soups, a cast-iron skillet, a wok (which can do double duty as both a sauté pan and as a steamer base when paired with a bamboo steamer), two professional-grade half-sheet pans, and one large roasting pan.

All pots should have riveted metal handles and thick bottoms so they can go straight from the burner into the oven. A thick bottom is crucial for consistent temperature and even cooking.

Stainless-steel-lined pans with an aluminum core are the best all-around performers; they heat quickly and evenly and hold heat well.

And a note on nonstick pans: at Miraval, we generally don't use nonstick pans because it's nearly impossible to achieve a good sear. It's also very easy to compromise the coating, whether with a metal utensil or a scrub pad. (And once this happens, you could expose yourself to the toxic chemicals used to make the coating.)

However, most of us have a hard time making eggs without a nonstick pan, so if you have to have one, make sure to hand wash it (putting it in the dishwasher will shorten its life span) with warm soapy water, keep a close eye on the coating to watch for scratches, and don't overheat the pan.

MIXING BOWLS

A set of mixing bowls is invaluable. Options include stainless steel, ceramic, and glass. Glass bowls are practical because they are also microwave safe, but stainless steel is much more durable and won't chip. Make sure the sizes nest for easy storage.

VEGETABLE PEELER

There's no need to spend a lot of money on this item. One of the simple metal peelers from a grocery store will work just as well as an expensive one from a kitchen-equipment store.

MICROPLANE ZESTER

This tool is great for adding a burst of flavor to your food by easily zesting citrus, fresh coconut, gingerroot, hard cheeses, or fresh nutmeg or cinnamon into a dish. These zesters come in different sizes and shapes, each with a slightly different function. The one that looks like a long, thin hardware rasp with a handle is a good all-purpose version.

SILICONE BAKING MAT

These nonstick mats are an alternative to greasing or using parchment paper on a baking sheet. They don't retain flavors and are heat resistant to about 650° F. Each mat can be used thousands of times. Wash them well in warm soapy water after each use, allow them to dry, and store flat or rolled. Do not use knives or other sharp kitchen tools on them, or they will tear.

HANDHELD CITRUS JUICER OR CITRUS REAMER

This simple, inexpensive tool will help you squeeze every last drop of juice out of citrus fruit just as effectively as an electric juicer. And it's much easier to clean!

PLASTIC TRIGGER SPRAY BOTTLE

These can be found nearly everywhere—from your supermarket to home and garden stores. At Miraval, we consider spray bottles to be the single most important kitchen tool to help reduce calories. We fill our bottles with Miraval Oil Blend and use them to lightly coat pans for sautéing foods, roasting vegetables, and more.

Although the amount of oil released varies from bottle to bottle, each pull of the trigger should spray between ⅛ and ¼ teaspoon of oil, allowing you to easily reduce the amount of fat (oil) in each meal.

This item is often superior to aerosol pump spray bottles (misters) sold in most kitchen-equipment stores because it releases the oil in droplets instead of in a mist that cooks away quickly, and it won't clog. There's also no spring to break, unlike in aerosol pump bottles. While aerosol vegetable spray is listed in the pantry shopping list and called for in many baking recipes, we prefer to use the trigger spray bottle for sautéing and most other cooking needs.

HEAT-RESISTANT SILICONE SPATULAS

Silicone spatulas are great for mixing, cleaning out a mixing bowl, stirring risotto, or scrambling eggs. The best spatulas can handle heat up to 800° F and won't melt during cooking like cheaper models often do. They also won't crack, chip, or scratch nonstick pans.

METAL KITCHEN TONGS

We suggest having two lengths of tongs on hand—small and medium—both with scalloped edges. These are indispensable for turning hot foods on a grill or in a pan.

HEAVY-DUTY METAL KITCHEN SPOONS

Have at least one solid and one perforated metal spoon on hand for stirring stocks, soups, pastas, and such.

STAND MIXER

Advanced bakers and cooks may want to consider a stand mixer. KitchenAid is one of the best-known brands. Their mixers are used in many commercial kitchens, including ours.

MANDOLINE OR V-SLICER

It is nearly impossible to consistently slice very thin vegetables, fruits, and potatoes using a kitchen knife. A good mandoline allows almost any fruit or vegetable to be cut into uniform pieces, such as for French fries or chips. And using a slicer takes only a fraction of the time that it would take to do the work with a knife. These tools are extremely sharp and should be used with a hand guard or mesh safety glove.

BLENDER

A blender with a large container (1-quart or 2-quart) and a strong motor will effortlessly make smoothies, salad dressings, soups, and marinades. Vitamix is our preferred blender, because of its power, ease of use, and durability.

FOOD PROCESSOR

Food processors are essential to many tasks, from chopping vegetables and aromatics such as garlic, to making pesto sauce and pureeing tomatoes. A good food processor will have a strong but quiet motor, a pulse button in addition to an on/off switch, and a bowl large enough to handle whatever you are making—although the size for a nonprofessional processor is generally a one-quart capacity.

COFFEE GRINDER

The small one-cup-capacity model in the Miraval kitchen is indispensable! We use it to make custom spice blends and rubs for poultry, seafood, game, and vegetables. We also use ours to grind whole spices, such as black peppercorns, star anise, cumin and coriander seeds, and dried chilies.

DISPOSABLE VINYL OR NITRILE GLOVES

Available at any medical supply, grocery store, or pharmacy, these gloves are a great way to prevent strong odors (such as fish and onions) from sticking to your skin. These are also necessary to protect your skin when working with hot peppers.

PASTRY BAG AND STAR TIP

Also referred to as a cake-decorating bag, a pastry bag fitted with a star tip proves invaluable in food presentation. (You'll notice the butter on the Miraval breakfast buffet has been piped with a star tip.) Pipe anything from cake decorations to mashed potatoes for a special look.

In a pinch, you can use a one-gallon heavy-duty plastic bag instead of a pastry bag. Spoon the ingredients into the bag and cut one corner with scissors to pipe out the ingredients.

PLASTIC SQUEEZE BOTTLE AND TIP

Squeeze bottles are great for "painting" plates with pureed sauces and reductions for a more attractive presentation. You can find these in most supermarkets, and the bright red and yellow ones made for condiments work just as well as the clear ones. Clean them well after each use.

MINDFUL PANTRY SHOPPING LIST AND SOURCE GUIDE

BEANS AND LEGUMES

Adzuki beans

Anasazi beans

Black beans

Fava beans

Garbanzo beans

Great northern beans

Kidney beans

Lentils (brown, green, or red)

Navy beans

Pinto beans

Split green peas

RAW, UNSALTED NUTS AND SEEDS

Almonds

Cashews

Chia seeds

Flax seeds

Pecans

Pine nuts

Pistachios (shelled)

Pumpkin seeds

Sesame seeds (black and white)

Sunflower seeds

Walnuts

SWEETENERS, FLOURS, AND BAKING PRODUCTS

Agave syrup

All-purpose flour

Almond flour

Baker's (melting) white chocolate

Baking powder

Baking soda

Brown rice flour

Brown sugar

Cake flour

Confectioners' (powdered) sugar

Corn starch

Dark melting chocolate (64 percent or higher cacao content)

Garbanzo (chickpea) flour

Honey

Lentil flour

Maple syrup

Masa (corn flour)

Molasses

Phyllo dough

Potato starch

Powdered gelatin

Quinoa flour

Rye flour

Semisweet chocolate chips

Tapioca flour

Unrefined cane sugar

Unsweetened dark baker's cocoa powder (not Dutch processed)

Whole-wheat flour

Xanthan gum

DAIRY AND DAIRY SUBSTITUTES

Almond milk

Buttermilk (fat-free)

Coconut milk

Evaporated skim milk

Kefir

Rice milk

Skim and/or 2 percent milk

Soy milk

Yogurt (plain)

HERBS, SPICES, AND SEASONINGS

Ancho chili powder

Basil (assorted varieties)

Chili powder

Chipotle chilies (canned)

Chipotle powder

Chives

Cilantro

Coriander

Cream of tartar

Cumin

Dill

Garlic

Honey

Lavender

Oregano

Paprika

Rosemary

Sage

Sambal Oelek chili sauce

Sriracha hot chili sauce

Tarragon

Turmeric

Vanilla beans

Vanilla extract

FRUITS AND VEGETABLES

Always look for fresh, seasonal fruits and vegetables. When buying juices, choose fresh, low-sodium, unsweetened varieties.

Apples

Applesauce

Apricots

Bananas

Cherries

Cranberries

Currants

Dried fruits (not preserved with sulfur)

Figs

Mangoes

Mushrooms, fresh and dried (morel, porcini, portobello, shiitake, etc.)

Onions

Papaya

Pears

Pineapple

Prunes (canned)

Pumpkin (canned)

Raisins

Sugar-free juice concentrates

Sun-dried tomatoes, dehydrated

Tomatoes (canned, stewed, and diced)

Unsweetened frozen fruits

GRAINS AND RICE

- Arborio or carnaroli rice
- Bamboo rice
- Barley
- Bhutanese red rice
- Black forbidden rice
- Brown basmati rice
- Brown kalijira rice
- Brown rice, long- or short-grain
- Bulgur
- Kamut
- Jasmine rice
- Millet
- Oats, rolled and steel-cut
- Polenta, quick-cooking and traditional
- Quinoa
- Semolina
- Spelt or farro
- Teff
- Wehani rice
- Wheat berries
- Wheat bran
- White-corn hominy
- Wild rice
- Yellow and blue cornmeal

CHEESE

- Assorted aged cheeses
- Chèvre (goat cheese)
- Cotija
- Cottage cheese
- Feta
- Fresh mozzarella
- Mascarpone
- Neufchâtel
- Parmigiano-Reggiano
- Part-skim ricotta

MEATS, POULTRY, AND SEAFOOD

- Berkshire or Kurobuta pork tenderloin
- Duck breasts
- Free-range skinless chicken breasts and thighs
- Grass-fed ground chuck
- Omega-3-enhanced cage-free eggs
- Pasture-raised, lean cuts of grass-fed beef, buffalo, elk, lamb, and venison (NY strip, flank steaks, sirloin, tenderloin, etc.)
- Sustainably harvested wild or farmed seafood (arctic char, sockeye salmon, black cod, trout, sardines, anchovies, shrimp, scallops, halibut, mackerel, etc.)
- Turkey

OILS AND FATS

- Cold-pressed canola oil
- Cold-pressed extra-virgin olive oil
- Grape-seed oil
- Nonstick aerosol vegetable spray
- Sesame oil
- Unsalted butter
- Walnut oil
- White truffle oil

THE MINDFUL PANTRY SOURCE GUIDE

There are many ingredients in the Miraval pantry that probably won't be found at your local grocery store. Here are just a few vendors that can help you find these items:

MOUNT HOPE FOODS www.mounthopefoods.com
Dried herbs, spices, gluten-free breads, organic whole-grain cereals, dried fruits, exotic grains, sweeteners (such as agave syrup and stevia), flours, nuts and seeds, organic chocolate, Bragg Liquid Aminos, tamari, soy and whey protein powders, and more.

VALLEY GAME & GOURMET www.valleygame.com
Venison, North American elk, buffalo, duck, Berkshire pork, and more.

THE CHEF'S GARDEN www.chefs-garden.com
A great resource for specialty produce.

HONOLULU FISH COMPANY www.honolulufish.com
A great resource for seafood.

KANALOA SEAFOOD MARKET www.kanaloaseafood.com
A great resource for seafood.

MAYA TEA 877-629-2832 www.mayatea.com
Loose-leaf teas including white teas, herbal teas, oolong teas, black teas, and green teas.

NIMAN RANCH www.nimanranch.com
Beef, pork, lamb, and poultry.

DOUBLE CHECK RANCH 520-357-6515 www.doublecheckranch.com
Grass-fed beef.

BOB'S RED MILL 800-349-2173 www.bobsredmill.com
Offers a wide variety of grains, beans, seeds, cereals, and gluten-free mixes.

ARBUCKLE COFFEE ROASTERS 800-533-8278 www.arbucklecoffee.com
Coffee and teas.

VITAL CHOICE 800-608-4825 vitalchoice.com
Wild salmon, sablefish, shrimp, oils, vinegars, etc.

KNIFE SAFETY TIPS

KEEP YOUR KNIVES SHARP

You're more likely to cut yourself with a dull knife than a sharp one. Using a dull knife requires more downward pressure to cut and could result in the blade slipping and cutting you. Use one of the many good sharpening tools on the market or a professional knife-sharpening service.

USE A KNIFE FOR ITS INTENDED PURPOSE

Never try to open a can or bottle with a knife or use a knife as a screwdriver. Don't use your knives to cut string, boxes, bones, metal, or paper, as these materials will dull your knife, put nicks in the blade, or even break it.

ALWAYS USE A CUTTING BOARD

Never cut something while holding it in your hand! Use a cutting board and keep it in place on your work surface by placing a damp towel underneath it. This will keep the board from shifting or sliding while you use it. Make sure the board is free of clutter and big enough for the task at hand.

CHOOSE THE CORRECT KNIFE

Use a paring knife for peeling fruits and vegetables, a chef's knife or Asian-style cleaver for chopping and mincing, a serrated knife for slicing, and so forth.

HAND WASH KNIVES IN HOT SOAPY WATER

Never put knives in the dishwasher, as high heat and caustic detergents can corrode blades and swell handles over time. And don't put a knife into a sink filled with sudsy water—you could inadvertently cut yourself when you reach down to retrieve it.

ALWAYS HOLD A KNIFE BY ITS HANDLE

When cleaning, turn the blade away from your hand, and never run a cloth down its edge.

STORE KNIVES PROPERLY

A magnetic knife rack or wooden knife block is best. If you are storing knives in a drawer, keep them in a separate compartment. Line the area with a rubber mat or towel to prevent the knives from sliding into each other when you open and close the drawer.

PAY ATTENTION

Keep your eyes on your cutting board, your knife, your non-cutting hand, and whatever you're cutting or chopping. Don't allow yourself to be distracted by conversations, children, pets, or the television.

Always use caution. When chopping peppers, for instance, make sure that you've removed all the seeds from the cutting board, the pepper to be cut, your hands, and your knife. The slippery seeds often contribute to kitchen accidents involving knives.

And finally, if you drop a knife, ignore the instinct to catch it! Step back and wait until it comes to a complete rest before picking it up.

TIPS FOR WORKING WITH PHYLLO DOUGH

Phyllo dough is a great way to bring a light, crispy texture to your culinary creations. Use it to make "baskets" for savory or sweet recipes, as a replacement for puff pastry when making a strudel, or to make spanakopita.

Phyllo can also be used to make sweet napoleons. To do this, place two sheets of phyllo on top of one another (spray between the layers). Spray the top layer and fold the sheets in half lengthwise. Cut into 8 squares and then cut each square into two triangles. Spray and sprinkle with cinnamon and sugar.

Thaw frozen phyllo dough in its original packaging in the refrigerator overnight. Wrap unused dough in plastic wrap, and store it in the refrigerator for up to one week.

To prevent the delicate sheets from drying out while you work, cover the extra dough with a slightly dampened, lightweight kitchen towel.

STEP 1. Carefully remove one sheet at a time. Layer four sheets, one on top of the other, for a sturdy pastry. Coat all but the top layer with aerosol cooking spray to prevent tearing and encourage browning during the baking process. For extra flavor and enhanced appearance, sprinkle each layer of phyllo with fresh or dried chopped herbs and minced garlic, or with cinnamon or graham cracker crumbs.

STEP 2. Use a pizza cutter or knife to cut dough in half vertically, creating two long sections. Use an aerosol cooking spray to help repair any tearing that occurs while working. (Dampen tears, then gently press edges together.)

STEP 3. To make triangles: Working with one section at a time, drop a small amount of filling onto the bottom. Leave a one-inch border around the filling to allow for folding.

STEP 4. Gently fold pastry into a triangle: start at the filling end and fold forward in a flag pattern. Avoid wrapping too tightly, which can cause the filling to spill out during baking.

STEP 5. To make shells: cut the two long sections (from Step 2) into thirds to create six squares. Line a muffin tin and bake for 20 minutes, then fill and serve.

THE CHEF'S DEMONSTRATION KITCHEN

Our culinary team is passionate about creating mindful Miraval experiences for guests, and are devoted to the interactive and informative cooking demonstrations they lead every week in the cozy, fully equipped demonstration kitchen adjacent to the Cactus Flower Restaurant.

Some classes take participants through an entire meal from start to finish, with one of our chefs assembling a meal from scratch. Culinary details are explained, shortcuts are taught, and wines are chosen from the resort's extensive cellar.

Not only appetizing, these meals are a means of discovering innovative ways to approach healthful cooking and develop new culinary skills through our "insider tips."

THE BASICS

BALSAMIC REDUCTION

It's important to use very good quality vinegar for your reduction—that means no caramel coloring or added ingredients. The vinegar reduction will thicken as it cools, so be careful not to over-reduce it. If you're unsure about whether the reduction is finished, remove the pan from the heat and dip a spoon into it. The reduction is ready when it's thick enough to coat the back of the spoon.

MAKES ABOUT ¾ CUP; SERVING SIZE: 1 TBSP.

2 c. balsamic vinegar

PLACE the vinegar in a medium saucepan and bring to a low boil over medium heat. Reduce the heat and simmer gently until it's reduced by slightly more than half, 25 to 30 minutes.

CALORIES: 14; TOTAL FAT: 0 G; CARBOHYDRATE: 3 G; DIETARY FIBER: 0 G; PROTEIN: 0 G

BASIC BLACK BEANS

MAKES 1 QUART; SERVING SIZE: ½ CUP

2 c. black beans, picked over for broken beans and pebbles, and rinsed well

8 c. Vegetable Stock (page 24), canned vegetable broth, or water

PLACE the beans in a large saucepan, add the vegetable stock, cover, and bring to a simmer. Cook, stirring occasionally, until the beans are tender but still retain their shape, about 2 hours.

REMOVE from heat and serve, or use as directed.

CALORIES: 114; TOTAL FAT: 1 G; CARBOHYDRATE: 20 G; DIETARY FIBER: 7 G; PROTEIN: 7 G

BASIC GRILLED CHICKEN

MAKES 4 SERVINGS

4 four-ounce boneless skinless chicken breasts
⅛ tsp kosher salt
Pinch fresh ground black pepper
¼ tsp. Miraval Oil Blend

COMBINE all ingredients in small mixing bowl, and toss to evenly coat chicken breasts.

PREHEAT grill on high heat for 15 minutes.

PREHEAT oven to 400° F.

PLACE chicken on grill and cook for 2 minutes on each side. Place on baking sheet, and bake in the oven until each breast is cooked through and reaches an internal temperature of 165° F, about 10 minutes.

CALORIES: 130; TOTAL FAT: 3 G; SODIUM: 130 MG;
CARBOHYDRATE: 0 G; DIETARY FIBER: 0 G; PROTEIN: 24 G

BASIC JASMINE RICE

MAKES 2 CUPS; SERVING SIZE: ½ CUP

1½ c. Vegetable Stock (page 24), canned
vegetable broth, or water
¾ c. jasmine rice

COMBINE rice and vegetable stock in a medium saucepan and bring to a boil over high heat. Reduce the heat to low, cover, and simmer until the rice is tender and the liquid is absorbed, 10 to 12 minutes.

REMOVE the pan from the heat and let stand for at least 5 minutes. Fluff with a fork and serve.

CALORIES: 150; TOTAL FAT: 0 G; CARBOHYDRATE: 33 G; DIETARY
FIBER: 2 G; PROTEIN: 3 G

BASIC LENTILS

MAKES 3 CUPS; SERVING SIZE: ½ CUP

1 c. brown lentils, picked over for broken beans and pebbles
3 c. Vegetable Stock (page 24), canned
vegetable broth, or water

PLACE the lentils in a large saucepan, add the liquid, cover, and bring to a simmer. Cook, stirring occasionally, until the beans are tender but still retain their shape, about 25 minutes.

REMOVE from the heat and serve or use as directed.

CALORIES: 140; TOTAL FAT: 0 G; CARBOHYDRATE: 27 G; DIETARY
FIBER: 6 G; PROTEIN: 11 G

BASIC MASHED POTATOES

MAKES ABOUT 2 CUPS; SERVING SIZE: ½ CUP

2 medium russet potatoes, peeled and sliced
2 tsp. extra-virgin olive oil
⅛ tsp. kosher salt
⅛ tsp. freshly ground black pepper

PLACE the potatoes in a medium saucepan, and add enough cold water to cover them by an inch. Bring to a boil over high heat. Reduce the heat, and cook at a low boil until the potatoes are fork tender but not falling apart, 17 to 20 minutes.

DRAIN the potatoes well, place in a medium bowl, and mash with a potato masher. (Alternatively, turn the potatoes through a ricer into a bowl.) Stir in the olive oil, salt, and pepper; mix well. Serve immediately.

CALORIES: 142; TOTAL FAT: 3 G; CARBOHYDRATE: 28 G; DIETARY
FIBER: 4 G; PROTEIN: 2 G

BASIC MASHED SWEET POTATOES

MAKES 2 CUPS; SERVING SIZE: ½ CUP

22 oz. sweet potatoes, peeled and cut into ½-inch thick slices

8 oz. russet potatoes, peeled and cut into ½-inch thick slices

3 Tbsp. crumbled Cotija or feta cheese

1 Tbsp. extra-virgin olive oil

½ tsp. kosher salt

Pinch of freshly ground black pepper

PLACE the sweet potatoes in one medium saucepan and the russet potatoes in a second saucepan, and add enough cold water to both pans to cover the potatoes by an inch. Bring both pans to a boil over high heat. Reduce the heat, and cook at a low boil until the potatoes are fork tender but not falling apart, 17 to 20 minutes.

DRAIN the potatoes well, combine in a medium bowl, and mash together with a potato masher. (Alternatively, turn the potatoes through a ricer into a bowl.) Stir in the cheese, olive oil, salt, and pepper; and mix well. Serve immediately.

CALORIES: 110; TOTAL FAT: 2.5 G; CARBOHYDRATE: 19 G; DIETARY FIBER: 2 G; PROTEIN: 2 G

BASIC PINTO BEANS

MAKES 1 QUART; SERVING SIZE: ½ CUP

2 c. pinto beans, picked over for broken beans and pebbles, and rinsed well

9 c. Vegetable Stock (page 24), canned vegetable broth, or water

PLACE the beans in a large saucepan, add the vegetable stock, cover, and bring to a simmer. Cook, stirring occasionally, until the beans are tender but still retain their shape; about one hour.

REMOVE from heat and serve, or use as directed.

CALORIES: 122; TOTAL FAT: TRACE; CARBOHYDRATE: 23 G; DIETARY FIBER: 8 G; PROTEIN: 8 G

BASIC WHITE BEANS

MAKES 1 QUART; SERVING SIZE: ½ CUP

2 c. white beans (picked over for broken beans and pebbles, and rinsed well)

11 c. Vegetable Stock (page 24), canned vegetable broth, or water

PLACE the beans in a large saucepan, add the vegetable stock, cover, and bring to a simmer. Cook, stirring occasionally, until the beans are tender but still retain their shape; about 1½ hours.

REMOVE from heat and serve, or use as directed.

CALORIES: 127; TOTAL FAT: TRACE; CARBOHYDRATE: 23 G; DIETARY FIBER: 9 G; PROTEIN: 8 G

BASIC QUINOA

Nutritional note from Junelle Lupiani: "Notice that the 10- to 12-minute cooking time here is about the same length of time it takes to cook refined grains such as pasta and white rice. Choose the healthier alternative rather than the usual go-to grain when time is tight.

"Also, experiment with the recipe. And double the recipe and refrigerate the leftovers so that another meal can be made quickly. Not only is quinoa easy to prepare, but it reheats well, too."

There is a naturally occurring resin on quinoa that needs to be removed before the grain can be cooked. At Miraval, we toast quinoa before cooking either in the oven or on the stove top, such as in this recipe. This method also helps to more fully develop the grain's flavor. Alternatively, you can place the quinoa in a fine mesh strainer and rinse it under cold running water until the water runs clear.

MAKES 3 CUPS; SERVING SIZE: ½ CUP

2 c. Vegetable Stock (page 24), canned vegetable broth, or water

1 c. quinoa

PLACE the stock and quinoa in a medium saucepan and bring to a boil. Reduce the heat to low, cover, and simmer until tender, 10 to 12 minutes.

REMOVE the pan from the heat, fluff the quinoa with a fork, and serve immediately.

CALORIES: 120; TOTAL FAT: 2 G; CARBOHYDRATE: 22 G; DIETARY FIBER: 3 G; PROTEIN: 4 G

BASIC ROASTED PEPPERS

MAKES 1 PEPPER

1 medium bell pepper, about 6 oz., including stem and seeds

TURN gas burner on high.

USING a pair of tongs, carefully place the pepper on the burner. Leave pepper on the flame until skin is charred completely black and no original color is left. Rotate to the next side and repeat until the entire pepper is charred black, about 24 minutes.

USE the tongs to remove the pepper from the flame and place in a Ziploc or paper bag. Seal the bag to make sure that no steam can escape, and let the pepper rest for 8 to 10 minutes. This will allow the hot steam inside of the pepper to slowly loosen the charred skin as it cools. Please note that the pepper, and therefore the bag, will be extremely hot after being removed from the flame. Even after the pepper is cool to the touch, there may still be steam inside of the pepper hot enough to burn you.

ONCE the pepper is cool enough to touch, lightly massage it through the bag to remove most of the skin. Once the skin has been removed, take the pepper out of the bag and remove the stem and seeds. Reserve for use.

CALORIES: 35; TOTAL FAT: 0 G; CARBOHYDRATE: 7 G; DIETARY FIBER: 2 G; PROTEIN: 1 G

BASIC ROASTED SWEET POTATOES

MAKES 2 CUPS; SERVING SIZE: ½ CUP

2 six- to eight-ounce sweet potatoes
¼ tsp. Miraval Oil Blend (page 19) or canola oil
Pinch kosher salt
Pinch freshly ground black pepper
Chopped parsley, optional garnish
Shredded purple cabbage, optional garnish

PREHEAT the oven to 400° F.

PLACE the potatoes on a small baking sheet or in a baking dish. Spray with the oil and turn to coat on all sides. Season with salt and pepper, and roast until very tender and the skins start to split; 45 to 50 minutes.

REMOVE the potatoes from the oven and allow them to cool slightly on the baking sheet.

CUT each potato in half on the bias, add garnish if desired, and serve.

CALORIES: 45; TOTAL FAT: 0 G; CARBOHYDRATE: 10 G; DIETARY FIBER: 1 G; PROTEIN: 1 G

BLACKENING SPICE BLEND

MAKES 2 CUPS; SERVING SIZE: 1 TSP.

7 Tbsp. onion powder
7 Tbsp. paprika
6 Tbsp. ground black pepper
6 Tbsp. dried oregano
6 Tbsp. dried, crushed thyme
4 Tbsp. garlic powder
3½ Tbsp. kosher salt
3 Tbsp. ground white pepper
2 tsp. cayenne pepper

COMBINE all the ingredients in a mixing bowl and stir well to blend. Use as desired. Can be stored in an airtight container in your spice cabinet for up to three months.

CALORIES: 10; TOTAL FAT: 0 G; CARBOHYDRATE: 2 G; DIETARY FIBER: 1 G; PROTEIN: 0 G

MIRAVAL OIL BLEND

This is a kitchen staple that's used in many of the recipes in this book. By combining the two oils, the higher heat-resistant properties of the canola oil help to preserve the flavor of the more delicate extra-virgin olive oil.

MAKES 1 CUP; SERVING SIZE: 1 TBSP.

¾ cup canola oil
¼ cup cold-pressed extra-virgin olive oil

COMBINE in a spray bottle or mister and use to sauté food.

CALORIES: 144; TOTAL FAT: 17.5 G; CARBOHYDRATE: 0 G; DIETARY FIBER: 0 G; PROTEIN: 0 G

CHICKEN STOCK

MAKES 2 QUARTS

1 bay leaf

1 tsp. fresh thyme leaves

2 Tbsp. whole black peppercorns

1 c. yellow onions, chopped

½ c. celery ribs, chopped (no leaves)

3 lbs. chicken bones or 3 carcasses, thoroughly washed, excess fat removed

3 qt. cold water

IN a large stockpot, combine all ingredients. Add enough cold water to cover the bones and the vegetables. Bring contents to a boil, reduce heat, and simmer uncovered for 4 hours.

USING a slotted spoon, skim off any impurities such as foam and fat throughout the cooking process.

STRAIN stock through a colander lined with cheesecloth or through a fine mesh strainer, discarding bones and vegetables.

USE stock immediately or cool down in an ice bath. Once the stock is cool (below 40° F), store in the refrigerator in an airtight container for up to one week or freeze for about one month.

PER 1 CUP: CALORIES: 60; TOTAL FAT: 1 G; SATURATED FAT: 0 G; CARBOHYDRATE: 11 G; DIETARY FIBER: 2 G; PROTEIN: 3 G

HERB OIL

At Miraval we use this as a dip for our freshly baked bread, or as a garnish for a flatbread or an entrée.

MAKES A GENEROUS ⅓ CUP; SERVING SIZE: 2 TSP.

¼ c. loosely packed fresh flat-leaf parsley

¼ c. loosely packed fresh basil

¼ c. loosely packed fresh chives

⅓ c. canola oil or vegetable oil

1 Tbsp. extra-virgin olive oil

BRING a medium pot of water to a boil.

PREPARE an ice bath and set aside.

PLACE the herbs in a fine mesh strainer, immerse in the boiling water for 20 seconds, and immediately shock in the ice bath.

SQUEEZE the herbs dry and place in the bowl of a blender. Add the canola and olive oils and blend on low speed until well combined, scraping down the sides of the bowl as needed.

TRANSFER to an airtight container and refrigerate until ready to use. (The oil will keep refrigerated for up to seven days.)

CALORIES: 47; TOTAL FAT: 5 G; CARBOHYDRATE: 0 G; DIETARY FIBER: 0 G; PROTEIN: 0 G

HOUSE PICKLED GINGER

Pickled ginger is delicious served with grilled tuna and other seafood dishes. And use the gingered syrup that's left over from the cooking process to flavor dressings, marinades, or even cocktails!

MAKES ABOUT 1 CUP; SERVING SIZE: 1 TBSP.

¾ c. rice wine vinegar

½ c. cane sugar

½ tsp. kosher salt

1¼ c. peeled, very thinly sliced fresh ginger (about ½ lb.)

COMBINE the vinegar, sugar, and salt in a medium, non-reactive saucepan. Bring the mixture to a boil and cook, stirring occasionally, until the sugar is melted, 2 to 4 minutes. Remove the pan from the heat and add the ginger. Stir well, return to a simmer, and cook for 2 minutes. Remove the pan from the heat and let the mixture cool to room temperature.

STRAIN the liquid into a clean airtight container, and refrigerate for up to two weeks.

SERVE the ginger at room temperature, or place in a separate airtight container and refrigerate until ready to serve, for up to two weeks.

CALORIES: 13; TOTAL FAT: 0 G; CARBOHYDRATE: 3.5 G; DIETARY FIBER: 0 G; PROTEIN: 0 G

MIRAVAL MAYONNAISE

MAKES 4 CUPS; SERVING SIZE: 1 TBSP.

2 c. nonfat yogurt

2 c. soft tofu

2 Tbsp. rice wine vinegar

1 Tbsp. minced Roasted Garlic (page 22)

1 tsp. kosher salt

1 tsp. Worcestershire sauce

½ tsp. freshly ground black pepper

½ tsp. Tabasco sauce

LINE a colander or a strainer with cheesecloth. Place the yogurt in the colander set over a large bowl, and refrigerate until the excess liquid is drained; 1 to 2 hours. Discard the liquid.

PLACE the drained yogurt, tofu, vinegar, and garlic in a blender and process until the mixture is smooth, 45 seconds. Add the remaining ingredients and process on high speed until completely blended, 30 seconds.

USE immediately or transfer to an airtight container and refrigerate until ready to use. (The mayonnaise will keep refrigerated for up to two weeks.)

CALORIES: 10; TOTAL FAT: 0 G; CARBOHYDRATE: 2 G; DIETARY FIBER: 0 G; PROTEIN: 1 G

MIRAVAL PEANUT BUTTER

MAKES 2 CUPS; SERVING SIZE: 1 TBSP.

2 c. peeled, ¼-inch-thick sliced carrots
1 c. organic smooth or chunky peanut butter

BRING a small pot of water to a boil. Add the carrots and cook at a high simmer until they're very tender, 20 minutes. Drain well and cool to refrigerator temperature (37–39°F).

PLACE the carrots in the bowl of a food processor and blend on high speed until smooth. Add the peanut butter and process on high speed until very smooth.

TRANSFER to an airtight container and refrigerate until ready to use. (The peanut butter will keep refrigerated for up to seven days.)

CALORIES: 50; TOTAL FAT: 3 G; CARBOHYDRATE: 4 G; DIETARY FIBER: 1 G; PROTEIN: 2 G

ROASTED GARLIC

MAKES ABOUT ¼ CUP; SERVING SIZE: ¼ CUP

¼ c. peeled garlic cloves
¾ tsp. Miraval Oil Blend (page 19) or canola oil

PREHEAT the oven to 375° F.

PLACE the garlic in a small saucepan or baking dish, and lightly coat with the oil. Roast uncovered for 10 minutes and stir. Continue cooking until tender and lightly browned, an additional 10 to 12 minutes.

REMOVE from the oven and let cool before using. (The garlic will keep in an airtight container refrigerated for up to four days.)

CALORIES: 20; TOTAL FAT: 1 G; CARBOHYDRATE: 3 G; DIETARY FIBER: 0 G; PROTEIN: 1 G

ROASTED SHALLOTS

MAKES ABOUT ¼ CUP; SERVING SIZE: ¼ CUP

¼ c. peeled shallots, rough chopped
¾ tsp. Miraval Oil Blend (page 19) or canola oil

PREHEAT the oven to 375° F.

PLACE the shallots in a small saucepan or baking dish and lightly coat with the oil. Roast uncovered for 7 minutes and stir. Continue cooking until tender and lightly browned, an additional 5 to 6 minutes.

REMOVE from the oven and let cool before using. (The shallots will keep in an airtight container refrigerated for up to four days.)

CALORIES: 20; TOTAL FAT: 1 G; CARBOHYDRATE: 3 G; DIETARY FIBER: 0 G; PROTEIN: 1 G

SEDONA SPICE RUB

If you've been in search of "that extra something" to give emphasis to pork, chicken, elk, or fish entrées, Chef Chad's special Sedona Spice Rub is very likely it. Chamomile flowers can be found at your local health-food store.

MAKES ½ CUP; SERVING SIZE: 1 TSP.

1 tsp. chili powder

1 tsp. whole cumin seeds

3 whole pods star anise

1 Tbsp. whole black peppercorns

1 Tbsp. dried chamomile flower, whole

1 Tbsp. plus 2 tsp. garlic powder

1 Tbsp. plus 2 tsp. onion powder

1 Tbsp. dried orange peel

2 tsp. paprika

1½ tsp. kosher salt

PREHEAT the oven to 350° F.

SPREAD the chili powder and cumin seeds in a small baking dish and roast in the oven until fragrant (but not smoking) and the color changes, 5 to 6 minutes.

GRIND together the star anise and peppercorns in a spice grinder. Add the cumin and chili powder mixture and the chamomile and grind together. Add the remaining ingredients and grind to a fine powder.

STORE in an airtight container until ready to use. (The spice rub will keep at room temperature in an airtight container for up to one month.)

CALORIES: 5; TOTAL FAT: 0 G; CARBOHYDRATE: 1 G; DIETARY FIBER: 0 G; PROTEIN: 0 G

SIMPLE SYRUP

SERVING SIZE: 1 OZ.

2 c. sugar

2 c. water

HEAT the sugar and water in a medium saucepan over medium-high heat. Reduce the heat to medium-low and simmer, stirring occasionally, until the sugar is completely dissolved, about 2 minutes.

LET cool before using. (Simple syrup can be made in advance. Transfer the cooled syrup to an airtight container and store in refrigerator for up to two weeks.)

CALORIES: 50; TOTAL FAT: 0 G; CARBOHYDRATE: 14 G; DIETARY FIBER: 0 G; PROTEIN: TRACE

SWEETENED WHIPPED CREAM

MAKES 1½ CUPS; SERVING SIZE: 1 TBSP.

1 c. heavy cream, very cold

2 Tbsp. confectioners' sugar, sifted

IN the bowl of an electric mixer or with a handheld electric mixer, combine the cream and sugar and beat on high speed until soft peaks form. Serve immediately.

CALORIES: 90; TOTAL FAT: 9 G; CARBOHYDRATE: 2 G; DIETARY FIBER: 0 G; PROTEIN: 0 G

VEGETABLE STOCK

MAKES 3 CUPS; SERVING SIZE: ½ CUP

2 qt. water

3 c. roughly chopped, peeled yellow onion

2 c. roughly chopped tomato

1½ c. roughly chopped celery

1½ c. roughly chopped carrots

½ c. roughly chopped cremini or shiitake mushrooms

2 tsp. black peppercorns

5 sprigs fresh thyme

COMBINE all the ingredients in a small stockpot and bring to a boil. Reduce the heat and simmer uncovered for 2 hours.

REMOVE from heat and strain through a fine mesh strainer or a colander lined with cheesecloth into a clean container. Let cool to room temperature, and transfer to airtight containers. Refrigerate until ready to use. (The stock will keep refrigerated for up to five days and frozen for up to one month.)

CALORIES: 25; TOTAL FAT: 0 G; CARBOHYDRATE: 6 G; DIETARY FIBER: 1 G; PROTEIN: 1 G

THICKENED VEGETABLE STOCK

MAKES 1⅔ CUPS; SERVING SIZE: ½ CUP

3 c. Vegetable Stock

4 Tbsp. cornstarch

3 Tbsp. cold water

PLACE the stock in a medium saucepan and bring to a boil.

COMBINE the cornstarch and water in a bowl and whisk to make a thick slurry.

WHISK 1 Tbsp. of the cornstarch slurry into the hot stock and cook at a low boil, whisking constantly, until well incorporated. Add another 1 Tbsp. of the slurry, whisking constantly, and simmer until well incorporated. Add an additional 1 Tbsp. cornstarch slurry, whisking. Lower the heat and cook at a low simmer, whisking constantly, for 1 minute. Add the remaining 1 Tbsp. slurry, whisking, and cook until the stock is thickened and heavily coats the back of a spoon, 2 to 3 minutes.

REMOVE from heat and let cool to room temperature. Transfer to an airtight container and store in the refrigerator until ready to use. (The stock will keep refrigerated for up to two weeks.)

CALORIES: 20; TOTAL FAT: 0 G; CARBOHYDRATE: 5 G; DIETARY FIBER: 1 G; PROTEIN: 0 G

VEAL STOCK

MAKES 1 GALLON

5 lb. veal knuckle bones, cut

1½ c. burgundy or cabernet sauvignon wine

1 tsp. fresh thyme sprigs

1 bay leaf

1 tsp. whole black peppercorns

1 c. yellow onion, peeled and chopped

1 c. carrots, peeled and chopped

1 c. celery, chopped (no leaves)

⅓ c. tomato paste

1½ gallons cold water

PREHEAT the oven to 400° F.

RINSE the bones and place in a roasting pan. Place the pan in the oven and roast the bones for about 1 hour, or until a deep brown color. Using tongs, carefully remove the bones from pan and place in a large bowl.

ADD the wine to the hot roasting pan and scrape off the sediments from the bottom of pan for additional flavor. Reserve this mixture.

HEAT a large stockpot over medium heat and add the vegetables. Sauté, stirring occasionally to prevent scorching, until vegetables are softened, 3 to 5 minutes. Stir in the tomato paste and red wine mixture. Stir to fully incorporate. Add the thyme, bay leaf, peppercorns, bones, and water. Bring to a boil, reduce heat, and simmer for 24 hours.

USING a slotted spoon, skim off any impurities such as foam and fat throughout the cooking process. As the stock cooks, check the water level. You may need to add additional cold water to maintain the liquid volume in the stockpot. Toward the end of the cooking period, let the stock reduce by about one-third of the original amount.

STRAIN stock through a colander lined with cheesecloth or a fine mesh strainer, discarding bones and vegetables.

USE stock immediately or cool down in an ice bath. Store in the refrigerator in an airtight container for up to one week or freeze in large Ziploc bags for about one month.

PER 1 CUP: CALORIES: 70; TOTAL FAT: 1 G; SATURATED FAT: 0 G; CARBOHYDRATE: 9 G; DIETARY FIBER: 0 G; PROTEIN: 4 G; CHOLESTEROL: 10 MG; SODIUM: 110 MG

THE CACTUS FLOWER RESTAURANT & COYOTE MOON

Miraval is a place to reconnect and relax, whether in a group or by yourself. The Cactus Flower Restaurant is the center of cuisine at Miraval and is a perfect environment for mindfully enjoying a meal. The view from our spacious dining room or breezy patio is transformative, with the expansive Catalina Mountains and the wild Sonoran Desert spread in the distance. It's easy to be focused in this comfortable setting and relearn eating habits—remembering to put down your fork, digest, and enjoy the space between bites rather than eating quickly.

A handcrafted fireplace anchors one side of the room, while two adjacent French doors open onto the wide flagstone terrace for alfresco dining. Arizona's mild climate means that guests are able to dine outside nearly year round, both day and night. The Cactus Flower also adjoins the Coyote Moon dining room and our intimate chef demonstration kitchen, where Chef Chad inspires guests with technique and creativity.

We carefully craft menus that are inventive and satisfying—not what one might generally consider "spa food." We believe that choice is paramount, and learning how to make sound choices is part of practicing mindfulness. For instance, healthy breads are served at every meal—from English muffins and banana bread at the breakfast buffet to freshly baked Italian-style loaves at night…complete with choices of butters, spreads, and flavored oils. And desserts? Every guest happily enjoys the flavorful cuisine they desire, while learning healthy habits to take home.

The warm and inviting Coyote Moon dining room adjoins the Cactus Flower Restaurant. Its focal point is an exhibition window into our bustling kitchen, which provides nightly entertainment for diners watching our talented team work in harmony to create gorgeous, healthy cuisine.

For the modern comfort of many guests, we've added a communal table that inspires a mix of solo travelers and couples—guests of all ages and backgrounds—to gather and share their Miraval experiences over an extraordinary meal.

BREAKFAST
FAVORITES

BREAKFAST PARFAIT

Begin your morning with one of our classic Miraval recipes. Make this healthy and easy-to-prepare breakfast parfait your own by incorporating colorful seasonal fruits from your farmers' market. Our chefs love it with sweet oranges and tangy tangerines.

MAKES 4 SERVINGS

½ c. fresh blueberries
½ c. chopped, stemmed strawberries
½ c. chopped cantaloupe
1 c. Miraval Granola (page 43) or prepared granola
2 c. fat-free yogurt

PLACE four footed, clear parfait or martini glasses on your work surface. Layer the fruit, granola, and yogurt into each glass, making three layers per serving of each ingredient. Serve immediately.

CALORIES: 200; TOTAL FAT: 3.5 G; CARBOHYDRATE: 34 G; DIETARY FIBER: 3 G; PROTEIN: 9 G

BREAKFAST BURRITO

Farm-fresh eggs, off-the-vine tomatoes, and just-cut cilantro. Separately, these ingredients are delicious, but together they are divine. We recommend drizzling your favorite salsa on top to highlight the flavors.

MAKES 2 SERVINGS

2 large eggs
¼ tsp. Miraval Oil Blend (page 19)
2 Tbsp. chopped fresh tomatoes
2 tsp. chopped fresh cilantro
1 tsp. crumbled Cotija or feta cheese
2 Tbsp. Miraval Salsa (page 221)
One 12" whole-wheat tortilla

OVER a medium flame, heat the tortilla until warmed through, turning twice, 20 seconds per side. (Alternately, heat in a large dry skillet over medium heat.)

BEAT the eggs in a small bowl until airy.

HEAT a 6-inch skillet over medium heat. Add the oil and when hot, add the eggs and reduce the heat to low. Cook, stirring with a rubber spatula or wooden spoon, to desired doneness, 1 to 2 minutes. Add the tomatoes and cilantro; cook, stirring for 30 seconds. Remove from the heat and stir in the cheese.

PLACE the tortilla on a work surface and spoon the egg mixture into the center of the bottom third. Fold the sides toward the center over the eggs and roll up to completely enclose the eggs. Place the flap-side down and cut on the bias in half.

PLACE one half on each of two serving plates, and drizzle one tablespoon of salsa over each half. Serve immediately.

CALORIES: 250; TOTAL FAT: 9 G; CARBOHYDRATE: 29 G; DIETARY FIBER: 2 G; PROTEIN: 11 G

CACTUS FLOWER OMELET

Put a spin on this dish by incorporating salsa. Some of our favorites are Miraval Salsa, Roasted Green Chili Sauce, and Tomato Pico de Gallo. Remember, this is your art to create! Be sure to use freshly grated cheese—it makes such a flavorful difference.

MAKES 1 SERVING

2 large eggs

½ tsp. Miraval Oil Blend
(page 19) or canola oil

1 tsp. finely chopped red onion

1 Tbsp. chopped red bell pepper

1 Tbsp. chopped asparagus

¼ c. baby spinach, rinsed and spun dry

1 Tbsp. Basic Lentils (page 15)

1 tsp. freshly grated
Parmigiano-Reggiano

Salt, optional

Freshly ground black pepper, optional

1 Tbsp. Miraval Salsa (page 221), optional

1 Tbsp. Roasted Green Chili
Sauce (page 131), optional

WHISK the eggs in a small bowl until frothy. Set aside.

HEAT a small skillet over medium-high heat. Add the oil and when hot, add the onion and cook, stirring for 15 seconds. Add the asparagus and bell pepper, and cook, stirring for 15 seconds. Add the spinach and stir well. Add the lentils and cook, stirring for 30 seconds. Reduce the heat to low. Add the eggs and cook undisturbed until they start to set and pull away from the sides of the pan, 45 seconds to 1 minute.

USING a rubber spatula, gently pull the eggs away from the sides of the pan and tip the pan to allow the uncooked eggs to run underneath. Cook the eggs to desired doneness, 4 to 6 minutes. Carefully slip a spatula under the eggs, flip onto the other side, and cook for 15 seconds.

PLACE a plate over the pan and invert the pan, releasing the omelet onto the plate. Top the omelet with the cheese. Add salt, pepper, and salsas, as desired. Serve immediately.

CALORIES: 190; TOTAL FAT: 12 G; CARBOHYDRATE: 6 G; DIETARY FIBER: 2 G; PROTEIN: 15 G

CARAMELIZED GRAPEFRUIT

1 large Ruby Red grapefruit, halved crosswise

2 tsp. agave syrup (see Source Guide), or honey

RUN a small sharp paring knife around each grapefruit section to release the membranes. Arrange each half on a salad plate, and drizzle with 1 teaspoon of the syrup.

USING a blowtorch, carefully work the flame over the tops of the grapefruit halves until the syrup bubbles and caramelizes. Serve immediately.

CALORIES: 60; TOTAL FAT: 0 G; CARBOHYDRATE: 14 G; DIETARY FIBER: 1 G; PROTEIN: 1 G

CINNAMON KASHA

MAKES 4 SERVINGS; SERVING SIZE: ½ CUP

1 c. kasha

1½ c. water

¼ c. dried fruit (such as raisins, dried cherries, apricots, or cranberries)

¼ tsp. ground cinnamon

⅛ tsp. kosher salt

COMBINE the kasha, salt, and water in a medium saucepan and bring to a gentle simmer over low-medium heat. Add the dried fruit and cinnamon, and stir well. Simmer uncovered, stirring occasionally until the liquid is absorbed and the grain is no longer crunchy, about 15 minutes. Serve hot.

CALORIES: 170; TOTAL FAT: 1 G; CARBOHYDRATE: 37 G; DIETARY FIBER: 5 G; PROTEIN: 5 G

CHICKEN BREAKFAST SAUSAGE PATTIES

MAKES 4 TO 6 SERVINGS

1 c. russet potato, peeled and
cut into ½-inch cubes

1 lb. boneless, skinless chicken
breast, cut into 1-inch pieces

2 large egg whites

1 tsp. kosher salt

½ tsp. freshly ground black pepper

⅓ c. minced red onion

3 Tbsp. finely chopped
green bell peppers

3 Tbsp. finely chopped red bell peppers

3 Tbsp. finely chopped yellow bell
peppers

2 Tbsp. chopped assorted soft herbs,
such as basil, oregano, parsley, or thyme

1 tsp. Miraval Oil Blend
(page 19) or canola oil

PLACE the potatoes in a small saucepan and cover with water by one inch. Bring to a low boil and cook until the potatoes are fork tender but not falling apart, about 6 minutes. Drain well and let cool before using.

PREHEAT the oven to 350° F.

PLACE the chicken in a food processor and pulse until roughly chopped. Add the egg whites, salt, and pepper and process on high speed to a smooth puree.

TRANSFER the mixture to a large bowl. Fold in the remaining ingredients, except the oil, and stir with a rubber spatula until well combined but the potatoes still retain their shape.

SCOOP the chicken mixture into 2-ounce cakes using a quarter-cup measuring cup, and place on a plate lined with plastic wrap or wax paper.

HEAT a large skillet over medium-high heat. Add ½ tsp. of the oil and 5 chicken patties; and cook until well browned, 1 to 2 minutes per side. Transfer the patties to a baking sheet and repeat with the remaining oil and patties. Bake the chicken patties until cooked through, 5 to 6 minutes.

REMOVE from the oven and serve immediately.

CALORIES: 70; TOTAL FAT: 1 G; CARBOHYDRATE: 3 G; DIETARY FIBER: 0 G; PROTEIN: 10 G

CORNFLAKE-CRUSTED BANANA-STUFFED FRENCH TOAST

Our chefs agree that there is something positively nostalgic about the smell of cinnamon and vanilla. Ripe bananas make it all the more memorable. From our table to yours, enjoy this back-to-scratch approach to French toast. It's the ideal dish for a relaxed Sunday morning.

MAKES 2 SERVINGS

1 Tbsp. sliced almonds
1 c. corn cereal, such as Corn Flakes
2 egg whites
1 large egg
½ tsp. cinnamon
½ tsp. pure vanilla extract
4 slices whole-wheat bread
¼ c. mashed very ripe bananas
1 tsp. canola or vegetable oil

PREHEAT the oven to 400° F.

PLACE the almonds in an ovenproof dish and cook until fragrant and golden brown, about 6 minutes. Remove from the oven, and place in a shallow dish large enough to hold one slice of bread.

PLACE the cereal in a food processor and pulse to make fine crumbs. Add the cornflakes to the almonds and set aside.

WHISK together the egg whites, egg, cinnamon, and vanilla extract in a medium bowl.

ONE at a time, dip the bread slices into the egg mixture until saturated on both sides and then coat on both sides with the cornflake-almond mixture. Set on a rack or clean plate while coating the remaining bread.

SPREAD 2 Tbsp. of the mashed banana on 2 slices of the bread and top with the remaining 2 slices, pressing to adhere.

PREHEAT a large skillet or griddle pan over medium-high heat. Add the oil and when hot, add the French toast and cook until the crust is golden brown, 3 to 3½ minutes. Turn and cook until the second side is golden brown and the inside is warmed through, 2½ to 3 minutes. Serve immediately.

CALORIES: 300; TOTAL FAT: 5 G; CARBOHYDRATE: 49 G; DIETARY FIBER: 9 G; PROTEIN: 15 G

COWBOY BREAKFAST BURRITO

MAKES 1 SERVING

One 12" whole-wheat tortilla

2 large eggs

½ tsp. Miraval Oil Blend (page 19), canola, or vegetable oil

2 Tbsp. seeded and minced tomatoes

1½ Tbsp. minced red onions

1 tsp. minced, seeded jalapeños

3 Tbsp. sweet potatoes

3 Tbsp. Basic Black Beans (page 14)

2 tsp. minced fresh cilantro

⅛ tsp. kosher salt

Pinch freshly ground black pepper

3 Tbsp. shredded cheddar cheese

Fresh cilantro leaves, as garnish

Miraval Salsa (page 221), optional

OVER a medium flame, heat the tortilla until warmed through, turning twice, 20 seconds per side. (Alternatively, heat in a large dry skillet over medium heat.)

BEAT the eggs in a small bowl until airy.

HEAT a 6-inch skillet over medium heat. Add ¼ tsp. of the oil and when hot, add the tomatoes, onions, and jalapeños; cook, stirring until the veggies start to wilt, 45 seconds. Add the sweet potatoes and black beans and cook, stirring for 1 minute. Add the remaining oil and stir. Add the eggs, cilantro, salt, and pepper; reduce the heat to low; and cook, stirring with a rubber spatula or wooden spoon to desired doneness, 1 to 2 minutes. Remove from the heat, and stir in the cheese.

PLACE the tortilla on a work surface and spoon the egg mixture into the center of the bottom third. Fold the sides toward the center over the eggs and roll up to completely enclose the eggs. Place flap-side down and cut on the bias in half.

PLACE one half on each of two serving plates, garnish with cilantro, and drizzle one tablespoon of salsa over each half, if desired. Serve immediately.

CALORIES: 310; TOTAL FAT: 12 G; CARBOHYDRATE: 34 G; DIETARY FIBER: 6 G; PROTEIN: 17 G

FRUIT YOGURT

MAKES 3 CUPS

1 c. frozen blueberries or strawberries with their juice

2 c. plain nonfat yogurt

2 Tbsp. honey or agave syrup (see Source Guide)

PLACE the berries and their juice in a medium bowl and roughly break apart with the bottom of a heavy whisk or fork without mashing completely.

ADD the yogurt and honey (or agave), and whisk until smooth.

SERVE immediately, or transfer to an airtight container and refrigerate for up to three days.

CALORIES: 90; TOTAL FAT: 0 G; CARBOHYDRATE: 20 G; DIETARY FIBER: 1 G; PROTEIN: 4 G

GARDEN QUICHE

Our very definition of simple, wholesome food. This crustless quiche is a recipe you'll love to prepare and serve for years to come. Your friends and family will delight in this dish as much as we do—even if they are gluten intolerant.

MAKES 6 TO 12 SERVINGS, DEPENDING ON THE PORTION SIZE DESIRED

12 large egg whites

3 large eggs

1 packed c. baby spinach, rinsed and cut into chiffonade

⅓ c. chopped shiitake or crimini mushrooms

⅓ c. chopped tomatoes

¼ c. freshly grated Parmigiano-Reggiano

3 Tbsp. chopped red bell pepper

1 Tbsp. chopped green onions

1 tsp. chopped fresh tarragon

Pinch salt

Pinch freshly ground black pepper

PREHEAT the oven to 350° F.

LIBERALLY coat the bottom of a 10-inch baking dish with vegetable cooking spray and set aside.

WHISK together the egg whites and eggs in a large bowl until well blended. Add the remaining ingredients and whisk to combine. Pour into the prepared pan and bake until the eggs are set, 23 to 25 minutes.

REMOVE the quiche from the oven and let cool on a wire rack for 30 minutes before serving. Slice into 6 to 12 equal portions to serve.

CALORIES: 90; TOTAL FAT: 3.5 G; CARBOHYDRATE: 3 G; DIETARY FIBER: 0 G; PROTEIN: 12 G

HUEVOS RANCHEROS

Expand your culinary boundaries with this classic Mexican breakfast that's filling and flavorful. We enhance our eggs with a Roasted Green Chili Sauce (page 131) to give it some extra zest. Be sure to warm the tortillas on the skillet rather than in the microwave to preserve the taste and texture.

MAKES 4 SERVINGS

1 c. Basic Black Beans (page 14)

4 corn tortillas

1 tsp. Miraval Oil Blend
(page 19) or canola oil

8 medium eggs

1 c. Roasted Green Chili Sauce (page 131)

1 c. thinly shredded red
cabbage, optional

1 tsp. Cotija cheese or feta cheese

HEAT the black beans in a small saucepan over medium-low heat. Set aside.

HEAT the tortillas in a dry large skillet one at a time until softened, about 30 seconds each, turning once. Stack on a clean plate to keep warm.

HEAT ¼ tsp. of the oil in a small nonstick skillet over medium-high heat. Add the eggs, lower the heat to medium, and cook undisturbed until the whites begin to set, 1½ minutes. Lower the heat and continue cooking until the yolks and whites both are set and to desired doneness, 3 to 4 minutes. (Alternatively, use two medium pans to cook 4 eggs each, using ½ tsp. oil in each pan.)

PLACE one tortilla in the center of each of four large plates and top each with ¼ cup of the warm beans. Arrange two eggs over each serving of beans and top each portion with ¼ cup of the green chili sauce. Divide with the cabbage and cheese between the four portions and serve immediately.

CALORIES: 280; TOTAL FAT: 12 G; CARBOHYDRATE: 25 G; DIETARY FIBER: 5 G; PROTEIN: 17 G

MIRAVAL GRANOLA

MAKES 4 CUPS; SERVING SIZE: ½ CUP

¼ c. sliced almonds

¼ c. pumpkin seeds

3 c. rolled oats

1½ c. oat bran

¾ c. agave syrup (see Source Guide), or honey

1 vanilla bean, split in half lengthwise and seeds scraped out (reserve halves for another use)

1½ c. apple juice

¼ c. diced dried apricots

¼ c. raisins

¼ c. dried cherries

¼ c. dried cranberries

PREHEAT the oven to 400° F.

SPREAD the almonds and pumpkin seeds on a small baking sheet or in a large skillet and bake until lightly toasted and fragrant, 7 to 8 minutes. Set aside.

SPREAD the oats on one large baking sheet and the oat bran on a small sheet pan and bake each until golden brown and fragrant, 8 to 9 minutes. Set aside.

LOWER the oven to 350° F.

COMBINE the agave syrup and vanilla-bean seeds in a small saucepan, and bring to a simmer. Cook while whisking until fragrant, about 1 minute. Remove from the heat and let cool.

COMBINE the apple juice, apricots, raisins, cherries, and cranberries; and bring to a simmer. Cook until the fruit is plumped and tender, about 2 minutes. Drain the fruit in a strainer, and discard the cooking liquid.

COMBINE all the ingredients in a large bowl, scraping the agave-vanilla mixture with a rubber spatula, and stir well to coat the dry ingredients. Spread the oat mixture on a large baking sheet and bake on the middle rack in the oven until crisp, stirring occasionally with a spatula, until the mixture turns an even golden brown, 30 to 35 minutes.

REMOVE the granola from the oven and let cool on the baking sheet, stirring occasionally. Store the cooled granola in an airtight container until ready to serve. (The granola will keep for up to one week in an airtight container at room temperature.)

CALORIES: 210; TOTAL FAT: 4 G; CARBOHYDRATE: 43 G; DIETARY FIBER: 5 G; PROTEIN: 6 G

MIRAVAL MUESLIX

Nutritional note from Junelle Lupiani: "This is by far Miraval guests' favorite breakfast food, and it is so easy to prepare. You can use soy milk and soy yogurt for a vegan version." If you don't want to make Miraval Granola, purchase prepared granola to make this delicious breakfast treat.

MAKES 2½ CUPS; SERVING SIZE: ½ CUP

2 c. Miraval Granola (page 43), or prepared granola

1 c. nonfat plain yogurt

¾ c. peeled, cored, seeded, and chopped apples

¾ c. hulled and sliced fresh strawberries

¼ c. raisins

½ c. nonfat milk

1 tsp. agave syrup (see Source Guide), or honey

COMBINE all the ingredients in a large bowl and stir well. Let sit until the granola is soft and the liquid is absorbed, about 30 minutes. (Alternatively, let the cereal sit, covered, in the refrigerator to serve cold.)

SERVE immediately.

CALORIES: 370; TOTAL FAT: 6 G; CARBOHYDRATE: 77 G; DIETARY FIBER: 8 G; PROTEIN: 12 G

HONEY-LIME YOGURT

Nutritional note from Junelle Lupiani: "Flavoring your own yogurt is easy to do and tastes great, but beyond taste, it's also a terrific way to be aware of the ingredients in your food. Nowadays, many prepared foods use artificial flavorings, and yogurt is a prime example. Buy yogurt that contains as few ingredients as possible, and then get creative with the flavoring in your kitchen. Soy yogurt works well here, too."

MAKES 2 HEAPING CUPS; SERVING SIZE: ½ CUP

2 c. plain nonfat yogurt

2 Tbsp. honey or agave syrup (see Source Guide)

2 Tbsp. fresh lime juice

½ tsp. finely grated lime zest

COMBINE the ingredients in a medium bowl and whisk until smooth.

SERVE immediately, or transfer to an airtight container and refrigerate for up to three days.

CALORIES: 80; TOTAL FAT: 0 G; CARBOHYDRATE: 19 G; DIETARY FIBER: 0 G; PROTEIN: 5 G

SALMON BREAKFAST PATTIES

MAKES 6 SERVINGS

½ c. russet potato, peeled and cut into ½-inch cubes

8 oz. skinless, deboned salmon

1 large egg white

¾ tsp. freshly ground black pepper

½ tsp. kosher salt

½ c. chopped seedless green or red grapes

¼ c. chopped green onions

1 Tbsp. chopped fresh chervil, parsley, dill, or cilantro

1 tsp. Miraval Oil Blend (page 19) or canola oil

PLACE the potatoes in a small saucepan and cover with water by one inch. Bring to a low boil and cook until the potatoes are fork tender but not falling apart, about 6 minutes. Drain well and let cool before using.

PREHEAT the oven to 350° F.

PLACE the salmon in a food processor and pulse until roughly chopped. Add the egg whites, pepper, and salt and process on high speed to a smooth puree.

TRANSFER the mixture to a large bowl. Fold in the remaining ingredients, except the oil, and stir with a rubber spatula until well combined but the potatoes still retain their shape.

SCOOP the salmon mixture into 2-ounce cakes using a quarter-cup measuring cup, and place on a plate lined with plastic wrap or wax paper.

HEAT a large skillet over medium-high heat. Add ½ tsp. of the oil and 3 salmon patties, and cook until well browned, 1 to 2 minutes per side. Transfer the patties to a baking sheet and repeat with the remaining oil and patties. Bake the salmon patties until cooked through, 5 to 6 minutes.

REMOVE from the oven and serve immediately.

CALORIES: 80; TOTAL FAT: 2.5 G; CARBOHYDRATE: 5 G; DIETARY FIBER: 0 G; PROTEIN: 8 G

WARM TEFF CEREAL WITH DRIED FRUIT

MAKES 2 CUPS; SERVING SIZE: ½ CUP

1 c. teff

1 c. apple juice

1 c. water

¼ c. dried fruit (such as raisins, dried cherries, apricots, or cranberries)

⅛ tsp. kosher salt

COMBINE teff, apple juice, and water in a medium saucepan and bring to a low simmer, stirring occasionally for about 15 minutes. Add the fruit and salt, and stir to incorporate. Simmer gently, uncovered, stirring occasionally, until liquid is mostly absorbed and the grains are no longer crunchy, another 15 minutes. Serve hot.

CALORIES: 200; TOTAL FAT: 1.5 G; CARBOHYDRATE: 41 G; DIETARY FIBER: 6 G; PROTEIN: 6 G

POACHED EGGS FLORENTINE

One recipe Florentine Sauce

One recipe Poached Eggs

TO SERVE, spoon one-quarter cup of the sauce into the center of four plates and top with one or two eggs, as desired. Serve immediately.

CALORIES: 110; TOTAL FAT: 8 G; CARBOHYDRATE: 4 G; DIETARY FIBER: 1 G; PROTEIN: 12 G

FLORENTINE SAUCE

MAKES 1 CUP

¼ c. dry white wine

1 Tbsp. minced shallots

1 tsp. minced garlic

⅓ c. low-fat cottage cheese

¼ c. skim milk

2 Tbsp. grated Parmigiano-Reggiano

2 Tbsp. Neufchâtel cheese or low-fat cream cheese

2 Tbsp. sour cream

⅛ tsp. nutmeg

Pinch kosher salt

Pinch freshly ground black pepper

3 c. chiffonade fresh baby spinach

COMBINE the wine, shallots, and garlic in a small saucepan and simmer until reduced to about 1 Tbsp. in volume, 3 minutes. Remove from the heat and set aside.

COMBINE the remaining ingredients except the spinach in a blender and process until smooth. Transfer to the saucepan with the reduced wine mixture and fold in the spinach. Bring to a simmer over medium heat. Reduce the heat to medium-low and gently simmer, stirring occasionally, until thick, 12 to 14 minutes.

REMOVE from the heat and cover to keep warm until ready to serve.

POACHED EGGS

Rest assured, the process of poached eggs really is quite simple…and worthy of your efforts! While this recipe calls for 8 eggs, any number of eggs—from 2 to 12—can be made using the same amount of water and the same procedure.

MAKES 4 TO 8 SERVINGS

3 c. water

½ tsp. white vinegar

Pinch kosher salt

8 large eggs

BRING the water, vinegar, and salt to a simmer in a large saucepan or pot over high heat.

CRACK an egg into a saucer and slide it gently into the water. Repeat with 3 more eggs in quick succession. Return the water to a simmer and cook until the egg whites are firm and the yolks are still soft, 2 to 2½ minutes.

DRAIN the cooked eggs on a clean kitchen towel and repeat with remaining eggs.

STEEL-CUT OATS

Tried and true, this quintessential recipe is your opportunity to stay on track with a balanced breakfast, even on the most hectic morning. You can prepare a large batch of oatmeal, let it cool, and keep it refrigerated in an airtight container for up to five days. Reheat the individual servings as needed, and add your favorite seasonal fruits, nuts, and yogurt toppings.

Find your preferred texture: at Miraval, we cook less for a slightly more toothsome texture, although you might prefer to cook it longer for softer, milkier grains.

MAKES 3¼ CUPS; SERVING SIZE: ½ CUP

1 c. steel-cut oats

1 3-inch cinnamon stick

3½ c. water

⅛ tsp. kosher salt

PLACE in a medium saucepan over medium heat and dry roast until the oats begin to turn light golden brown, about 3 minutes. Add the cinnamon stick and continue toasting, shaking the pan occasionally, until fragrant, 2 to 3 minutes. Add the water and salt, and bring to a boil. Lower the heat and cook at a medium simmer, stirring occasionally until starting to thicken, about 15 minutes. Lower the heat and cook at a low simmer, stirring occasionally, to desired doneness, 15 to 25 minutes.

SERVE immediately.

CALORIES: 80; TOTAL FAT: 1.5 G; CARBOHYDRATE: 15 G; DIETARY FIBER: 2 G; PROTEIN: 3 G

BAKED GOODS

MIRAVAL MULTIGRAIN NUTRITION BAR

Nutritional note from Junelle Lupiani: "This bar is a perfect mid-afternoon snack to bring with you to work or for your children." The oats and cereal provide whole-grain goodness, and the nuts and seeds provide plant protein and fat. Flaxseed meal is included here for its nutritional punch, but it's optional.

MAKES 30 BARS

2 c. rolled oats

¼ c. sesame seeds

2 Tbsp. almonds, chopped

1 Tbsp. cashews, chopped

1 Tbsp. flaxseed meal, optional

½ c. water

½ c. 7-grain cereal

¾ c. creamy organic peanut butter

½ c. honey

1 c. mixed dried fruit (raisins, cranberries, cherries, apricots), cut into ½-inch pieces if large

Pinch kosher salt

PREHEAT the oven to 350° F. Lightly grease an 8" by 8" baking sheet or cake pan with vegetable cooking spray and set aside.

SPREAD the oats, seeds, nuts, and flaxseed meal on a sheet pan and bake until very light golden brown and fragrant, 10 to 12 minutes. Transfer to a large bowl.

BRING the water to a boil in a medium saucepan. Remove from the heat and add the 7-grain cereal; set aside until the water is absorbed, 2 minutes. Add the peanut butter and honey, stir well, and place over medium-low heat. Cook, stirring constantly, until the mixture is thick and glossy and pulls away from the sides of the pan, 1½ to 2 minutes.

SPOON the fruit and salt into the hot peanut-butter mixture and immediately pour into the bowl with the grains. With a large rubber spatula, work the peanut butter–fruit mixture into the grains until evenly coated. (The mixture will become very sticky; it may be necessary to work the mixture with your hands.)

TRANSFER the mixture to the prepared pan, working it out to the edges with your fingers and pressing to a uniform ½-inch thickness. Refrigerate until firm, at least 2 hours.

CUT the cooled cake into bars measuring 1½" by 1¼" and serve immediately, or wrap individually in plastic wrap. (The bars will keep at room temperature for up to two days, and refrigerated for up to four days.)

CALORIES: 110; TOTAL FAT: 4.5 G; CARBOHYDRATE: 14 G; DIETARY FIBER: 2 G; PROTEIN: 3 G

PUMPKIN CORNMEAL BREAD

MAKES 2 LOAVES

1 c. warm water, not above 110° F

4½ tsp. active dry yeast

⅛ tsp. sugar

1 c. buttermilk, at room temperature

5 Tbsp. canola oil or vegetable oil

⅓ c. light molasses

½ c. canned pumpkin puree

5 c. all-purpose flour, plus more as needed for working the dough

1½ c. yellow cornmeal, plus more for the baking sheet

1 Tbsp. kosher salt

COMBINE the water, yeast, and sugar in the bowl of an electric mixer with a dough-hook attachment and let sit until the yeast blooms and becomes foamy, 5 minutes. Add the buttermilk, oil, molasses, and pumpkin puree; and mix on low speed until combined, 1 minute.

ADD the flour, cornmeal, and salt and mix on low speed until the dough comes together in a ball and has a smooth, silken texture, 7 to 10 minutes. (Note: Depending upon kitchen temperature and humidity, the dough may become sticky and require extra flour during the kneading process. Add additional flour as needed, ¼ tsp. at a time, until the dough no longer sticks to the sides of the bowl. Alternatively, this dough can be made by hand; the time required to work the dough will be doubled.)

LIGHTLY coat the inside of a medium bowl with cooking spray. Transfer the dough to the bowl, cover with plastic wrap, and set aside in a warm place until doubled in size, 1½ hours.

TURN the dough out onto a work surface, and with a sharp knife, cut into 2 equal portions. Roll each portion into a large ball and dust the tops lightly with flour.

COVER a large baking sheet with parchment paper and lightly dust with cornmeal. Transfer the dough to the baking sheet, cover loosely with plastic wrap, and let rise until almost doubled in size and spongy to the touch, 45 minutes.

PREHEAT the oven to 350° F.

CUT slits in the top of each loaf and bake until it's cooked through and makes a hollow sound when tapped on the bottom, 50 to 55 minutes; turn the racks 180 degrees halfway through the cooking time.

REMOVE from the oven. Transfer the loaves to a wire rack, and let cool for 1 hour before serving.

CALORIES PER SLICE: 60; TOTAL FAT: 1 G; CARBOHYDRATE: 10 G; DIETARY FIBER: 0 G; PROTEIN: 1 G

STRAWBERRY CRUNCH BAR

MAKES 2 LOAVES

2 c. all-purpose flour

2 c. rolled oats

1¼ c. light brown sugar

2 tsp. ground cinnamon

4 Tbsp. unsalted butter, melted

½ c. unsweetened applesauce

⅔ c. strawberry jam or preserves

PREHEAT the oven to 350° F. Line an 8" by 8" baking sheet or cake pan with parchment paper, lightly grease with vegetable cooking spray, and set aside.

COMBINE the flour, oats, sugar, and cinnamon in a large bowl and stir well. Add the butter and applesauce, and mix until slightly wet crumbs form.

PRESS two-thirds of the oats mixture into the prepared pan, pressing to a uniform half-inch thickness. Spread the jam over the top of the layer, using a small offset spatula or the back of a spoon to evenly spread onto the oats. Crumble the remaining oats mixture over the jam to form a uniform thickness. Bake until the top is golden brown, 30 minutes.

REMOVE from the oven and place on a wire rack to cool completely before cutting.

CUT the cooled cake into bars measuring 1½" by 1¼" and serve immediately, or wrap individually in plastic wrap. (The bars will keep at room temperature for up to two days, and refrigerated for up to four days.)

CALORIES: 120; TOTAL FAT: 2 G; CARBOHYDRATE: 24 G; DIETARY FIBER: 1 G; PROTEIN: 2 G

TEFF BANANA BREAD

A delightful option for a mid-morning snack or brunch, our Teff Banana Bread is also gluten-free and dairy-free. We slice ours with a serrated knife, first lengthwise down the middle and then across into 12 slices, for a total of 24 one-ounce servings per loaf.

MAKES ONE 9-INCH LOAF

3 large very ripe bananas, peeled and broken into pieces

½ c. canola oil or vegetable oil

1 c. sugar

2 large eggs

1 tsp. pure vanilla extract

¼ c. teff flour

⅓ c. rice flour

¼ c. plus 1 Tbsp. tapioca flour

¼ c. potato starch

½ tsp. xanthan gum

1 tsp. baking soda

PREHEAT the oven to 350° F. Lightly grease a 9" by 4" loaf pan with nonstick cooking spray.

IN the bowl of a standing mixer fitted with a paddle attachment or with an electric mixer, puree the bananas on medium speed. Add the oil and blend on low speed for 30 seconds. Add the sugar and blend on medium speed until well combined, 1 minute. Add the eggs and vanilla extract and blend on medium speed for 1 minute.

STIR together the remaining ingredients in a large bowl. Add the wet ingredients to the dry ingredients, working the batter with a large whisk to combine and make a slightly elastic batter, 3 minutes.

POUR the batter into the prepared pan and bake until the cake pulls away from the sides of the pan and a tester inserted into the center comes out clean, about 55 minutes.

LET the bread cool in the pan for 15 minutes, and then turn out onto a wire rack to finish cooling before slicing. Serve warm or at room temperature.

CALORIES PER SLICE: 110; TOTAL FAT: 5 G; CARBOHYDRATE: 16 G; DIETARY FIBER: 1 G; PROTEIN: 1 G

VEGAN WHOLE-WHEAT MUFFINS

Add a half cup of fresh blueberries or dried fruit, such as raisins or cranberries, to these beautifully textured muffins for a burst of sweetness and color. If you aren't on a vegan diet, one large egg can be substituted for the flaxseed and water mixture, buttermilk for the soy milk, honey for the agave syrup, and butter for canola oil.

MAKES 24 MINI-MUFFINS, OR 12 REGULAR-SIZE MUFFINS

2 Tbsp. water

1 Tbsp. flaxseed meal

1 c. rolled oats

1 c. whole-wheat flour

⅓ c. light brown sugar

1½ tsp. baking powder

1 tsp. baking soda

½ tsp. kosher salt

¼ tsp. ground cinnamon

1¼ c. soy milk

¼ c. canola oil or mashed ripened bananas

¼ c. agave syrup (see Source Guide)

½ c. fresh blueberries or dried fruit, optional

PREHEAT the oven to 350° F. Lightly spray one 24-cup 1-ounce muffin tin (or one 12-cup 2-ounce muffin tin) with nonstick cooking spray and set aside.

PLACE the water and flaxseed meal in a medium bowl and stir to combine. Let rest for 5 minutes until thick.

COMBINE the oats, flour, sugar, baking powder, baking soda, salt, and cinnamon in a large bowl and stir with a whisk to break up the sugar and mix the ingredients.

ADD milk, oil, and agave syrup to the flaxseed mixture and stir well. Add the wet ingredients to the dry ingredients and stir well to combine. Stir in berries, if desired.

DIVIDE the batter among the prepared muffin tin cups and bake until risen, golden brown, and pulled away from the sides of the pan, 12 to 14 minutes for small muffins, and 18 to 19 minutes for regular muffins.

REMOVE from the oven and let cool in the muffin tins for 10 minutes. Serve warm or at room temperature.

(The cooled muffins can be stored in an airtight container at room temperature for up to 3 days, and refrigerated for up to 7 days.)

CALORIES: 80; TOTAL FAT: 3 G; CARBOHYDRATE: 13 G; DIETARY FIBER: 1 G; PROTEIN: 2 G

WHOLE-WHEAT CHALLAH

MAKES 1 LOAF

1 c. warm water, not to exceed 110°F

5 tsp. active dry yeast

½ c. plus ⅛ tsp. granulated sugar

4 large eggs

¼ c. melted unsalted butter

¼ c. canola oil or vegetable oil

1½ c. whole-wheat flour

3½ c. all-purpose flour, plus as needed

2 tsp. salt

2 Tbsp. nonfat milk

1½ tsp. white sesame seeds

COVER a large baking sheet with a silicone baking mat or parchment paper and set aside.

COMBINE the water, yeast, and ⅛ tsp. of the sugar in the bowl of an electric mixer fitted with a dough hook and let sit until the yeast blooms and becomes foamy, 5 minutes.

ADD 3 of the eggs, the butter, and canola oil and mix on low speed for 30 seconds. Add the whole-wheat and all-purpose flours, the remaining ½ cup sugar, and the salt and mix on low speed until the dough comes together in a ball and has a smooth, silken texture, 7 to 10 minutes. (Note: Depending upon kitchen temperature and humidity, the dough may become sticky and require extra flour during the kneading process. Add additional all-purpose flour ¼ tsp. at a time until the dough no longer sticks to the sides of the bowl.)

LIGHTLY coat the inside of a medium bowl with cooking spray. Transfer the dough to the bowl, cover with plastic wrap, and set aside in a warm place until doubled in size, 1 to 1½ hours.

TURN the dough out onto a lightly floured work surface and with a sharp knife, cut into 3 equal portions. Roll each portion into a 12-inch strip.

LAY the strips side by side on the prepared baking sheet, and braid together. Lightly spray the top of the dough with nonstick cooking spray and cover with a clean kitchen cloth or plastic wrap. Let rise in a warm place until nearly doubled in size and spongy to the touch, 45 minutes to 1 hour.

PREHEAT the oven to 350°F.

BEAT the remaining egg and the nonfat milk in a small bowl to make an egg wash. Using a pastry brush, cover the top and sides of the bread with the egg wash and sprinkle the top and sides lightly with the sesame seeds. Bake until the bread is baked through and makes a hollow sound when tapped on the bottom, about 40 to 45 minutes.

REMOVE from the oven and cool the bread on a wire rack for 1 hour before serving. Serve warm or at room temperature.

CALORIES PER SLICE: 70; TOTAL FAT: 2.5 G; CARBOHYDRATE: 11 G; DIETARY FIBER: 1 G; PROTEIN: 2 G

APPETIZERS

ASIAN PORK LETTUCE CUPS

MAKES 4 SERVINGS

¼ tsp. Miraval Oil Blend
(page 19) or canola oil

¼ tsp. sesame oil

½ tsp. garlic, minced

½ tsp. ginger, minced

1 c. ground pork (boneless
loin, tenderloin, or butt)

1 c. red onion, minced

6 Tbsp. Anaheim chili peppers,
seeded and minced

1½ c. Asian Sauce (page 122)

12 large Bibb lettuce leaves, rinsed
clean and spun or shaken dry

¼ c. cucumbers, peeled, seeded,
and finely chopped

2 Tbsp. fresh mint leaves, thinly sliced

1 c. carrots, peeled and thinly sliced

1 c. daikon radish, peeled and
thinly sliced

HEAT the oils in a medium-heavy skillet over medium heat. Add the garlic and ginger and cook, stirring for 20 seconds. Add the pork and cook, stirring until evenly browned, 4 minutes. Add the onion and chili peppers and cook, stirring for 15 seconds. Add ½ cup of the Asian Sauce, increase the heat to high, and cook, stirring until the liquid is reduced by half, 3 to 4 minutes.

REMOVE from the heat.

ARRANGE three lettuce leaves on each of the four large plates. Spoon a heaping ¼ cup of the meat mixture onto the center of each leaf and top with 1 tsp. of the cucumber and a pinch of the mint. Arrange ¼ cup of the carrots and ¼ cup of the radishes on the side of each plate.

DIVIDE the remaining cup of Asian Sauce among four decorative ramekins or shallow dishes and place one dish on each plate. Serve immediately.

CALORIES: 130; TOTAL FAT: 3.5 G; CARBOHYDRATE: 11 G; DIETARY FIBER: 3 G; PROTEIN: 15 G

BLUE-CORN CRAB CAKES WITH AVOCADO-CORN SALSA

MAKES 8 CRAB CAKES, OR 4 SERVINGS

1¾ tsp. Miraval Oil Blend
(page 19) or canola oil

3 tsp. chopped yellow onion

4 tsp. chopped green bell pepper

4 tsp. chopped red bell pepper

8 oz. lump crabmeat, picked
over for shell and cartilage

2 large egg whites

2 Tbsp. plus 1 tsp. Dijon mustard

1½ Tbsp. prepared horseradish

2 tsp. Worcestershire sauce

¾ tsp. garlic powder

¾ tsp. baking powder

¼ tsp. Tabasco sauce, or other
hot red-pepper sauce

Pinch kosher salt

¾ c. panko bread crumbs

2 Tbsp. blue cornmeal

Avocado-Corn Salsa (recipe follows)

PREHEAT the oven to 400° F.

HEAT ¼ tsp. of the oil in a small skillet over medium-high heat. Add the onion and bell peppers, and cook, stirring until fragrant and soft, 2 minutes. Spread onto a plate to cool while assembling the other ingredients.

COMBINE the remaining ingredients except the oil, panko, salsa, and blue cornmeal in a large bowl, and fold together gently so as to not break up the lumps of crabmeat. Add the onions, peppers, and panko; and fold just to incorporate. Divide in eight portions and form the crab cakes.

SPREAD the cornmeal on a clean plate. One at a time, place the cakes in the meal, turning to lightly coat on both sides. Place the cakes on a clean plate until ready to cook. (The crab cakes can be assembled up to this point, covered with plastic wrap, and kept refrigerated for up to four hours.)

HEAT a medium skillet over medium-high heat. Add ¾ tsp. of the oil and four of the crab cakes, and lower the heat to medium. Cook until the crab cakes are golden brown, 2 minutes. Turn and cook for 1½ minutes and transfer to a baking sheet or baking dish.

HEAT the remaining ¾ tsp. of oil in the skillet over medium-high heat. Add the remaining four crab cakes, lower the heat, and cook the same way as the first batch. Transfer to the baking sheet with the other crab cakes and bake until cooked through and hot, 5 to 6 minutes.

REMOVE the crab cakes from the oven and place two on each of four plates. Arrange the salsa to the side of the crab cakes and serve immediately.

CALORIES: 240; TOTAL FAT: 8 G; CARBOHYDRATE: 25 G; DIETARY FIBER: 4 G; PROTEIN: 18 G

AVOCADO-CORN SALSA

MAKES 1 CUP; SERVING SIZE: ¼ CUP

¼ tsp. Miraval Oil Blend
(page 19) or canola oil

¼ c. fresh or frozen corn kernels

¾ c. avocado, chopped

1 Tbsp. red onion, minced

2 tsp. fresh lime juice

1 tsp. cilantro, minced

Pinch kosher salt

Pinch freshly ground black pepper

HEAT the oil over medium-high heat in a small skillet. Add the corn and cook, stirring, until starting to turn golden brown, 1½ minutes. Spread the corn on a clean plate to cool.

COMBINE the remaining ingredients and the cooled corn in a small bowl and mix well.

SERVE immediately. (The salsa can be made up to four hours in advance, tightly covered, and kept refrigerated until ready to serve.)

SEARED DIVER SCALLOPS WITH ROASTED CORN AND POBLANO CHILI RELISH

MAKES 4 ONE-SCALLOP SERVINGS

2 Tbsp. minced poblano pepper

2 tsp. Miraval Oil Blend
(page 19) or canola oil

¼ c. fresh corn kernels

2 Tbsp. red onion, minced

½ c. jicama, finely chopped

2 Tbsp. red bell peppers, finely chopped

2 Tbsp. fresh cilantro, chopped

4 large scallops, about 2
oz. each, wiped dry

Pinch kosher salt

Pinch freshly ground black pepper

2 tsp. prickly pear syrup
(see Source Guide)

HEAT a small skillet over medium-high heat. Add the poblano peppers and cook, stirring, until they start to make a popping noise and jump across the bottom of the pan, 1½ to 2 minutes. Add 1 tsp. of the oil and the corn; stir and cook until the corn starts to wilt, 45 seconds to 1 minute. Add the red onion and cook for 45 seconds, stirring occasionally. Add the jicama and bell peppers and cook, stirring for 1 minute. Add the cilantro, stir well, and remove from the heat.

SEASON the scallops lightly on both sides with the salt and pepper.

HEAT a clean medium skillet over high heat until very hot. Add the remaining 1 tsp. oil and swirl to coat the bottom of the pan. Add the scallops and cook until well seared, 1½ to 2 minutes. Turn the scallops and cook until seared and nearly cooked through, 1½ to 2 minutes.

TRANSFER the scallops to four medium plates. Spoon about 1 tsp. of the corn relish on top of each scallop and 2 Tbsp. of the relish around the sides. Drizzle ½ tsp. of the prickly pear syrup around the edge of each plate and serve immediately.

CALORIES: 80; TOTAL FAT: 3 G; CARBOHYDRATE: 6 G; DIETARY FIBER: 1 G; PROTEIN: 7 G

DIVER SCALLOPS WITH
FLAT-LEAF PARSLEY PUREE

MAKES ½ CUP

1 tsp. Miraval Oil Blend
(page 19) or canola oil

4 large fresh scallops, about
2 oz. each, wiped dry

Pinch of kosher salt

Pinch of freshly ground black pepper

½ c. Parsley Puree (recipe follows)

1 c. microgreens

2 tsp. truffle oil

SEASON the scallops lightly on both sides with the salt and pepper.

HEAT a clean medium skillet over high heat until very hot. Add the oil and swirl to coat the bottom of the pan. Add the scallops and cook until well seared, 1½ to 2 minutes. Turn the scallops and cook until seared and nearly cooked through, 1½ to 2 minutes. Remove from the heat.

SPOON 2 Tbsp. of the Parsley Puree into four shallow bowls and top each portion with one scallop. Arrange microgreens on top of scallop and garnish each serving with ½ tsp. of the truffle oil.

SERVE immediately.

CALORIES: 180; TOTAL FAT: 8 G; CARBOHYDRATE: 18 G; DIETARY FIBER: 1 G; PROTEIN: 10 G

PARSLEY PUREE

MAKES ½ CUP

2 bunches flat-leaf parsley

¼ c. Miraval "Monte au Beurre"
(recipe is on the next page)

BRING a medium pot of water to a boil. Add the parsley and cook for 20 seconds. Quickly remove using tongs or a slotted spoon, and place in an ice bath to stop the cooking process.

PLACE the leaves and top one inch of the stems in the bowl of a blender, and puree to a smooth paste on high speed.

TRANSFER the mixture to a small saucepan with the Miraval "Monte au Buerre" sauce and cook, stirring, over medium-low heat until thick and creamy.

REMOVE from the heat and cover to keep warm until ready to serve.

MIRAVAL "MONTE AU BUERRE"

MAKES 2 CUPS; SERVING SIZE: 2 TBSP.

This mixture is our take on the traditional thickening agent used in French cooking. It will keep up to five days refrigerated, and can be used to finish and thicken all manner of sauces, including demi-glaces and traditionally cream-based sauces, like the saffron sauce on our black-cod dish.

¼ c. raw almonds or cashews   1 qt. rice milk

PREHEAT oven to 350° F.

PLACE the nuts in a small dish and bake until fragrant and lightly toasted, 5 minutes. Remove from the oven.

COMBINE the nuts and rice milk in a medium saucepan, and bring to a low boil over medium-high heat. Cook until the milk is reduced by half in volume, about 25 minutes.

TRANSFER the mixture to the bowl of a blender or food processor, and process on high speed until smooth, 30 seconds.

SET aside until ready to use. (The sauce can be kept refrigerated in an airtight container for up to three days.)

TAMARIND MARINATED BEEF SATAY
WITH SPICY PEANUT SAUCE

Either use thin metal or bamboo skewers, six to eight inches long, to cook the satay. Soak the wooden ones in water for 30 minutes before using to prevent them from splintering or igniting on the grill or under the broiler. If you are not a beef eater, substitute thinly sliced chicken breasts or large peeled shrimp for the beef, and adjust the cooking time accordingly.

MAKES 4 SERVINGS

12 oz. beef sirloin, cut into one-ounce strips, about two inches long and one inch wide

1 recipe Tamarind Marinade (recipe follows)

¼ c. Spicy Peanut Sauce (page 127)

4 sprigs fresh mint, optional garnish

PLACE the beef strips in the marinade, stirring with a spoon to evenly coat the meat. Cover and refrigerate for 30 minutes to 1 hour.

PREHEAT a grill or broiler to high heat.

REMOVE the beef from the marinade, and one at a time, thread onto 12 metal or bamboo skewers.

IN batches, cook the satays on the grill (or on a broiler pan under the broiler) until medium rare, 1 to 2 minutes per side, watching carefully and turning so the meat does not burn.

TO serve, spoon 1 Tbsp. of the peanut sauce into the center of each of four plates and arrange three skewers on each plate next to the sauce. Garnish each plate with one mint sprig and serve immediately.

CALORIES: 190; TOTAL FAT: 7 G; CARBOHYDRATE: 6 G; DIETARY FIBER: 0 G; PROTEIN: 25 G

TAMARIND MARINADE

MAKES 1 CUP

1⅔ Tbsp. tamarind pulp

¼ c. dark-brown sugar

3 Tbsp. shallots, chopped

2 Tbsp. garlic, chopped

2 Tbsp. fresh ginger, chopped

1 Tbsp. low-sodium soy sauce or tamari

2 tsp. canola oil

1 tsp. kosher salt

1 tsp. crushed red pepper

¼ tsp. ground turmeric

⅛ tsp. ground coriander

COMBINE the tamarind pulp and 3 Tbsp. warm water in a medium bowl and whisk to combine. Add the remaining ingredients and whisk until smooth.

USE a directed as a marinade for beef or chicken.

MUSSELS WITH WINE, TOMATOES, AND HERBS

MAKES 4 SERVINGS

¼ tsp. Miraval Oil Blend
(page 19) or canola oil

3 Tbsp. shallots, minced

2 tsp. garlic, minced

1 four-ounce portobello mushroom,
wiped clean, stemmed, gills removed,
and chopped

2 c. cherry tomatoes, halved

12 black mussels, scrubbed and bearded

1 tsp. fresh oregano, minced

1 tsp. fresh parsley, minced

1 tsp. fresh thyme, minced

2 c. dry white wine

2 tsp. unsalted butter

½ tsp. kosher salt

¼ tsp. freshly ground black pepper

1 recipe Toasted Pita Chips (page 222)

SUBMERGE mussels in clean, cold water for 20 minutes after bearding and scrubbing so that they will spit out any sand within.

HEAT a large skillet or sauté pan over high heat. Add the oil, shallots, and garlic, and cook, stirring, until fragrant and the shallots start to turn golden brown, 1½ minutes. Add the mushroom and cook, stirring, until it starts to give off its liquid, 2 minutes. Add the tomatoes, stir, and cook for 15 seconds.

ADD the mussels, shake the pan well, and cook until they start to open, 20 to 30 seconds. Add the herbs, stir well to incorporate, and cook for 10 seconds. Add the wine, stir well, and bring to a boil. Add the butter, stir to incorporate, reduce the heat to medium, and cook uncovered until the mussels open and the liquid is reduced by one-quarter in volume, 2½ to 3½ minutes.

REMOVE the pan from the heat. Season the mussels with the salt and pepper and stir well.

DIVIDE the mussels and the wine and tomato sauce between four large soup bowls. Serve immediately with Toasted Pita Chips.

CALORIES: 140; TOTAL FAT: 2.5 G; CARBOHYDRATE: 9 G; DIETARY FIBER: 1 G; PROTEIN: 2 G

SAMBAL WILTED GREENS

Prepared with water spinach instead of bok choy at cafés throughout Vietnam, this dish is loved by our guests, even those who don't typically like spicy foods. For timid palates, add more thickened vegetable stock for a milder flavor. The thickened stock also reduces the amount of sesame oil needed.

MAKES 4 HALF-CUP SERVINGS

¼ c. Thickened Vegetable Stock (page 24)

2 Tbsp. sambal red chili garlic sauce

1 Tbsp. green onion, thinly sliced on the bias

1 Tbsp. low-sodium soy sauce

2 tsp. garlic, very finely sliced

1½ tsp. fresh lemon juice

1 tsp. sesame oil

1 tsp. sugar

¼ tsp. Miraval Oil Blend (page 19) or canola oil

6 oz. baby bok choy, cored and roughly chopped

5 large black-kale leaves, cored and roughly chopped

2 Tbsp. Vegetable Stock (page 24) or water

COMBINE the thickened stock, chili sauce, green onion, soy sauce, garlic, lemon juice, sesame oil, and sugar in a medium bowl and whisk well to combine.

HEAT a large heavy skillet or wok over high heat. Add the Miraval Oil Blend and swirl to coat the bottom of the pan. Add the bok choy and kale and cook, stirring, until slightly wilted, 1½ minutes. Add the sauce and cook, stirring, for 30 seconds. Add the vegetable stock and cook, stirring, for 15 seconds.

REMOVE from the heat and divide the stir-fry among four plates. Serve immediately as an appetizer or side dish.

CALORIES: 35; TOTAL FAT: 1.5 G; CARBOHYDRATE: 5 G; DIETARY FIBER: 1 G; PROTEIN: 2 G

Shrimp and Mango Ceviche

SHRIMP AND MANGO CEVICHE

½ c. fresh mango, chopped and peeled

½ c. fresh lime juice

1 Tbsp. red onion, minced

1 Tbsp. red bell pepper, minced

1 Tbsp. fresh cilantro, chopped

2 tsp. garlic, minced

1½ tsp. jalapeño, minced

1 tsp. hot red-pepper sauce, such as Cholula Hot Sauce

⅛ tsp. kosher salt

8 oz. shrimp, peeled, deveined, and cut into quarter-inch pieces

COMBINE all of the ingredients except the shrimp in a medium nonreactive bowl, and stir well.

ADD the shrimp and toss to coat with the marinade. Cover and refrigerate, stirring every 30 minutes, until the shrimp is opaque in color, 45 to 90 minutes.

ARRANGE the ceviche in a decorative bowl or martini glass and serve chilled.

CALORIES: 60; TOTAL FAT: 0.5 G; CARBOHYDRATE: 6 G; DIETARY FIBER: 0 G; PROTEIN: 8 G

GRILLED VEGETABLE BRUSCHETTA

Come together with your loved ones and enjoy our take on this Italian staple. We serve bruschetta with grilled, in-season vegetables, choosing the most vibrant as the toppings to obtain the highest nutritive value and freshest flavor.

8 ½-inch thick diagonal slices French or Italian bread

1 tsp. Miraval Oil Blend (page 19)

½ recipe Grilled Vegetables (page 140)

PREHEAT a grill to high heat. (Alternatively, preheat the broiler.)

LIGHTLY coat both sides of the bread with the oil and grill or broil, turning once, until light golden brown.

LET the bread cool slightly before topping with the grilled vegetables. Serve at room temperature.

CALORIES: 70; TOTAL FAT: 1 G; CARBOHYDRATE: 13 G; DIETARY FIBER: 1 G; PROTEIN: 2 G

SPA FALAFEL

Our secret to making falafel patties turn out just right is a batter that is neither too wet nor too dry. And because these falafels are not deep-fried, we maintain their creamy texture and ensure that the garbanzo and lemon flavors shine.

MAKES 6 SERVINGS

2 c. canned garbanzo beans, rinsed and drained

3 Tbsp. fresh lemon juice

2 Tbsp. boxed falafel mix

1 Tbsp. tahini

½ tsp. ground cumin

¾ tsp. Miraval Oil Blend (page 19)

¾ c. Lime Raita (page 126)

COMBINE beans, lemon juice, falafel mix, tahini, and cumin in the bowl of a food processor and process until smooth, scraping down the sides of the bowl as needed.

DIVIDE the batter into 12 portions using a 2-ounce scoop, and flatten slightly into half-inch thick patties.

HEAT the oil in a medium skillet over high heat. Add the falafel patties, lower the heat to medium-high, and cook until golden brown and firm, 2½ to 3 minutes. Turn and cook until golden brown on the second side and cooked all the way through, 3 minutes.

ARRANGE two patties on each of six small plates and spoon 2 Tbsp. of the Lime Raita on each plate. Serve immediately.

CALORIES: 290; TOTAL FAT: 6 G; CARBOHYDRATE: 46 G; DIETARY FIBER: 12 G; PROTEIN: 15 G

SOUPS

BUTTERNUT SQUASH SOUP

Miraval's approach to the classic Butternut Squash Soup channels the warmth and essence of autumn. We incorporate reduced cinnamon-infused rice milk to balance the butternut squash, which adds a completely different dimension of flavor to the dish.

Please note: Soups pureed in a blender have a richer texture. While the butternut squash mixture can be pureed with a food processor or stick blender, the texture and yield will be different from that made in a blender.

Always be careful when blending hot liquids. Do not fill the blender container more than halfway full, and hold down the top with a kitchen towel as you turn on the machine. These safeguards prevent the lid from blowing off and hot liquids flying, which can result in dangerous burns.

MAKES 6 CUPS; SERVING SIZE: ½ CUP

¼ tsp. Miraval Oil Blend (page 19) or vegetable oil

1 c. chopped yellow onion

1 c. chopped celery

½ tsp. chopped garlic

5 c. peeled, one-inch cubes butternut squash

¼ tsp. ground nutmeg

1 bay leaf

½ tsp. kosher salt

⅛ tsp. freshly ground black pepper

5 c. Vegetable Stock (page 24) or canned vegetable broth

1½ c. rice milk

2 whole cinnamon sticks

HEAT a large saucepan over medium-high heat. Add the oil and swirl to coat the bottom of the pan. Add the onion and celery and cook, stirring, for 2 minutes. Add the garlic and cook, stirring, for 1 minute. Add the squash, nutmeg, bay leaf, and salt and pepper; cook until the squash starts to turn brown, 3 to 4 minutes. Add the stock and bring to a boil. Reduce the heat and cook until the squash is fork tender, about 20 minutes.

IN a small saucepan, bring the rice milk and cinnamon sticks to a boil. Reduce the heat and cook, whisking occasionally, until light caramel in color and reduced to ¼ cup in volume, 18 to 20 minutes. Remove the cinnamon sticks and cool completely.

IN batches, transfer the butternut squash mixture to a blender and puree on high speed until smooth. Transfer to a clean container, stir, and cover to keep warm until ready to serve.

TO serve, ladle half-cup portions into small soup bowls. Decoratively drizzle 1 tsp. of the rice milk into the center of each serving and serve immediately.

CALORIES: 50; TOTAL FAT: 0 G; CARBOHYDRATE: 12 G; DIETARY FIBER: 1 G; PROTEIN: 1 G

CUCUMBER-AVOCADO SOUP

This is a refreshing summer soup that can easily be doubled for an impressive garden-party starter. We recommend serving this soup in small coffee cups or teacups.

MAKES 5 CUPS; SERVING SIZE: ½ CUP

2 c. fat-free plain yogurt

1 c. Vegetable Stock (page 24) or canned vegetable broth

¾ c. chopped, peeled, and seeded cucumber

½ c. chopped avocado

1 Tbsp. chopped fresh cilantro

¾ tsp. minced garlic

⅛ tsp. kosher salt

⅛ tsp. ground white pepper

3½ Tbsp. minced peeled and seeded cucumber, for garnish

COMBINE all of the ingredients except the minced cucumber in the bowl of a blender and process until smooth.

TRANSFER to an airtight container and refrigerate until ready to serve, or up to 12 hours.

TO serve, pour half cup of the soup into individual small serving bowls or decorative cups, and garnish each serving with 1 tsp. of the minced cucumber.

CALORIES: 35; TOTAL FAT: 1 G; CARBOHYDRATE: 4 G; DIETARY FIBER: 0 G; PROTEIN: 3 G

EGG DROP SOUP

MAKES 6 CUPS; SERVING SIZE: ½ CUP

¼ tsp. Miraval Oil Blend (page 19) or vegetable oil

½ c. green onions

3 Tbsp. chopped and peeled lemongrass

1½ Tbsp. chopped and peeled ginger

1 Tbsp. chopped garlic

1 Tbsp. seeded and minced jalapeño

6 c. Chicken Stock (page 20) or canned low-sodium chicken broth

3 Tbsp. low-sodium soy sauce

¼ c. cornstarch or arrowroot

¼ c. water

4 large egg whites

1 large egg

¼ tsp. sesame oil

HEAT a large saucepan over medium-high heat. Add the oil and onions and cook, stirring for 2 minutes. Add the lemongrass, ginger, and garlic; and cook, stirring until aromatic, 1 minute. Add the jalapeño and cook, stirring for 45 seconds. Add the chicken stock and soy sauce, and bring to a boil. Reduce the heat to low and simmer until very aromatic, 10 minutes, skimming the surface from time to time to remove any foam that might form on the surface.

REMOVE the pan from the heat and carefully strain through a fine mesh strainer into a clean pot.

COMBINE the cornstarch and water in a small ramekin and stir to make a slurry.

PLACE the pot over high heat and when the soup comes to a boil, whisk in the slurry, and boil for 2 minutes. Reduce the heat to medium-low and simmer until glossy, 5 minutes.

BEAT together the egg whites, whole egg, and sesame oil in a medium bowl.

RETURN the soup to the boil and whisk aggressively to create a whirlpool in the center of the liquid. Slowly dribble the beaten egg mixture into the center of the whirlpool, and cook until the eggs form long ribbons, 5 seconds.

REMOVE the pot from the heat and serve immediately.

CALORIES: 80; TOTAL FAT: 2.5 G; CARBOHYDRATE: 9 G; DIETARY FIBER: 0 G; PROTEIN: 4 G

GREEN CHILI POSOLE

The ultimate expression of Southwestern flavors, this stew finds its way onto the Miraval menu frequently, regardless of the time of year. While we recommend fresh poblano chilies, you can easily substitute canned green chilies that have been rinsed, adding them at the same time as the stock. Canned tomatillos can also be substituted for fresh ones. Be sure to wash fresh tomatillos carefully after husking to rinse off their sticky resin.

MAKES 6 CUPS; SERVING SIZE: ½ CUP

2 Tbsp. Miraval Oil Blend
(page 19) or vegetable oil

1 c. chopped yellow onions

½ c. chopped celery

¼ c. chopped garlic

1 c. chopped poblano pepper

1 lb. lean boneless pork
loin, cut into ¾" cubes

1½ c. chopped fresh tomatillo, or canned

1 c. canned hominy, rinsed
well and drained

¼ c. chopped fresh cilantro

4 tsp. chili powder

4 tsp. ground cumin

1 tsp. kosher salt

½ tsp. freshly ground black pepper

6 c. Chicken Stock (page 20) or canned
low-sodium, nonfat chicken broth

¼ c. thinly sliced red cabbage, garnish

3 tsp. crumbled Cotija, feta, or
Parmesan cheese, for garnish

1½ tsp. finely grated fresh
lime zest, for garnish

HEAT a large saucepan over high heat. Add 1 Tbsp. of the oil and swirl to coat the bottom of pan. Lower the heat to medium-high, add the onions, and cook, stirring for 1 minute. Add the celery, stir, and cook for 45 seconds. Add the garlic and cook, stirring for 45 seconds. Add the pepper and cook, stirring for 1 minute.

ADD the remaining 1 Tbsp. of oil and stir well. Add the pork and cook, stirring to sear on all sides, about 3 minutes. Add the tomatillo, hominy, 2 Tbsp. of the cilantro, the chili powder, cumin, salt, and pepper; stir well and cook for 1 minute. Add the stock, stirring to scrape any bits from the bottom of the pan. Increase the heat and bring to a high simmer. Reduce the heat to medium-low and simmer until the meat is tender and cooked through, 40 minutes.

REMOVE from the heat and stir in the remaining 2 Tbsp. cilantro. Divide the stew among 12 serving bowls (half cup per serving). Garnish each portion with 1 tsp. of the cabbage, ¼ tsp. of the cheese, and ⅛ tsp. of the lime zest; and serve immediately.

CALORIES: 190; TOTAL FAT: 5 G; CARBOHYDRATE: 27 G; DIETARY FIBER: 7 G; PROTEIN: 13 G

GAZPACHO

MAKES 1 CUP; SERVING SIZE: ½ CUP

¾ c. low-sodium vegetable
juice, such as V8

5 Tbsp. tomato juice

5 Tbsp. seeded and chopped tomato

¼ c. peeled, seeded, and diced cucumber

2 Tbsp. finely chopped green bell pepper

2 Tbsp. finely chopped red onion

1¾ c. finely chopped fresh cilantro

1½ tsp. finely grated lemon zest

1¼ tsp. extra-virgin olive oil

¼ tsp. minced, seeded jalapeño

¼ tsp. Tabasco sauce

¼ tsp. Worcestershire sauce

⅛ tsp. ground cumin

Pinch kosher salt

Pinch freshly ground black pepper

COMBINE all the ingredients in a large measuring cup and stir well.

COVER and chill until ready to serve. (The soup can be made up to one day in advance and kept refrigerated.)

CALORIES: 50; TOTAL FAT: 3 G; CARBOHYDRATE: 5 G; DIETARY FIBER: 3 G; PROTEIN: 1 G

LENTIL SOUP

There's nothing quite as satisfying as a warm bowl of lentil soup. Cooking times for lentils can vary drastically depending upon their age; the longer lentils have been on the shelf, the longer they will take to cook. For bolder, richer flavor, and as a gluten-free alternative to soy sauce or tamari sauce, we recommend Bragg Liquid Aminos—a natural all-purpose seasoning derived from soybeans.

MAKES 6 CUPS; SERVING SIZE: ½ CUP

½ tsp. Miraval Oil Blend (page 19) or vegetable oil

½ c. finely chopped carrots

½ c. finely chopped celery

½ c. finely chopped yellow onion

2 tsp. minced garlic

2 c. green, brown, or red lentils

6 c. Vegetable Stock (page 24) or canned vegetable stock

1 Tbsp. minced fresh oregano

1 Tbsp. minced fresh thyme leaves

2 Tbsp. plus 2 tsp. Bragg Liquid Aminos (see Source Guide)

1 tsp. freshly ground black pepper

HEAT a large saucepan over medium-high heat. Add the oil, carrots, celery, onion, and garlic and cook, stirring until soft, about 3 minutes. Add the lentils and cook, stirring for 20 seconds. Add the stock and bring to a boil. Reduce the heat and simmer for 7 minutes. Add the oregano and thyme, stir well, and continue cooking for an additional 7 minutes. Stir in the liquid aminos and pepper, and continue cooking until the lentils are tender, an additional 15 to 18 minutes.

SERVE immediately.

CALORIES: 60; TOTAL FAT: 0 G; CARBOHYDRATE: 12 G; DIETARY FIBER: 4 G; PROTEIN: 4 G

NAVAJO LAMB STEW WITH TOASTED TORTILLA CHIPS

MAKES 4 SERVINGS

1 tsp. Miraval Oil Blend
(page 19) or canola oil

1 lb. boneless lamb leg or loin,
trimmed and cut into ½-inch cubes

1 Tbsp. ground coriander

1 Tbsp. ground cumin

1 Tbsp. dried oregano

1 Tbsp. smoked paprika

1 Tbsp. red chili powder

1 Tbsp. dried thyme

1 Tbsp. kosher salt

1 c. chopped poblano peppers

1 c. fresh or thawed frozen corn kernels

1 c. red grape or cherry tomatoes,
cut in half

½ c. red wine, such as Cabernet
Sauvignon or Merlot

1 c. Red Wine Demi-Glace (page 130)
or canned low-sodium beef broth

2 c. tomato juice

2 c. Vegetable Stock (page 24)

1 six-ounce russet potato, peeled
and cut into half-inch pieces

1 recipe Toasted Tortilla Chips (page 227)

HEAT ½ tsp. of the oil in a medium pot over medium-high heat. Add the meat and sear on all sides, 1 to 2 minutes. Add the seasoning and cook, stirring until fragrant, 45 seconds. Add the poblano peppers and cook, stirring for 30 seconds. Add the corn and tomatoes, and cook, stirring for 2 minutes.

ADD the red wine and cook, stirring to deglaze the bottom of the pan and until the liquid is reduced by half, 1½ minutes. Add the demi-glace, tomato juice, vegetable stock, and potato; stir well and bring to a boil. Reduce the heat and simmer until the meat is tender, the stew is thick, and the liquid is reduced by half, 50 minutes to 1 hour.

SERVE immediately with 1 tortilla chip per bowl.

CALORIES: 360; TOTAL FAT: 9 G; CARBOHYDRATE: 31 G; DIETARY FIBER: 4 G; PROTEIN: 29 G

PEACH-CHAMPAGNE BISQUE

We prefer frozen peaches in this recipe to fresh peaches. Aside from being available in any season, frozen peaches are picked and individually quick-frozen at the height of their freshness and ripeness, which means that they are consistently flavorful. Frozen peaches are also ideal for blended drinks, such as smoothies.

MAKES 4 CUPS; SERVING SIZE: ½ CUP

4 c. frozen, skinless, freestone peaches

1 c. apple juice concentrate, not frozen

½ c. champagne or good-quality sparkling wine

4 fresh blackberries or raspberries

⅛ tsp. Miraval Oil Blend (page 19) or canola oil

¼ tsp. sugar

¼ tsp. chili powder

1 tsp. chiffonade mint

COMBINE the peaches, apple juice, and champagne in a blender and pulse to mix. Blend on high speed until smooth.

TOSS the berries with the oil in a small bowl. Add the sugar and chili powder, and toss to coat the berries.

TO serve, divide the soup among four shallow bowls. Place one berry in the center of each bowl and arrange the mint around the berry. Serve immediately.

CALORIES: 50; TOTAL FAT: 0 G; CARBOHYDRATE: 12 G; DIETARY FIBER: 1 G; PROTEIN: 1 G

SAVORY ONION SOUP

We add interest to this classic by serving the soup in large onions. Our chefs carefully cut the top from the onions and scoop them out, leaving a half-inch outer layer and skin as a shell to hold the soup. When you prepare to serve the soup, nestle the "onion bowls" in oven safe bowls filled with rock salt so they won't tip over when filled.

MAKES 6 CUPS; SERVING SIZE: ½ CUP

1½ tsp. Miraval Oil Blend
(page 19) or canola oil

8 c. thinly sliced yellow onions

4 tsp. whole fresh thyme leaves

½ c. Bragg Liquid Aminos
(see Source Guide)

½ c. brandy

7 c. Vegetable Stock (page 24)
or canned vegetable broth

3 large slices whole-wheat
bread, for garnish

3 Tbsp. thinly sliced roasted red
bell pepper, for garnish

3 Tbsp. thinly sliced roasted
yellow bell pepper, for garnish

3 Tbsp. thinly sliced roasted
poblano pepper, for garnish

12 one-ounce slices of Gruyere,
Swiss, or provolone cheese

HEAT a large saucepan over high heat. Add the oil and when hot, add the onions and stir well. Cook the onions without stirring until they start to brown, about 2 minutes. Stir as the onions brown more to prevent them from sticking to the bottom of the pan. (Leave the onions undisturbed as much as possible during the cooking process in order for them to caramelize.) Cook for an additional 2½ minutes. Add the thyme and cook, stirring occasionally, for 30 seconds. Add the liquid aminos and cook for 30 seconds. Remove the pan from the heat, add the brandy, and very carefully ignite the mixture with a match to burn off the alcohol.

RETURN the pan to the heat, add the vegetable stock, and bring to a boil. Reduce the heat to medium-low and simmer uncovered until savory and slightly thickened, 18 to 20 minutes.

TO make the croutons, toast the bread and let cool slightly. Cut twelve 1-inch rounds with a cookie cutter. (Alternatively, toast the bread, remove the crusts, and cut into quarters.)

TO serve, layer the ingredients into each bowl: ¾ tsp. red bell pepper, ¾ tsp. yellow bell pepper, ¾ tsp. poblano pepper, and ½ cup onion soup. Top with a crouton and slice of cheese. Serve immediately.

CALORIES: 290; TOTAL FAT: 19 G; CARBOHYDRATE: 16 G; DIETARY FIBER: 5 G; PROTEIN: 9 G

SEAFOOD GAZPACHO

Our team prefers the rich, creamy quality of diver scallops for this dish, but plump, fresh bay scallops can easily be used.

MAKES 6 CUPS; SERVING SIZE: 1 CUP

3½ oz. fresh diver scallops, chopped

3½ oz. peeled and deveined shrimp, chopped

1 qt. tomato juice

¼ c. red onion, finely chopped

¼ c. jicama, finely chopped

¼ c. tomatillos, finely chopped

¼ c. green bell pepper, finely chopped

¼ c. celery, finely chopped

2 Tbsp. fresh cilantro, chiffonade

1 Tbsp. extra-virgin olive oil

1 Tbsp. fresh lemon juice

1 Tbsp. red wine vinegar

¾ tsp. chili powder

½ tsp. jalapeño, minced and seeded

¼ tsp. minced garlic

Pinch cayenne

¼ tsp. kosher salt

¼ tsp. freshly ground black pepper

BRING a small pot or pan of water to a boil. Add the scallops and shrimp, and cook until opaque and just cooked through, 1 to 1½ minutes. Immediately drain in a colander, rinse under cold water, and drain well. Place in a bowl, cover, and refrigerate until ready to serve. (The seafood can be cooked in advance, covered tightly, and refrigerated up to 24 hours in advance.)

COMBINE the remaining ingredients in a mixing bowl and stir well. Cover and chill for 2 hours before serving.

TO serve, ladle the soup into six bowls or decorative cups and top with the seafood. Serve immediately.

CALORIES: 45; TOTAL FAT: 1.5 G; CARBOHYDRATE: 5 G; DIETARY FIBER: 1 G; PROTEIN: 3 G

SOUTHWESTERN CHICKEN TORTILLA SOUP

¼ tsp. Miraval Oil Blend
(page 19) or canola oil

¼ c. chopped carrot

¼ c. chopped celery

¼ c. chopped red onion

¼ c. chopped Roasted Red
Bell Pepper (page 18)

2 Tbsp. chopped roasted poblano chili
pepper or canned poblano pepper

1½ tsp. minced garlic

½ c. chopped seeded tomato

1 tsp. ground cumin

1 tsp. chili powder

½ tsp. dried oregano

½ tsp. dried thyme

½ tsp. paprika

½ tsp. kosher salt

⅛ tsp. freshly ground black pepper

Pinch cayenne pepper

1 qt. Chicken Stock (page 20) or
canned low-sodium chicken broth

1 c. chopped, roasted, or
grilled chicken breast

4 tsp. chopped avocado, for garnish

4 tsp. chopped fresh cilantro, for garnish

4 tsp. grated pepper jack or
Cotija cheese, for garnish

4 lime wedges, for garnish

12 Toasted Tortilla Chips
(page 227), for garnish

HEAT a medium pot over medium-high heat. Add the oil and when hot, add the carrot, celery, onion, bell pepper, poblano pepper, and garlic; cook, stirring until soft, 3 minutes. Add the tomato, cumin, chili powder, oregano, thyme, paprika, salt, black pepper, and cayenne; cook, stirring for 1 minute. Add the stock and chicken, stir well, and bring to a boil.

REDUCE the heat and cook until the carrots are tender and the flavors have married, 10 minutes.

TO serve, ladle a half cup of the soup into each of four bowls. Garnish each serving with the avocado, cilantro, cheese, lime wedges, and three tortilla chips. Serve immediately.

CALORIES: 200; TOTAL FAT: 8 G; CARBOHYDRATE: 12 G; DIETARY FIBER: 1 G; PROTEIN: 21 G

TOMATO-HERB SOUP

Our kitchen loves the seasonal versatility of this soup—served warm and savory during autumn and winter, and then chilled and bright as a cool summer soup. To serve cold, simply refrigerate until well chilled and add a pinch more fresh herbs to each portion before serving. This recipe is a delicious opportunity to visit your farmers' market to stock up on fresh herbs, garlic, and tomatoes.

MAKES 1 QUART; SERVING SIZE: 1 CUP

¼ tsp. Miraval Oil Blend (page 19) or canola oil

1 c. chopped yellow onion

¼ c. chopped celery

1 Tbsp. chopped garlic

14 oz. fresh tomatoes, cored and quartered

2 c. canned stewed tomatoes and their juices

2 tsp. chopped fresh basil

1½ tsp. chopped fresh oregano

1½ tsp. chopped fresh thyme

¼ tsp. plus ⅛ tsp. sugar or agave syrup (see Source Guide)

½ tsp. salt

⅛ tsp. freshly ground black pepper

1 c. Vegetable Stock (page 24), canned vegetable broth, or water

½ tsp. low-sodium soy sauce

HEAT the oil in a large pot over medium-high heat. Add the onion, celery, and garlic and cook, stirring until starting to soften, 3 minutes. Add the fresh and canned tomatoes and their juices and cook, stirring for 30 seconds. Reduce the heat to medium, add 1 tsp. of the basil, ½ tsp. of the oregano, ½ tsp. of the thyme, the sugar, salt, and pepper; and stir well. Add the stock, and bring to a boil. Reduce the heat and simmer until the tomatoes are very tender and start to break apart, and the liquid is reduced by about one-quarter in volume, 18 minutes.

TRANSFER to a blender and blend on high speed until smooth. Add the soy sauce and remaining 1 tsp. each of basil, oregano, and thyme; blend to incorporate.

SERVE immediately.

CALORIES: 35; TOTAL FAT: 0 G; CARBOHYDRATE: 8 G; DIETARY FIBER: 1 G; PROTEIN: 1 G

VEGETARIAN CHILI

Another Southwestern favorite, this chili is a popular request during lunchtime with a variety of optional accompaniments, including sour cream; grated cheddar, Cotija, and Monterey Jack cheeses; chopped green onions; and diced tomatoes. Serve yours with any of these options, or devise your own.

MAKES 4½ QUARTS; SERVING SIZE: 1 CUP

1 tsp. Miraval Oil Blend (page 19) or extra-virgin olive oil

2 c. chopped yellow onions

2 c. chopped carrots

1 c. chopped celery

½ c. chopped red bell peppers

½ c. chopped yellow or orange bell peppers

1 Tbsp. minced garlic

1 c. chopped yellow squash

1 c. chopped zucchini

2 c. one-inch broccoli florets

1 c. fresh or frozen corn kernels

¾ c. Basic Black Beans (page 14)

¾ c. Basic Pinto Beans (page 17)

¾ c. Basic White Beans (page 17)

1 Tbsp. chili powder

1 Tbsp. ground cumin

2 tsp. ground coriander

½ c. tomato paste

2 Tbsp. chopped fresh basil

1 tsp. chopped fresh oregano

5½ c. low-sodium tomato juice

2 c. diced stewed tomatoes

2 c. Vegetable Stock (page 24) or canned vegetable broth

1 tsp. salt

½ tsp. freshly ground black pepper

HEAT the oil in a large pot over high heat. Add the onions and cook, stirring for 1 minute. Add the carrots and cook, stirring for 1 minute. Add the celery and cook, stirring for 1 minute. Add the bell peppers and cook, stirring for 1 minute. Add the garlic and cook, stirring for 30 seconds. Add the squash and zucchini and cook, stirring for 1 minute. Add the broccoli and corn and cook, stirring for 1½ minutes. Add the black, pinto, and white beans, chili powder, cumin, and coriander; cook, stirring for 1 minute. Add the tomato paste and cook, stirring until no lumps remain and it is well incorporated, 30 seconds. Add the remaining ingredients (except salt and pepper) and bring to a boil. Reduce the heat and simmer until the vegetables are tender, 20 to 25 minutes.

REMOVE the pot from the heat, stir in the salt and pepper, and serve immediately; or cool the leftovers down in a shallow casserole dish as quickly as possible (needs to be chilled down below 45° F within 90 minutes) and then store covered in the refrigerator for up to a week.

CALORIES: 60; TOTAL FAT: 0 G; CARBOHYDRATE: 7 G; DIETARY FIBER: 2 G; PROTEIN: 6 G

SALADS

ARTICHOKE AND PROSCIUTTO SALAD

1 c. canned artichoke hearts in water, rinsed and well drained

1 oz. prosciutto, cut into thin chiffonade (about 2 Tbsp.)

¼ c. cherry or grape tomatoes, cut in half if large

¼ c. baby arugula, rinsed and spun dry

¼ c. red onions, thinly sliced

¼ c. yellow or orange bell peppers, thinly sliced

1 Tbsp. fresh basil leaves, cut into chiffonade

1 Tbsp. grated Parmigiano-Reggiano

2 tsp. drained capers

2 tsp. white balsamic vinegar or red wine vinegar

½ tsp. extra-virgin olive oil

Pinch of minced garlic

Pinch of kosher salt

⅛ tsp. freshly ground black pepper

COMBINE all the ingredients in a large bowl and mix well.

COVER and refrigerate for at least one hour (and up to four hours) before serving.

CALORIES: 90; TOTAL FAT: 3.5 G; CARBOHYDRATE: 11 G; DIETARY FIBER: 7 G; PROTEIN: 7 G

BEEF AND GLASS-NOODLE SALAD WITH SPICY PEANUT SAUCE

Choose this recipe when you have time to savor the entire process of creating it. Glass noodles are also called "rice sticks" or "vermicelli." We get the best results if the noodles are softened first in warm water for 20 minutes and then cooked in boiling water.

To cut lemongrass, trim the tough bottom a quarter inch from the stem and peel the tough outer layers away to reveal the soft inner core, which is what you want to include in your recipe.

MAKES 4 HALF-CUP SERVINGS

2 oz. glass noodles

1 tsp. Sriracha hot-chili sauce

1 tsp. chopped garlic

1 tsp. fresh lime juice

1 tsp. sesame oil

1 tsp. low-sodium soy sauce

8 oz. beef steak, such as sirloin or New York strip

1 four-ounce Anjou or Bosc pear, peeled, cored, and thinly sliced

1 tsp. chopped lemongrass

¼ tsp. plus 1 Tbsp. Miraval Oil Blend (page 19) or canola oil

½ c. rice wine vinegar

1 Tbsp. Thickened Vegetable Stock (page 24)

½ c. peeled carrot, cut into three-inch julienne strips

½ c. red bell pepper, cut into three-inch julienne strips

1 tsp. chopped fresh cilantro, plus 8 sprigs for garnish

4 Tbsp. Spicy Peanut Sauce (page 127)

PLACE noodles in a medium bowl and cover with warm water. Let soak at room temperature until softened and the strands are easy to separate, about 20 minutes.

COMBINE the Sriracha, garlic, lime juice, sesame oil, and soy sauce in a medium bowl. Add the meat and turn to coat evenly. Let marinate for 20 minutes at room temperature, turning occasionally. (The meat can be marinated, covered and refrigerated for up to four hours. Bring to room temperature before cooking.)

TO make the dressing, heat a medium skillet or saucepan over high heat. Add the lemongrass and cook until fragrant, 45 seconds. Add ¼ tsp. of the oil and reduce the heat to medium. Add the pears and cook, stirring until caramelized on all sides, 3½ to 4 minutes. Add the rice wine vinegar and reduce the heat to low. (The vinegar will boil aggressively.) Cook until the mixture is slightly reduced, 3 minutes. Transfer to the bowl of a blender and add the Thickened Vegetable Stock and remaining 1 Tbsp. oil. Blend on high speed until smooth.

PREPARE an ice bath in a medium bowl.

BRING a medium pot of water to a boil. Add the soaked noodles and cook just until tender, 3 minutes. Quickly transfer to the prepared ice bath to cool for 2 minutes. Drain well in a colander and transfer to a large bowl.

ADD the carrots, bell peppers, and cilantro to the noodles and toss with the dressing to coat evenly. Set aside.

HEAT a medium skillet over high heat. Place the meat in the hot pan and cook until seared on the first side, 1 minute. Reduce the heat to medium-high and cook for an additional 2 minutes. Turn and cook, moving the meat occasionally to prevent it from sticking to the pan, 3 minutes. Turn the meat to cook on the sides, 2 minutes. (For a total cooking time of 8 minutes for rare, or cook to desired doneness.) Remove from the pan and let rest for 4 minutes before slicing.

TO plate, spoon 1 Tbsp. of the Spicy Peanut Sauce on the bottom of each of 4 serving plates. Divide the noodles among the plates, and arrange 2 slices of beef on each serving.

CALORIES: 220; TOTAL FAT: 6 G; CARBOHYDRATE: 22 G; DIETARY FIBER: 2 G; PROTEIN: 17 G

BULGUR WHEAT–GAZPACHO SALAD

MAKES 4 HALF-CUP SERVINGS

1 c. bulgur wheat
¼ c. chopped, canned stewed tomatoes and their juices
¼ c. red wine vinegar
4 tsp. thinly sliced green onions
4 tsp. chopped fresh cilantro
4 tsp. minced garlic
4 tsp. pine nuts
½ c. peeled, seeded, and finely chopped cucumber
4 tsp. crumbled feta cheese
½ tsp. salt
¼ tsp. freshly ground black pepper
4 c. mesclun greens, washed and spun dry

PLACE the bulgur wheat in a large heatproof bowl.

BRING 2 cups of water to a boil in a small saucepan and pour over the bulgur wheat. Cover and let rest until the grains are plumped and the water is absorbed, 5 to 10 minutes.

ADD the tomatoes and their juices, the vinegar, green onions, cilantro, and garlic to the bulgur; and stir well. Cover and let rest for 5 minutes.

STIR the bulgur mixture, cover, and refrigerate until well chilled, 1 to 2 hours.

HEAT a small skillet over high heat. Add the pine nuts and cook until fragrant and lightly browned, 2 minutes. Place on a plate to cool.

STIR the cucumber, feta, pine nuts, salt, and pepper into the bulgur mixture.

ARRANGE 1 cup of the greens on each of 4 large salad plates. Divide the bulgur among the 4 plates and serve immediately.

CALORIES: 100; TOTAL FAT: 3 G; CARBOHYDRATE: 15 G; DIETARY FIBER: 4 G; PROTEIN: 4 G

BLACK KALE SALAD

Known by various names including Dinosaur Kale and Lacinato Kale, Black Kale is a hardy green with leaves that need to be thoroughly saturated with dressing. Serve immediately after composing as the garlic and lemon juice will break down the leaves, causing them to wilt. Since kale holds up exceptionally well, we recommend making a little extra for just-as-fresh leftovers the next day.

MAKES 4 HALF-CUP SERVINGS

¼ c. panko bread crumbs, toasted to golden brown

¼ c. extra-virgin olive oil

1–2 average-sized lemons (use your Microplane to zest one of the lemons before juicing)

2 Tbsp. fresh lemon juice

1 Tbsp. minced garlic

½ tsp. crushed red-pepper flakes

6 c. black kale, ribs removed, rinsed well, spun dry, and chopped

¼ c. finely grated Parmigiano-Reggiano

PREHEAT the oven to 375° F.

SPREAD the bread crumbs on a small baking sheet and lightly toast in the oven until golden brown, 4 to 5 minutes. Remove from the oven, and transfer into a cool dish to avoid overcooking.

COMBINE the lemon juice and garlic in a blender and blend over medium speed until mixed. Increase the blender speed to high, and slowly drizzle in the oil until smooth and thick. Ideally, this dressing will be very lemony and garlicky. Adjust flavors to your taste using additional lemon juice or fresh minced garlic.

PLACE the kale in a large bowl and toss with the dressing, coating well; let rest for 10 to 15 minutes, or until the leaves begin to wilt slightly. Add 2 Tbsp. of the cheese and all but 2 tsp. of the bread crumbs to the kale; toss and let rest for 5 minutes.

DIVIDE the salad among four plates, and top each serving with 1½ tsp. of the remaining cheese, ½ tsp. of the bread crumbs, a pinch of fresh lemon zest, and a pinch of the crushed red-pepper flakes. Serve immediately.

CALORIES: 230; TOTAL FAT: 16 G; CARBOHYDRATE: 16 G; DIETARY FIBER: 2 G; PROTEIN: 6 G

BLACK RICE AND EDAMAME
BEAN SALAD

If preparing simple, wholesome food is what you desire, this is a good recipe to master. To achieve the best results, we suggest precisely measuring the water when cooking the rice, and use a large pot instead of a medium one so that it cooks evenly and retains its crunch.

MAKES 4 HALF-CUP SERVINGS

3½ c. water

¼ tsp. kosher salt

2 c. black rice

1 c. fresh or thawed frozen edamame beans

½ tsp. Miraval Oil Blend (page 19)

1 c. thinly sliced shiitake mushrooms

Pinch freshly ground black pepper

½ c. thinly sliced green onions, tops only

½ cup roughly chopped fresh cilantro

¼ c. low-sodium soy sauce

2 Tbsp. rice wine vinegar

1 Tbsp. agave syrup (see Source Guide) or honey

1½ tsp. sesame oil

PLACE the water and salt in a large pot and bring to a boil. Add the rice, cover, and cook uncovered until the liquid is absorbed and the rice is just tender but still al dente, 20 minutes. Drain well in a fine mesh strainer and rinse under cold running water until the water runs clear and the rice is cooled, 1 to 2 minutes. Drain well.

BRING a small pot of lightly salted water to a boil. Add the beans and lightly blanch, 1 minute. Drain the beans well, reserving 2 Tbsp. of the cooking water, and rinse the beans under cold running water. Drain the beans well, transfer to a large bowl, and set aside.

HEAT a medium skillet over medium-high heat. Add the oil, mushrooms, and pepper; stir well to combine and cook for 30 seconds. Add the reserved cooking water and cook until the mushrooms start to wilt but retain their shape, 1 to 2 minutes. Place the mushrooms in the bowl with the beans and add the drained rice, green onions, and cilantro.

TO make the dressing, whisk together the soy sauce, rice wine vinegar, agave syrup, and sesame oil in a small bowl.

ADD the dressing to the rice mixture, and stir well to combine. Serve immediately.

CALORIES: 200; TOTAL FAT: 3.5 G; CARBOHYDRATE: 40 G; DIETARY FIBER: 4 G; PROTEIN: 7 G

CARNE ASADA SALAD WITH RED CHILI VINAIGRETTE

For a dish that can be used as a light main course, all signs point to our Carne Asada Salad. While the marinade imparts flavor to the steak, be careful not to marinate for more than an hour, as the acid will begin to break down the proteins and change the meat's texture.

MAKES 4 SERVINGS

4 c. mesclun greens, washed and spun dry

1 c. thinly sliced Roasted Red Bell Peppers (page 18)

1 c. thinly sliced Roasted Yellow Bell Peppers (page 18)

1 tsp. crumbled Cotija cheese

1 recipe Marinated and Grilled Sirloin (recipe follows)

¼ c. Red Chili Vinaigrette (recipe follows)

1 recipe Cumin-Scented Corn Tortilla Strips (page 218)

COMBINE the ingredients in a large bowl and toss well.

DIVIDE the salad among four large plates and serve immediately.

CALORIES: 210; TOTAL FAT: 4.5 G; CARBOHYDRATE: 26 G; DIETARY FIBER: 7 G; PROTEIN: 12 G

RED CHILI VINAIGRETTE

MAKES ¾ CUP; SERVING SIZE: 2 TBSP.

½ tsp. cumin seeds

⅔ c. Thickened Vegetable Stock (page 24)

¼ c. rice wine vinegar

2 Tbsp. Bueno Red Chile Puree (see Source Guide) or Thai sweet red chili sauce

1 Tbsp. roughly chopped cilantro

1 tsp. fresh jalapeño

½ tsp. chopped garlic

½ tsp. chopped shallot

½ tsp. agave syrup (see Source Guide) or honey

Pinch kosher salt

Pinch freshly ground black pepper

1 tsp. extra-virgin olive oil

HEAT a small skillet over medium-high heat. Add the cumin seeds and cook, stirring until fragrant and lightly toasted, 45 seconds to 1 minute.

TRANSFER the seeds to the bowl of a blender and add the remaining ingredients, except the olive oil, and puree on high speed. With the machine running on medium speed, add the oil and blend until emulsified, 30 seconds.

TRANSFER to an airtight container and refrigerate until ready to use, or for up to five days.

MARINATED AND GRILLED SIRLOIN (CARNE ASADA)

MAKES 4 SERVINGS

8 oz. beef sirloin

6 oz. (¾ c.) Mexican beer, such as Pacifico or Corona

1 Tbsp. fresh lime juice

1 tsp. chili powder

½ tsp. ground cumin

½ tsp. dried oregano

½ tsp. minced garlic

COMBINE the beer, lime juice, chili powder, cumin, oregano, and garlic in a medium baking dish. Add the beef and turn to coat with the mixture. Cover and refrigerate for 30 minutes and up to 1 hour.

PREHEAT a grill to high heat, or the oven to 400° F.

GRILL the meat until medium rare, turning once, about 4 minutes per side.

(ALTERNATIVELY, preheat a medium-heavy ovenproof skillet over high heat. Add the oil and the meat and sear on the first side, about 1 minute. Turn the meat and sear on the second side for 1 minute. Transfer the pan to the oven and cook for 5 minutes. Turn the meat, return to the oven, and cook until medium rare, about 3 minutes.)

TRANSFER to a cutting board to rest for 5 minutes before serving.

THINLY slice the meat against the grain and serve.

GREEK PASTA SALAD

MAKES 4 HALF-CUP SERVINGS

1 c. whole-wheat penne or
bowtie pasta (2 oz.)

2 Tbsp. red wine vinegar

2 Tbsp. rice wine vinegar

1½ tsp. fresh lemon juice

½ tsp. extra-virgin olive oil

½ c. thinly sliced red bell pepper

½ c. thinly sliced yellow bell pepper

½ c. roughly chopped skinned
and seeded cucumber

¼ c. thinly sliced red onion

¼ c. canned artichoke hearts, quartered

¼ c. chopped tomato

1 Tbsp. crumbled feta cheese

1 Tbsp. minced fresh basil

1 Tbsp. minced fresh oregano

1½ tsp. finely chopped kalamata olives

Pinch freshly ground black pepper

BRING a medium-heavy pot of salted water to a boil. Add the pasta, return to the boil, and cook until al dente, 10 to 12 minutes.

DRAIN in a colander and rinse under cold running water to cool. Drain well and place in a large mixing bowl.

TO make the dressing, in a small bowl, whisk together the red wine and rice wine vinegars, lemon juice, and olive oil.

ADD the remaining ingredients to the pasta and the dressing to the pasta; toss well to combine.

SERVE immediately.

CALORIES: 90; TOTAL FAT: 2 G; CARBOHYDRATE: 14 G; DIETARY FIBER: 2 G; PROTEIN: 3 G

TUNA SALAD

MAKES 4 HALF-CUP SERVINGS

3 Tbsp. fat-free plain yogurt

10 oz. canned albacore tuna,
packed in water, drained

¼ c. plus 1 Tbsp. finely chopped
Granny Smith apple, skin on

¼ c. finely chopped celery

¼ c. finely chopped red onion

1 Tbsp. reduced-fat mayonnaise

1 tsp. fresh lemon juice

Pinch of ground black pepper

PLACE the yogurt in a small fine mesh strainer, place over a small bowl, and let sit for 20 minutes to drain the excess liquid. Discard the excess liquid.

PLACE the drained yogurt in a medium bowl, add the remaining ingredients, and toss well to combine.

SERVE immediately, or cover and refrigerate for one hour to chill before serving.

CALORIES: 120; TOTAL FAT: 3.5 G; CARBOHYDRATE: 5 G; DIETARY FIBER: 1 G; PROTEIN: 17 G

GRILLED VEGETABLE AND QUINOA SALAD

MAKES 4 HALF-CUP SERVINGS

2 c. Vegetable Stock (page 24)
or canned vegetable stock

1 c. quinoa

1 recipe Grilled Vegetables (page 140)

¼ c. crumbled Cotija or feta cheese

¼ tsp. kosher salt

⅛ tsp. freshly ground black pepper

PLACE the stock and quinoa in a medium saucepan and bring to a boil. Reduce the heat to low, cover, and simmer until tender, 10 to 12 minutes.

CAREFULLY transfer the hot quinoa to a baking dish and spread evenly across the bottom to stop the cooking process. Let cool to room temperature, stirring occasionally. Refrigerate until well chilled.

COMBINE the quinoa, Cotija cheese, salt, pepper, and vegetables; stir until well combined and coated with the dressing (the marinade of the grilled veggies will serve as the dressing). Serve immediately. (The salad can be made in advance and kept refrigerated in an airtight container for up to two days.)

CALORIES: 120; TOTAL FAT: 4 G; CARBOHYDRATE: 16 G; DIETARY FIBER: 3 G; PROTEIN: 4 G

CHERRY TOMATO AND PROVOLONE SALAD

MAKES 5 HALF-CUP SERVINGS

1½ c. halved cherry tomatoes

1 c. provolone cheese, cut
into half-inch cubes

1 Tbsp. minced red onion

1 Tbsp. chiffonade fresh basil

1 Tbsp. balsamic vinegar

1 tsp. extra-virgin olive oil

⅛ tsp. kosher salt

Pinch freshly ground black pepper

PLACE all the ingredients in a medium bowl and stir well to combine.

COVER and refrigerate until well chilled before serving, at least 30 minutes and up to 4 hours.

TOSS the salad before serving.

CALORIES: 110; TOTAL FAT: 8 G; CARBOHYDRATE: 3 G; DIETARY FIBER: 1 G; PROTEIN: 7 G

MICHAEL'S CORN SALAD

This is an ideal accompaniment to serve alongside grilled fish, scallops, and chicken.

MAKES 4 HALF-CUP SERVINGS

½ c. raw walnut pieces

2½ c. fresh corn kernels, about 5 ears

½ tsp. Miraval Oil Blend (see page 19)

½ tsp. kosher salt

⅛ tsp. freshly ground black pepper

1 c. diced red bell pepper

¼ c. crumbled Cotija cheese

1 tsp. minced fresh jalapeño

2 Tbsp. fresh lime juice

1 tsp. extra-virgin olive oil

PREHEAT the oven to 400° F.

SPREAD the walnuts on a small baking sheet or in a baking dish, and roast until fragrant and lightly colored, about 5 minutes. Remove from the oven and let cool.

PREHEAT a heavy, medium-sized skillet over high heat. Add the Miraval Oil Blend and the corn, and a pinch each of the salt and the pepper and stir well. Reduce the heat to medium-high, and cook, stirring occasionally, until tender and beginning to color, 3½ to 4 minutes. Spread the corn on a large plate and refrigerate until well chilled, 20 minutes.

COMBINE the corn and the remaining ingredients in a large bowl and stir well to combine. Adjust the seasoning to taste and serve immediately.

CALORIES: 150; TOTAL FAT: 11 G; CARBOHYDRATE: 11 G; DIETARY FIBER: 2 G; PROTEIN: 4 G

MIRAVAL FRUIT SALAD

MAKES 4 HALF-CUP SERVINGS

¾ c. diced Granny Smith Apple

¾ c. diced Gala apple, or other sweet red apple

2 Tbsp. quartered fresh strawberries

1 tsp. minced fresh mint

1 Tbsp. fresh blueberries

1 Tbsp. fresh blackberries

2 Tbsp. red grapes

1 Tbsp. fresh lemon juice

½ tsp. finely grated lemon zest

1 tsp. agave syrup (see Source Guide) or honey

COMBINE all the ingredients in a large bowl and stir together. Refrigerate for 30 minutes before serving.

CALORIES: 80; TOTAL FAT: 0 G; CARBOHYDRATE: 20 G; DIETARY FIBER: 3 G; PROTEIN: 1 G

MIRAVAL CAESAR SALAD

This is a delicious, healthy alternative to the traditionally calorie-, fat-, and cholesterol-laden Caesar salad. The texture and flavor is so close to the original full-fat recipe that your family and friends will never guess that it's good for them!

MAKES 4 HALF-CUP SERVINGS

1 head romaine lettuce, cored, washed, dried, and torn into bite-sized pieces

1 recipe Cumin-Scented Corn Tortilla Strips (page 218)

1 recipe Parmesan Crisps (recipe follows)

¼ c. Miraval Chipotle-Caesar Dressing (page 119)

Zest from 1 lemon and 1 lime

2 tsp. Parmigiano-Reggiano cheese, finely grated (use your Microplane)

PLACE the lettuce in a large bowl, and toss with the dressing. Garnish with one Parmesan crisp, ¼ of Cumin-Scented Tortilla Strips, Parmigiano-Reggiano, and freshly zested lemon and lime peels. Serve immediately.

CALORIES: 45; TOTAL FAT: 1.5 G; CARBOHYDRATE: 5 G; DIETARY FIBER: 2 G; PROTEIN: 3 G

PARMESAN CRISPS

MAKES 4 SERVINGS

4 tsp. finely grated Parmesan cheese

PREHEAT oven to 350° F. On a baking sheet lined with a nonstick silicone baking mat, sprinkle 1 tsp. of cheese into a small pile, and press down with your fingertips in a light circular motion to create a round about the size of a 50-cent piece. Bake until golden brown and crispy, 6–8 minutes. Cool completely before removing from pan.

CALORIES: 14; TOTAL FAT: 1 G; CARBOHYDRATE: TRACE; DIETARY FIBER: 0 G; PROTEIN: 1.25 G

NOPALITO CACTUS, JICAMA, AND ORANGE SALAD

An Arizona tradition and specialty, fresh nopalito cactus has become available in gourmet markets in many parts of the country. Use canned nopalito cactus from the ethnic section of the supermarket when fresh is not available.

MAKES 4 HALF-CUP SERVINGS

1½ tsp. cumin seeds

2 Valencia or navel oranges

¼ c. peeled jicama sticks, 2-inch long by ¼-inch thick

¼ cup fresh or canned nopalito cactus (drain first if using canned)

1 Tbsp. chopped red bell pepper

1 tsp. minced fresh cilantro

2 tsp. rice wine vinegar

½ tsp. chili powder

Pinch kosher salt

PLACE the cumin seeds in a small skillet and lightly toast over medium-high heat until fragrant, 45 seconds to 1 minute. Remove from the heat and let cool.

ONE at a time, cut the bottoms and tops from the oranges. Stand the orange upright and carefully cut away the peel, turning the orange as you work to expose the inner segments. Carefully hold the orange in your hand with a large bowl underneath. Using a sharp paring knife, cut around the membranes of each segment to release the segments into the bowl. Discard the membrane pieces.

ADD the cactus, jicama, cumin, red bell pepper, and cilantro to the orange segments.

IN a small bowl, whisk together the vinegar, chili powder, and salt.

ADD the vinegar mixture to the cactus mixture, and stir well to combine.

SERVE immediately.

CALORIES: 70; TOTAL FAT: 0 G; CARBOHYDRATE: 17 G; DIETARY FIBER: 7 G; PROTEIN: 2 G

PORTOBELLO-CAPRESE SALAD

MAKES 4 HALF-CUP SERVINGS

½ c. balsamic vinegar

2 Tbsp. extra-virgin olive oil

1 tsp. minced garlic

¼ tsp. freshly ground black pepper

2 large portobello mushrooms, about 8 oz., stems removed

4 oz. fresh Buffalo mozzarella cheese, cut into slices

1 four-ounce red tomato, cored and cut into 4 slices

1 four-ounce yellow tomato, cored and cut into 4 slices

2 tsp. Herb Oil (page 20)

2 tsp. Balsamic Reduction (page 14)

2 tsp. chiffonade fresh basil

⅛ tsp. kosher salt

⅛ tsp. freshly ground black pepper

TO make the marinade, combine the vinegar, olive oil, garlic, and pepper in a baking dish.

USING the edge of a spoon, scrape the gills from the mushrooms and discard. Wipe the mushrooms with a clean, damp towel. Place the mushrooms in the marinade, turning occasionally to evenly coat, for at least 20 minutes and up to 30 minutes.

PREHEAT a grill to high heat.

PREHEAT the oven to 400° F.

GRILL the mushrooms, 2 minutes per side. Transfer to a baking sheet and roast until tender, 6 to 8 minutes. Place the mushrooms on a plate and refrigerate until well chilled, 15 to 30 minutes.

TO serve, drizzle ½ tsp. of the Herb Oil around each of four plates. Stack the mushrooms, cheese, red tomato and yellow tomato slices in alternating colors on each plate. Drizzle the balsamic reduction around the vegetables and garnish each serving with ½ tsp. of basil and a pinch each of salt and pepper.

SERVE immediately.

CALORIES: 190; TOTAL FAT: 14 G; CARBOHYDRATE: 9 G; DIETARY FIBER: 1 G; PROTEIN: 8 G

SHAVED ASPARAGUS AND ARUGULA SALAD

Placing the "shaved" or peeled asparagus spears in cold water causes them to curl up into a very eye-appealing shape. White asparagus has a distinct flavor that we prefer for this salad. However, green asparagus will actually curl up better than the white.

MAKES 4 HALF-CUP SERVINGS

1 small parsnip, peeled and roughly chopped

1 bunch white asparagus, woody stems trimmed

1½ c. baby arugula

4 figs

1 c. good quality red wine, such as Cabernet Sauvignon or Merlot

6 Tbsp. White Balsamic Vinaigrette (recipe follows)

2 Tbsp. crumbled Stilton cheese

WHITE BALSAMIC VINAIGRETTE
MAKES 1 CUP; SERVING SIZE: 2 TBSP.

¾ c. white balsamic vinegar

½ c. Thickened Vegetable Stock (page 24)

1 Tbsp. honey or agave syrup (see Source Guide)

3 Tbsp. extra-virgin olive oil

1½ tsp. Dijon mustard

TO MAKE THE VINAIGRETTE: add all ingredients except the olive oil into a small mixing bowl. Slowly whisk in the oil.

PLACE the parsnip in a small saucepan, cover with water by half-inch, and bring to a low boil. Cook until the parsnip is just fork tender, about 5 minutes. Reserving the cooking liquid, place the parsnip pieces in the bowl of a blender or food processor, and blend with just enough cooking liquid to make a smooth paste.

TRANSFER the parsnip puree to a small bowl, and set aside until ready to use.

PLACE the asparagus flat on a work surface, and one at a time, run a vegetable peeler from the tip nearly three-quarters of the way down to the bottom. Turn the spear over and repeat on the other side. Place the peeled asparagus in a bowl of cold water and repeat with the remaining spears. (The peeled asparagus can be made and kept refrigerated for up to 24 hours in advance.)

PLACE the figs and wine in a medium saucepan and bring to a boil over medium-high heat. Cook until the figs are soft, about 5 minutes. Remove the figs from the pan with a slotted spoon and refrigerate until ready to serve. Continue cooking the wine until reduced to a thick syrup, 1 to 2 Tbsp., about 10 minutes. Remove from the heat and let the syrup cool before using.

TO assemble the salad, drain the asparagus curls and pat dry on a clean cloth. Combine the arugula and asparagus in a medium bowl and toss with the vinaigrette.

SPOON 1 tsp. of the parsnip puree into the center of four salad plates and place one-quarter of the salad on top. Sprinkle 1½ tsp. of the cheese over each salad.

CUT each fig in half and place 2 halves on each salad. Drizzle each plate with the red wine reduction and serve.

ANY leftover dressing may be kept refrigerated for up to 5 days and used on salad greens of your choice.

CALORIES: 140; TOTAL FAT: 2.5 G; CARBOHYDRATE: 17 G; DIETARY FIBER: 4 G; PROTEIN: 4 G

ROASTED CORN AND BLACK-BEAN SALAD

At Miraval, we utilize two tricks to ensure the success of our often-requested Roasted Corn and Black-Bean Salad. While this salad can be served at room temperature, we find it tastes best when served chilled, when the raspberry vinegar has a chance to marry with the other ingredients for an hour. We also insist upon using fresh corn, as the flavor and texture cannot be replicated by frozen kernels.

MAKES 2¾ CUPS, OR 4 SERVINGS

1 c. fresh corn kernels

1 tsp. chili powder

1 tsp. ground coriander

1 tsp. ground cumin

1 tsp. Miraval Oil Blend (page 19) or vegetable oil

1⅓ c. Basic Black Beans (page 14) or canned black beans, rinsed and drained

¼ c. finely chopped red onions

¼ c. finely chopped red bell peppers

2 Tbsp. minced cilantro

PREHEAT the oven to 400° F.

COMBINE the corn, chili powder, coriander, and cumin in a small bowl; and toss with the oil to coat. Place on a small baking sheet and roast until fragrant, 10 to 12 minutes.

SPREAD the corn on a plate and cool to room temperature.

COMBINE the remaining ingredients in a medium bowl, add the cooled corn, and stir. Cover and refrigerate for 1 hour before serving.

CALORIES: 100; TOTAL FAT: 1.5 G; CARBOHYDRATE: 17 G; DIETARY FIBER: 5 G; PROTEIN: 5 G

SMOKED SALMON POTATO SALAD

2 medium Red Bliss
Potatoes, about 4 oz.

1 medium Yukon Gold
Potato, about 4 oz.

1 medium Peruvian Purple
Potato, about 4 oz.

2 oz. haricots verts, or very thin fresh
green beans, stem ends trimmed

½ c. cold smoked salmon,
roughly chopped

¼ c. thinly sliced red onion

Pinch kosher salt

Pinch freshly ground black pepper

2 Tbsp. Thickened Vegetable
Stock (page 24)

2 Tbsp. mascarpone cheese

1 Tbsp. red wine vinegar

1½ tsp. extra-virgin olive oil

½ tsp. Dijon mustard

½ tsp. honey

PREHEAT the oven to 400° F.

COOK the potatoes until fork tender, 1 hour. Remove from the oven and let cool completely at room temperature. Refrigerate until well chilled, about 1 hour.

BRING a small pot of lightly salted water to a boil. Add the green beans and lightly blanch, 1 minute. Drain the beans well in a colander and rinse under cold running water. Drain the beans well, pat dry, and transfer to a large bowl.

CUT the potatoes into eighths and add to the bowl with the green beans. Add the salmon, onion, salt, and pepper; and toss lightly to combine, being careful not to break the potatoes.

TO make the dressing, whisk together the vegetable stock and mascarpone in a medium bowl until smooth. Add the remaining ingredients and whisk well to combine. Toss the dressing with the potato mixture until well coated.

SERVE immediately.

CALORIES: 170; TOTAL FAT: 9 G; CARBOHYDRATE: 18 G; DIETARY FIBER: 2 G; PROTEIN: 6 G

VIETNAMESE TORN CHICKEN AND CABBAGE SALAD WITH SPICY MINT VINAIGRETTE

To create a dish that looks as gorgeous as it tastes, Chef Justin uses a spiral vegetable slicer to cut the carrots into decorative swirls for this salad. These slicers are available both online and in specialty gourmet shops.

MAKES 4 HALF-CUP SERVINGS

¼ c. raw cashews

2 four-ounce boneless, skinless chicken breasts

¼ tsp. kosher salt

Pinch freshly ground black pepper

¼ tsp. Miraval Oil Blend (page 19) or canola oil

4 c. shredded napa cabbage

2½ c. spiral-cut or grated carrots

1 c. Spicy Mint Vinaigrette (page 121)

1 tsp. mixed black and white sesame seeds

PREHEAT the oven to 400° F.

SPREAD the cashews on a small baking sheet and toast until fragrant, 8 to 10 minutes. Remove from the oven and chop.

SEASON the chicken on both sides with the salt and pepper.

HEAT a medium ovenproof skillet on high heat. Add the oil and when hot, add the chicken and cook until golden brown, 2 to 3 minutes. Turn the chicken, transfer to the oven, and roast until cooked through, 7 to 8 minutes.

TRANSFER the chicken to a clean plate and let cool slightly. Cover and refrigerate until well chilled.

TO assemble the salad, toss the cabbage and carrots with 3 Tbsp. of the vinaigrette.

THINLY slice the chicken breasts lengthwise on the bias and divide between four salad plates. Lightly drizzle the chicken with additional vinaigrette, as desired. Top with cabbage and carrots, and garnish each serving with ¼ tsp. of the sesame seeds.

SERVE immediately.

CALORIES: 300; TOTAL FAT: 16 G; CARBOHYDRATE: 23 G; DIETARY FIBER: 4 G; PROTEIN: 19 G

MIRAVAL NIÇOISE SALAD

2 medium Red Bliss
Potatoes, about 6 oz.

2 medium Yukon Gold
Potatoes, about 6 oz.

1 oz. fresh green beans,
stem ends trimmed

½ c. well-drained, water-
packed albacore tuna

½ c. chopped tomato

¼ c. thinly sliced red onion

1½ tsp. minced kalamata olives

Pinch kosher salt

Pinch freshly ground black pepper

2 Tbsp. Thickened Vegetable
Stock (page 24)

1 Tbsp. red wine vinegar

1½ tsp. fresh lemon juice

1½ tsp. extra-virgin olive oil

½ tsp. Dijon mustard

½ tsp. honey

⅛ tsp. minced garlic

Pinch dried oregano

PREHEAT the oven to 400° F.

COOK the potatoes until fork tender, 1 hour. Remove from the oven and let cool completely at room temperature. Refrigerate until well chilled, about 1 hour.

BRING a small pot of lightly salted water to a boil. Add the green beans and lightly blanch, 1 minute. Drain the beans well in a colander and rinse under cold running water. Drain the beans well, pat dry, and transfer to a large bowl.

CUT the potatoes into eighths and add to the bowl with the green beans. Add the tuna, tomato, onion, olives, salt, and pepper; and toss lightly to combine, being careful not to break the potatoes.

TO make the dressing, combine the remaining ingredients in a small bowl and whisk well to blend.

TOSS the dressing with the tuna mixture, and stir until well coated. Serve immediately.

CALORIES: 170; TOTAL FAT: 3.5 G; CARBOHYDRATE: 25 G; DIETARY FIBER: 2 G; PROTEIN: 9 G

DRESSINGS, MARINADES, AND SAUCES

BALSAMIC VINAIGRETTE

A clever way to break out of a culinary rut, this easy-to-prepare dressing brings excitement to the simplest of salads. Because it's not an emulsification, it will not be smooth and needs to be whisked prior to using.

MAKES 2½ CUPS; SERVING SIZE: 2 TBSP.

2 c. Thickened Vegetable Stock (page 24)

3 Tbsp. Dijon mustard

2 Tbsp. honey or agave syrup
(see Source Guide)

1 Tbsp. minced Roasted Garlic (page 22)

1½ tsp. minced shallots

1 tsp. minced fresh basil

1 tsp. minced fresh oregano

¼ c. balsamic vinegar

2 Tbsp. extra-virgin olive oil

½ tsp. kosher salt

¼ tsp. freshly ground black pepper

COMBINE the stock, mustard, agave syrup, garlic, shallots, basil, and oregano in the bowl of a blender and process on high speed until well combined, 30 seconds. Lower the speed, and with the motor running, add the remaining ingredients and process until smooth, 30 to 45 seconds.

USE immediately, or transfer to an airtight container and refrigerate until ready to use. (The dressing will keep refrigerated for up to four days.)

CALORIES: 25; TOTAL FAT: 1 G; CARBOHYDRATE: 3 G; DIETARY FIBER: 0 G; PROTEIN: 0 G

BASIL-CABERNET VINAIGRETTE

This is a whisked dressing, not an emulsification. For this reason, it will not be smooth and will need to be whisked immediately prior to using.

MAKES 1½ CUPS; SERVING SIZE: 2 TBSP.

¼ c. Cabernet Sauvignon
¼ c. rice wine vinegar
¾ c. Thickened Vegetable Stock (page 24)
1 Tbsp. chopped fresh basil
1 Tbsp. chopped fresh oregano
1 Tbsp. fresh thyme leaves
1 Tbsp. agave syrup (see Source Guide) or honey
¼ c. extra-virgin olive oil

PLACE the wine and vinegar in the bowl of a blender and process on low speed until combined, 10 seconds. Add the stock and process until well combined, 15 seconds.

POUR the stock mixture into a medium bowl. Add the herbs and whisk in the agave syrup and oil. (The vinaigrette will appear separated. Whisk the dressing again immediately before serving.)

USE immediately, or transfer to an airtight container and refrigerate until ready to use. (The dressing will keep refrigerated for up to four days.)

CALORIES: 20; TOTAL FAT: 1.5 G; CARBOHYDRATE: 1 G; DIETARY FIBER: 0 G; PROTEIN: 0 G

BLACKBERRY VINAIGRETTE

MAKES 2½ CUPS; SERVING SIZE: 2 TBSP.

1 pint frozen blackberries
¼ c. balsamic vinegar
1 c. nonfat plain yogurt
1 Tbsp. agave syrup (see Source Guide) or honey
1 Tbsp. raspberry vinegar or red wine vinegar
Pinch kosher salt
Pinch freshly ground black pepper

PLACE the blackberries and vinegar in a medium bowl and thaw at room temperature.

LINE a small colander or a strainer with cheesecloth. Place the yogurt in the colander set over a large bowl and refrigerate until thick and the liquid is drained, 1 hour. Discard the liquid.

POUR the berries and their liquid into the bowl of a blender. Add the strained yogurt and remaining ingredients and process on high speed until smooth, 30 seconds.

USE immediately, or transfer to an airtight container and refrigerate until ready to use. (The dressing will keep refrigerated for up to seven days.)

CALORIES: 15; TOTAL FAT: 0 G; CARBOHYDRATE: 4 G; DIETARY FIBER: 1 G; PROTEIN: 1 G

CHIPOTLE VINAIGRETTE

MAKES 2 CUPS; SERVING SIZE: 2 TBSP.

1 c. rice wine vinegar

1 c. cored and quartered tomato

2 Tbsp. chopped cilantro

2 Tbsp. Thickened Vegetable Stock (page 24)

1 Tbsp. canned chipotle chili with adobo sauce

1 Tbsp. chili powder

1 Tbsp. Miraval Oil Blend (page 19) or canola oil

COMBINE all the ingredients except the oil in the bowl of a blender, and process on high speed to a smooth puree, 30 seconds. Lower the speed, and with the motor running, add the oil and process until smooth, 30 to 45 seconds.

USE immediately, or transfer to an airtight container and refrigerate until ready to use. (The dressing will keep refrigerated for up to three days.)

CALORIES: 210; TOTAL FAT: 11 G; CARBOHYDRATE: 5 G; DIETARY FIBER: 1 G; PROTEIN: 24 G

CITRUS VINAIGRETTE

MAKES 1 CUP; SERVING SIZE: 2 TBSP.

8 seedless orange segments

½ c. rice wine vinegar

¼ c. diced red onion

¼ c. diced seeded tomato

2 Tbsp. asparagus, sliced on the bias

2 Tbsp. sliced green onion

2 Tbsp. chopped fresh cilantro

2 Tbsp. water

2 tsp. fresh orange juice

1½ tsp. fresh lemon juice

¾ tsp. fresh lime juice

½ tsp. minced garlic

¼ tsp. extra-virgin olive oil

STIR together the ingredients in a medium bowl, cover, and refrigerate until ready to serve.

SERVE chilled. (The vinaigrette can be made up to two hours in advance and kept refrigerated.)

CALORIES: 270; TOTAL FAT: 2.5 G; CARBOHYDRATE: 36 G; DIETARY FIBER: 4 G; PROTEIN: 25 G

MIRAVAL CHIPOTLE-CAESAR DRESSING

MAKES ABOUT 2½ CUPS; SERVING SIZE: 2 TBSP.

1½ Tbsp. garlic, minced
2 Tbsp. lemon juice
2 Tbsp. lime juice
3 filets anchovies
½ chipotle pepper in adobo, canned
2 Tbsp. Dijon mustard
14 oz. (1 block) soft tofu, drained
1 Tbsp. Parmesan cheese, shredded
2 tsp. Worcestershire sauce
Pinch ground cumin, toasted

COMBINE all ingredients in a blender or food processor and puree.

ADJUST flavors as needed. Extra dressing may be kept refrigerated for up to five days.

CALORIES: 20; TOTAL FAT: 0.5 G; CARBOHYDRATE: 1 G; DIETARY FIBER: 0 G; PROTEIN: 1 G

MIRAVAL RANCH DRESSING

MAKES 2½ CUPS; SERVING SIZE: 2 TBSP.

2 c. Miraval Mayonnaise (page 21)
1 Tbsp. minced green onions
1 Tbsp. minced Roasted Garlic (page 22)
1 tsp. chopped fresh basil
1 tsp. chopped fresh oregano
1 tsp. chopped fresh parsley
1 tsp. minced fresh garlic
½ c. low-fat buttermilk
¼ tsp. kosher salt
⅛ tsp. freshly ground black pepper

COMBINE the mayonnaise, green onions, roasted garlic, herbs, and fresh garlic in the bowl of a blender and process on high speed until well combined, 30 to 45 seconds. Add the remaining ingredients and process on low speed until smooth, 30 seconds.

USE immediately, or transfer to an airtight container and refrigerate until ready to use. (The dressing will keep refrigerated for up to seven days.)

CALORIES: 20; TOTAL FAT: 0 G; CARBOHYDRATE: 1 G; DIETARY FIBER: 0 G; PROTEIN: 3 G

MIRAVAL FINE-HERB VINAIGRETTE

2 c. Thickened Vegetable Stock (page 24)

¼ c. chopped fresh basil

¼ c. chopped fresh cilantro

¼ c. chopped fresh oregano

¼ c. chopped fresh parsley

3 Tbsp. Dijon mustard

2 Tbsp. honey or agave syrup
(see Source Guide)

2 Tbsp. chopped Roasted Garlic (page 22)

1 Tbsp. chopped Roasted
Shallots (page 22)

1 Tbsp. chopped fresh rosemary

1½ tsp. minced fresh garlic

¼ c. apple juice

1 Tbsp. extra-virgin olive oil

¼ tsp. kosher salt

¼ tsp. freshly ground black pepper

PLACE the stock, basil, cilantro, oregano, parsley, mustard, honey, roasted garlic, roasted shallots, rosemary, and fresh garlic in the bowl of a blender and process on high speed until well blended, 30 seconds. Add the remaining ingredients and process on high speed until smooth, 20 to 30 seconds.

USE immediately, or transfer to an airtight container and refrigerate until ready to use. (The vinaigrette will keep refrigerated for up to four days.)

CALORIES: 30; TOTAL FAT: 1.5 G; CARBOHYDRATE: 4 G; DIETARY FIBER: 0 G; PROTEIN: 0 G

MIRAVAL HONEY-MUSTARD DRESSING

MAKES 2 CUPS; SERVING SIZE: 2 TBSP.

½ c. whole-grain mustard

½ c. honey

⅓ c. apple cider vinegar

¼ c. Dijon mustard

2 Tbsp. chopped Roasted
Shallots (page 22)

1 Tbsp. chopped Roasted Garlic (page 22)

1½ tsp. minced fresh garlic

½ c. Thickened Vegetable Stock (page 24)

1 Tbsp. extra-virgin olive oil

¼ tsp. kosher salt

⅛ tsp. freshly ground black pepper

PLACE the whole-grain mustard, honey, vinegar, Dijon mustard, roasted shallots, roasted garlic, and fresh garlic in the bowl of a blender and process on high speed until well combined, 30 seconds. Add the remaining ingredients and process on low speed until smooth, 30 to 45 seconds.

USE immediately, or transfer to an airtight container and refrigerate until ready to use. (The dressing will keep refrigerated for up to four days.)

CALORIES: 15; TOTAL FAT: 0 G; CARBOHYDRATE: 2 G; DIETARY FIBER: 0 G; PROTEIN: 0 G

SPICY MINT VINAIGRETTE

**MAKES A GENEROUS 1 CUP SERVING;
SERVING SIZE: 2 TBSP.**

½ c. fresh lime juice

2 Tbsp. fresh mint leaves

2 Tbsp. Thickened Vegetable
Stock (page 24)

2 tsp. roughly chopped garlic

1 Tbsp. roughly chopped jalapeño

2 tsp. sugar

1 tsp. sesame oil

½ tsp. fish sauce

COMBINE the lime juice, mint, vegetable stock, garlic, and jalapeño in a blender and pulse to combine. Blend on medium speed until the garlic and jalapeño are well chopped. Add the sugar, sesame oil, and fish sauce; and blend until well combined.

CALORIES: 33; TOTAL FAT: TRACE; CARBOHYDRATE: 7 G; DIETARY FIBER: 0 G; PROTEIN: 1.5 G

ACHIOTE-ORANGE MARINADE

Achiote is a common ingredient in Central American and Caribbean cooking. It has a slightly peppery flavor and bright orange color, and can be found in the international section of supermarkets.

We use this to marinate chicken breasts, but it's also superb for shrimp. If you do use this for seafood, avoid marinating for more than three hours, as the citric acid will break down the proteins and "cook" the seafood. For a sweeter marinade, use the optional agave syrup or honey in the ingredient list.

MAKES 1 CUPS; SERVING SIZE: 2 TBSP.

⅔ c. fresh orange juice

¼ c. fresh lime juice

2 Tbsp. adobo sauce

2 Tbsp. extra-virgin olive oil

1 Tbsp. achiote paste

1 to 2 tsp. agave syrup (see Source Guide) or honey to taste, optional

COMBINE the ingredients in the bowl of a blender and process on high speed until smooth.

TRANSFER to an airtight container and refrigerate until ready to use. (The marinade will keep refrigerated for up to seven days.)

CALORIES: 20; TOTAL FAT: 2 G; CARBOHYDRATE: 2 G; DIETARY FIBER: 0 G; PROTEIN: 0 G

ASIAN SAUCE

MAKES 1½ CUPS; SERVING SIZE 2 TBSP.

1¼ c. low-sodium soy sauce

½ c. fresh lime juice

1 Tbsp. Sriracha chili sauce

1½ tsp. pure cane sugar

COMBINE the ingredients in a medium bowl and mix well. Set aside until ready to use. (The sauce can be made in advance and kept refrigerated in an airtight container for up to five days.)

CALORIES: 130; TOTAL FAT: 3.5 G; CARBOHYDRATE: 11 G; DIETARY FIBER: 3 G; PROTEIN: 15 G

ALFREDO SAUCE

MAKES 2 CUPS; SERVING SIZE: ½ CUP

1 c. low-fat cottage cheese

¾ c. skim milk

¼ c. Neufchâtel cheese, or
low-fat cream cheese

¼ c. sour cream

¼ c. Parmigiano-Reggiano

½ tsp. ground nutmeg

⅛ tsp. kosher salt

⅛ tsp. freshly ground black pepper

1 Tbsp. Miraval Oil Blend
(page 19) or vegetable oil

1 Tbsp. minced shallots

1 Tbsp. minced garlic

¾ c. dry white wine

COMBINE the cottage cheese, milk, Neufchâtel cheese, sour cream, cheese, nutmeg, salt, and pepper in a blender and process until smooth.

HEAT a medium saucepan over medium heat. Add the oil and when hot, add the shallots and garlic; cook, stirring until soft and beginning to turn golden brown, 3 to 3½ minutes. Add the wine, increase the heat to medium-high, and simmer until the liquid is reduced to about 2 Tbsp., 8 to 10 minutes. Reduce the heat to medium and add the blended ingredients, whisking well to combine. Cook until the mixture reaches a simmer and thickens, stirring occasionally, about 8 minutes.

SERVE immediately on cooked pasta, chicken, or veal.

CALORIES: 45; TOTAL FAT: 2 G; CARBOHYDRATE: 2 G; DIETARY FIBER: 0 G; PROTEIN: 3 G

ANCHO CHILI, DRIED CHERRY, AND MANGO SALSA

This salsa is delicious with duck recipes!

MAKES ABOUT 1 CUP; SERVING SIZE: ¼ CUP

1½ c. mango, peeled, seeded, and diced small

1 Tbsp. dried ancho chili pepper, rehydrated and diced small

2 tsp. cilantro, chopped fine

4 tsp. kiln-dried cherries

1 tsp. mint leaves, chopped fine

¼ c. red onion, diced small

½ c. Roma tomato, diced small

½ tsp. garlic, minced

¾ tsp. sherry vinegar

¾ tsp. raspberry vinegar

SOAK the ancho chili in hot water until soft, about 10 minutes. Remove the stems, split open, and dip in water to remove seeds before dicing.

COMBINE with the remaining ingredients in a mixing bowl.

CALORIES: 34; TOTAL FAT: TRACE; CARBOHYDRATE: 8 G; DIETARY FIBER: 1 G; PROTEIN: TRACE

SMOKY HORSERADISH AIOLI

This mouthwatering aioli doubles as the sauce for the Pistachio-Crusted Beef Tenderloin and the Blackened Sirloin Tacos. A word of warning—this sauce is very spicy! Use less horseradish if you don't like spicy foods.

MAKES 1 CUP

1 c. Miraval Mayonnaise (page 21), low-fat mayonnaise, or mayonnaise

2 Tbsp. prepared horseradish, drained

2 Tbsp. Roasted Garlic (page 22)

½ tsp. extra-virgin olive oil

¼ tsp. chipotle powder

¼ tsp. kosher salt

⅛ tsp. freshly ground black pepper

COMBINE the ingredients in the bowl of a food processor and process on high speed until well blended.

TRANSFER to an airtight container and refrigerate until ready to use. (The aioli will keep refrigerated for up to seven days.)

CALORIES: 15; TOTAL FAT: 0 G; CARBOHYDRATE: 2 G; DIETARY FIBER: 0 G; PROTEIN: 1 G

CHIPOTLE-CILANTRO AIOLI

MAKES ¼ CUP; SERVING SIZE: 2 TBSP.

3 Tbsp. Miraval Mayonnaise (page 21) or low-fat mayonnaise

1 Tbsp. chopped fresh cilantro

2 tsp. fresh lime juice

1 tsp. drained, chopped chipotle peppers in adobo sauce

½ tsp. fresh garlic, minced

¼ tsp. cumin powder

⅛ tsp. salt

⅛ tsp. freshly ground black pepper

PLACE all the ingredients in a medium bowl and whisk to combine. Adjust the seasoning to taste, cover, and refrigerate until ready to serve.

CALORIES: 15; TOTAL FAT: 0.5 G; CARBOHYDRATE: 2 G; DIETARY FIBER: 0 G; PROTEIN: 1 G

GRANNY SMITH APPLE–CHIPOTLE CHUTNEY

MAKES 1 CUP; SERVING SIZE: 2 TBSP.

¾ c. peeled, seeded, cored, and chopped Granny Smith apple

2 Tbsp. thinly sliced dried apricot

2 Tbsp. thinly sliced red onion

2 Tbsp. packed light brown sugar

2 Tbsp. apple cider vinegar

2 Tbsp. fresh orange juice

1 tsp. minced canned chipotle chili in adobo sauce

Pinch mustard seeds

COMBINE all the ingredients in a heavy medium saucepan and bring to a boil over high heat. Reduce the heat to medium-low and simmer, stirring occasionally, until thick and the liquid is reduced by three-quarters in volume, about 15 minutes.

REMOVE from the heat and keep warm for service, or chill to use as a cold accompaniment.

CALORIES: 25; TOTAL FAT: 0 G; CARBOHYDRATE: 6 G; DIETARY FIBER: 0 G; PROTEIN: 0 G

LIME RAITA

Mindful and versatile, raita is an Indian yogurt salad that usually includes chopped cucumbers and mint, but can include other vegetables. We turn to this salad as a sauce or a cooling dip for spicy foods.

MAKES ABOUT 1 CUP; SERVING SIZE: ¼ CUP

¾ c. plain nonfat yogurt

3 Tbsp. peeled, seeded, and finely chopped cucumber

3 Tbsp. thinly sliced green onions

3 Tbsp. thinly sliced fresh mint

1 tsp. lime zest

Pinch kosher salt

Pinch ground white pepper

COMBINE the ingredients in a medium bowl and mix well.

COVER and refrigerate until ready to serve.

CALORIES: 45; TOTAL FAT: 0 G; CARBOHYDRATE: 8 G; DIETARY FIBER: 1 G; PROTEIN: 4 G

MARINARA SAUCE

MAKES 3 CUPS; SERVING SIZE: ¼ CUP

½ tsp. extra-virgin olive oil

2 Tbsp. minced garlic

32 oz. canned stewed tomatoes and their juices

2 Tbsp. roughly chopped fresh basil

½ tsp. sugar or agave syrup (see Source Guide)

½ tsp. kosher salt

⅛ tsp. freshly ground black pepper

HEAT the oil in a medium pot over medium-high heat. Add the garlic and cook, stirring, until starting to brown, 45 seconds. Add the remaining ingredients and bring to a boil. Reduce the heat and simmer until the tomatoes are very tender and start to break apart, and the liquid is reduced by about one-quarter in volume, 14 to 15 minutes.

TRANSFER to a blender and blend on high speed until smooth. Use as directed in recipes.

(The marinara sauce will keep refrigerated in an airtight container for up to four days. The sauce also can be frozen in an airtight container for up to one month.)

CALORIES: 50; TOTAL FAT: 0 G; CARBOHYDRATE: 10 G; DIETARY FIBER: 3 G; PROTEIN: 1 G

SPICY PEANUT SAUCE

Whether preparing a flavorful dish for a relaxing evening for two or surprising friends with your expanded culinary prowess, you can easily double this recipe with great results. We find that our Spicy Peanut Sauce complements several other Miraval recipes (such as the Tamarind Marinated Beef Satay), and is delicious with grilled or broiled chicken, beef, or shrimp.

MAKES ½ CUP; SERVING SIZE: ¼ CUP

⅓ c. rice wine vinegar

1 Tbsp. low-sodium soy sauce

1 tsp. Sriracha hot chili sauce

1 tsp. sesame oil

¼ c. low-fat, creamy peanut butter

PLACE the vinegar, soy sauce, Sriracha, and sesame oil in the bowl of a blender and blend on low speed. With the motor running, add the peanut butter a tablespoon at a time and blend until well combined, scraping down the sides of the bowl as needed.

SERVE immediately, or store refrigerated in an airtight container for up to seven days.

CALORIES: 220; TOTAL FAT: 6 G; CARBOHYDRATE: 22 G; DIETARY FIBER: 2 G; PROTEIN: 17 G

PRICKLY PEAR BARBECUE SAUCE

Use this as a basting sauce for chicken, pork, or tofu, or as you would any barbecue sauce.

MAKES ABOUT 2 CUPS; SERVING SIZE: 2 TBSP.

1 c. ketchup

½ c. prickly pear syrup (see Source Guide)

¼ c. apple cider vinegar

2 Tbsp. agave syrup (see Source Guide) or honey

2 Tbsp. molasses

¼ c. Blackening Spice Blend (page 19)

COMBINE all the ingredients in a heavy medium saucepan and bring to a simmer over medium heat. Simmer, stirring occasionally, until thick enough to coat the back of a spoon and the liquid is reduced by about a third, approximately 10 minutes.

REMOVE from the heat and serve immediately or cool down and store in refrigerator for later use, up to seven days.

CALORIES: 60; TOTAL FAT: 0 G; CARBOHYDRATE: 14 G; DIETARY FIBER: 1 G; PROTEIN: 0 G

PRICKLY PEAR MARINADE

MAKES 1 CUP; SERVING SIZE: 2 TBSP.

1½ tsp. cumin seeds

½ c. apple juice

2 Tbsp. prickly pear syrup
(see Source Guide)

2 Tbsp. Ruby Port

1 Tbsp. extra-virgin olive oil

1 Tbsp. low-sodium soy sauce

1 Tbsp. chopped shallot

2 tsp. chopped fresh cilantro

1½ tsp. apple cider vinegar

1½ tsp. canola oil

1½ tsp. cracked black pepper

½ tsp. chopped garlic

½ tsp. crushed red pepper

⅛ tsp. liquid smoke

⅛ tsp. dried thyme

⅛ tsp. chopped fresh rosemary

1 bay leaf

HEAT a small skillet over medium-high heat. Add the cumin seeds and cook, stirring until fragrant and lightly toasted, 30 to 45 seconds. Transfer the seeds to a medium bowl.

ADD the remaining ingredients to the bowl with the seeds and stir well to combine.

USE as a marinade for duck breasts or chicken. (About 10 percent of the marinade is absorbed into the meat when marinating, and the remainder is discarded.)

CALORIES: 5; TOTAL FAT: TRACE; CARBOHYDRATE: 1 G; DIETARY FIBER: 0 G; PROTEIN: TRACE

RATATOUILLE SAUCE

Our Ratatouille Sauce underlies several of our other dishes, including Miraval's vegetable lasagna and various cooked whole-grain pastas. Served either hot or chilled, it also makes a wonderful summer side staple. Keep in mind that the recipe doubles easily, which makes it ideal for dinner parties or holiday meals.

MAKES ABOUT 2 CUPS; SERVING SIZE: ½ CUP

¼ c. yellow zucchini, one-inch baton cuts

¼ c. green zucchini, one-inch baton cuts

¼ c. eggplant, one-inch baton cuts

2 Tbsp. bell pepper, julienne

2 Tbsp. portobello mushroom, large diced

1 Tbsp. black, green, or kalamata olives, halved lengthwise

1½ tsp. fresh basil chiffonade

2 tsp. fresh oregano, chopped

1½ tsp. fresh chopped garlic

½ c. canned diced tomatoes

½ c. tomato puree

¼ c. red onions, julienne

1½ tsp. Miraval Oil Blend (page 19)

PREHEAT medium saucepot over medium-high heat. Add oil and garlic, and sauté until it starts to brown, about 30 seconds.

STIR in basil and oregano, and sauté for about 20 seconds, or until you can just smell their aroma.

ADD all remaining ingredients except tomatoes and tomato puree (zucchini, onions, eggplant, peppers, mushroom, and olives) and sauté for one minute, or until the vegetables just begin to soften.

REDUCE heat to low-medium, and add in tomatoes and tomato puree. Simmer until sauce is heated, about 5 minutes, stirring often. Season to taste with salt and pepper if needed. Ladle over polenta, wild salmon, or your favorite pasta.

CALORIES: 12; TOTAL FAT: TRACE; CARBOHYDRATE: 3 G; DIETARY FIBER: TRACE; PROTEIN: TRACE

RED WINE DEMI-GLACE

MAKES 1 CUP; SERVING SIZE: 2 TBSP.

¼ c. sliced shallots

¾ tsp. whole black peppercorns

6 sprigs fresh thyme

2 c. Cabernet Sauvignon

3 c. Veal Stock (page 25) or store-bought beef stock

COMBINE the shallots, peppercorns, and thyme in a medium saucepan; place over high heat; and cook, stirring until the shallots start to soften, 1 to 2 minutes. Add the wine and bring to a boil. Reduce the heat to medium and simmer until reduced to about a quarter cup in volume, 14 to 15 minutes. Add the veal stock and cook until reduced to a syrup (thick enough to coat the back of a spoon), 25 to 30 minutes.

REMOVE from heat and serve hot.

CALORIES: 30; TOTAL FAT: 0 G; CARBOHYDRATE: 2 G; DIETARY FIBER: 0 G; PROTEIN: 0 G

RED WINE REDUCTION

A favorite standby to add flavorful polish to a plate, this is one recipe you will turn to time and again. Keep in mind that red wines are more astringent than others, particularly younger wines. If your reduction is slightly bitter, add agave syrup or sugar to taste.

MAKES 1 CUP; SERVING SIZE: 2 TBSP.

3 c. good-quality red wine, such as Cabernet Sauvignon or Merlot

PLACE the wine in a medium heavy saucepan pan and bring to a boil over high heat. Lower the heat to medium-high and cook until reduced to a thick syrup, reducing the heat as the liquid evaporates, 45 minutes.

POUR the reduction into a small ramekin until ready to serve. (The reduction will keep, covered in the refrigerator, for up to two weeks.)

CALORIES: 20; TOTAL FAT: 0 G; CARBOHYDRATE: TRACE; DIETARY FIBER: 0 G; PROTEIN: 0 G

ROASTED GREEN-CHILI SAUCE

You can substitute canned green chilies and tomatillos for the fresh ingredients called for in this recipe. Remember that canned items contain salt, and the recipe will need to be adjusted accordingly.

MAKES 3 CUPS

½ tsp. Miraval Oil Blend (page 19) or canola oil

1 c. chopped yellow onion

2½ tsp. chopped garlic

½ c. chopped celery

4 c. hulled, rinsed, and chopped tomatillos; or canned tomatillos, rinsed and drained

1 c. peeled, seeded, and chopped roasted poblano peppers; or canned green chilies, rinsed and drained

2 c. Vegetable Stock (page 24), canned vegetable broth, or water

2 tsp. chopped fresh basil

1½ tsp. chopped fresh thyme

1 tsp. chopped fresh oregano

⅛ tsp. kosher salt

Pinch freshly ground black pepper

HEAT the oil in medium saucepan over medium-high heat. Add the onion and cook, stirring, for 1 minute. Add the garlic and cook, stirring, for 45 seconds. Add the celery and cook, stirring, for 1 minute. Add the tomatillos and peppers and cook until the peppers begin to sweat, about 2 minutes. Add the stock, increase the heat, and bring to a rapid boil. Cook, stirring occasionally, over medium-high heat until the tomatillos begin to burst and the liquid is reduced to a half cup, 20 to 25 minutes. Add the herbs, salt, and pepper; and stir well. Reduce the heat to medium-low, and cook, stirring occasionally until thick and nearly all the liquid is gone, 5 to 7 minutes.

REMOVE the pan from the heat. Using a handheld immersion blender, or in batches in a food processor or blender, carefully puree the sauce. Serve immediately.

TO store this salsa, let it cool down as quickly as possible after cooking: pour into a shallow pan, cool at room temperature, and transfer immediately to an airtight container. Freezing is not recommended, but it will keep refrigerated for up to four days.

CALORIES: 25; TOTAL FAT: 0 G; CARBOHYDRATE: 4 G; DIETARY FIBER: 1 G; PROTEIN: 1 G

SIDE
VEGETABLES
& STARCHES

ASPARAGUS, RED BELL PEPPER, AND MUSHROOM RISOTTO

This can be a companion dish to virtually any of our meat, poultry, or fish recipes, as well as a satisfying vegetarian entrée on its own.

MAKES 4 SERVINGS

3¼ c. Vegetable Stock (page 24) or canned vegetable broth

½ tsp. Miraval Oil Blend (page 19) or canola oil

1 Tbsp. chopped yellow onion

¼ tsp. minced garlic

¾ c. arborio or carnaroli rice

½ c. dry white wine

½ tsp. minced fresh parsley

¼ tsp. minced fresh oregano

¼ tsp. minced fresh thyme

¾ tsp. kosher salt

¾ tsp. freshly ground black pepper

½ c. chopped red bell pepper

½ c. half-inch pieces asparagus

½ c. sliced shiitake mushrooms

1 Tbsp. grated Parmigiano-Reggiano

PLACE the vegetable stock in a small saucepan and bring to a simmer over medium-high heat. Remove from the heat and cover to keep warm until ready to use.

HEAT a ¼ tsp. of the oil in a medium saucepan over medium-high heat. Add the onion and garlic and cook, stirring until fragrant, 45 seconds. Add the rice and cook, stirring until lightly browned, about 2 minutes. Add the wine to deglaze the pan and cook until reduced by half, about 1 minute.

ADD the hot stock a ½ cup at a time and stir well. Cook at a low simmer, stirring occasionally, until nearly all the stock is absorbed and the rice is tender and almost al dente, about 22 minutes. Reserve ¼ cup of stock. Add the herbs, salt, and pepper and cook, stirring for 1½ minutes. Remove from the heat and cover to keep warm.

HEAT the remaining ¼ tsp. oil in a medium skillet over medium-high heat. Add the bell pepper and asparagus and cook, stirring for 2 minutes. Add the mushrooms and cook, stirring for 1½ minutes.

FOLD the vegetables into the risotto with the remaining ¼ cup stock, and cook over medium heat, stirring until the rice is warmed through and the stock is absorbed, 2 minutes. Add the cheese, stir well, and cook for 30 seconds.

REMOVE the pan from the heat, and serve immediately.

CALORIES: 140; TOTAL FAT: 0.5 G; CARBOHYDRATE: 27 G; DIETARY FIBER: 2 G; PROTEIN: 3 G

BASIC RISOTTO

MAKES 4 SERVINGS

2 c. Vegetable Stock (page 24)
or canned vegetable broth

¼ tsp. Miraval Oil Blend
(page 19) or canola oil

1 Tbsp. chopped yellow onion

¼ tsp. minced garlic

½ c. arborio or carnaroli rice

½ c. dry white wine

½ tsp. minced fresh parsley

¼ tsp. minced fresh oregano

¼ tsp. minced fresh thyme

¾ tsp. kosher salt

¾ tsp. freshly ground black pepper

1 Tbsp. grated Parmigiano-Reggiano

PLACE the vegetable stock in a small saucepan and bring to a simmer over medium-high heat. Remove from the heat and cover to keep warm until ready to use.

HEAT the oil in a medium saucepan over medium-high heat. Add the onion and garlic and cook, stirring until fragrant, 45 seconds. Add the rice and cook, stirring for 1 minute. Add the wine and cook until reduced by half, 1 to 1½ minutes.

ADD 1½ cups of the hot stock and stir well. Cook at a low simmer, stirring occasionally until nearly all the stock is absorbed, 6 to 7 minutes. Add the additional ½ cup stock and cook, stirring occasionally, for 2 minutes. Add the herbs, stir well, and cook for 2 minutes. Add the salt and pepper, stir well, and cook until all the liquid is absorbed, 1 to 1½ minutes. Add the cheese, stir well, and cook until melted, 30 seconds.

REMOVE the pan from the heat and serve immediately as an accompaniment for chicken, beef, fish, or vegetarian entrées.

CALORIES: 130; TOTAL FAT: 0.5 G; CARBOHYDRATE: 23 G; DIETARY FIBER: 2 G; PROTEIN: 2 G

BLACK BEANS CHARRO-STYLE

MAKES 2 CUPS; SERVING SIZE: ¼ CUP

½ tsp. extra-virgin olive oil

2 c. Basic Black Beans (page 14)

¼ c. onion, chopped

1 clove garlic, minced

¼ tsp. jalapeño, chopped

1 Tbsp. cilantro, chopped

⅛ tsp. kosher salt, or to taste

HEAT the oil in a small saucepan over medium heat. Add the onion, garlic, and jalapeño; and cook, stirring until soft, 4 minutes. Add the black beans and cook, stirring until warmed through, 4 to 5 minutes. Add the cilantro and salt, stir well, and adjust the seasoning to taste.

REMOVE from the heat and cover to keep warm until ready to serve.

CALORIES: 60; TOTAL FAT: 0.5 G; CARBOHYDRATE: 10 G; DIETARY FIBER: 4 G; PROTEIN: 4 G

BUTTERNUT SQUASH–PANCETTA RAVIOLI

MAKES 8 RAVIOLI

1 c. chopped, peeled butternut squash

¼ tsp. Miraval Oil Blend (page 19)

1 Tbsp. extra-virgin olive oil

¼ c. chopped pancetta
(about 2½ ounces)

2½ Tbsp. fine, dry bread crumbs

1 Tbsp. grated Parmigiano-Reggiano

1 tsp. finely grated lemon zest

1 tsp. chopped fresh sage

⅛ tsp. kosher salt

⅛ tsp. freshly ground black pepper

1 pinch freshly grated nutmeg

8 square wonton wrappers

1 large egg beaten with 2 tsp.
water to make an egg wash

PREHEAT oven to 400° F.

COMBINE squash and Miraval Oil Blend in a mixing bowl and toss to coat. Transfer to a baking sheet and bake until soft, about 25 minutes. Remove from oven. Reduce heat to 375° F.

TO PREPARE THE RAVIOLI: Heat ½ tsp. of the olive oil in a medium sauté pan over medium heat. Add the pancetta and cook, stirring until the pancetta is crisp, about 3 minutes. Drain well.

PLACE the pancetta, roasted butternut squash, and the remaining ingredients (except the wrappers and egg wash) in a food processor and puree until smooth. Alternately, place the squash in a medium mixing bowl and mash, then add in the pancetta and other ingredients, stirring well to combine.

LINE a baking sheet with parchment paper and set aside.

LAY one wonton wrapper on a work surface and spoon about 2 tsp. of the mixture into the center. Lightly dab a small amount of the egg wash around the edges of the wrapper and lay a second wrapper on top, pressing down to seal; place on the prepared baking sheet. Repeat with the remaining ingredients.

BAKE the ravioli until cooked through, lightly toasted, and fragrant, about 13 minutes.

REMOVE from the oven and place two ravioli on each plate. Serve with Rack of Lamb with Cinnamon-Peppercorn Sauce (page 159) or the entrée of your choice.

CALORIES: 200; TOTAL FAT: 8 G; CARBOHYDRATE: 13 G; DIETARY FIBER: TRACE; PROTEIN: 5 G

CARAMELIZED-ONION ORZO CAKES

MAKES 2 CUPS; SERVING SIZE: ½ CUP

½ tsp. Miraval Oil Blend
(page 19) or canola oil

⅔ c. thinly sliced yellow onion

1 c. orzo pasta

1⅓ c. Vegetable Stock (page 24),
canned vegetable broth, or water

½ tsp. kosher salt

½ tsp. chopped fresh flat-leaf parsley

½ tsp. chopped fresh oregano

¼ tsp. chopped fresh thyme

Pinch freshly ground black pepper

HEAT a large skillet over high heat. Add the oil and onion and cook, stirring until the onions start to caramelize and turn dark golden brown, 2 to 3 minutes. Lower the heat to medium and continue to cook, stirring occasionally until caramelized, 2 minutes. Add the orzo and cook, stirring to completely combine and to lightly toast the pasta, 30 to 45 seconds. Add the stock and cook, stirring until the pasta is tender, 7 to 9 minutes.

REMOVE from the heat and stir in the salt, herbs, and pepper.

LIGHTLY spray 4 four-ounce ramekins with nonstick cooking spray.

DIVIDE the orzo among the ramekins, filling each three-quarters full. Refrigerate the ramekins until well chilled so that they will hold their shape when turned out, 30 to 40 minutes.

TURN out the cakes onto a baking sheet that has been lightly sprayed with nonstick cooking spray, and roast until warmed through and the edges are beginning to turn brown, 12 to 14 minutes.

SERVE immediately.

CALORIES: 230; TOTAL FAT: 1.5 G; CARBOHYDRATE: 47 G; DIETARY FIBER: 3 G; PROTEIN: 8 G

CARAMELIZED THREE-ONION POLENTA

MAKES 2 CUPS; SERVING SIZE: ½ CUP

½ tsp. Miraval Oil Blend
(page 19) or canola oil

1½ Tbsp. thinly sliced red onion

1½ Tbsp. thinly sliced yellow onion

1½ Tbsp. sliced leek, well rinsed

2½ c. Vegetable Stock (page 24), canned
vegetable broth, rice milk, or water

1 tsp. kosher salt

½ tsp. freshly ground black pepper

¾ c. quick-cooking polenta

HEAT the oil in a large saucepan or medium pot over medium-high heat. Add the red and yellow onions and cook, stirring, until soft and starting to turn brown, about 2 minutes. Add the leeks and cook, stirring until soft and starting to turn brown, 1 minute. Add the liquid, salt, and pepper and bring to a boil over high heat.

ADD the polenta, lower the heat to medium-low and cook, whisking constantly until clumps are gone and polenta is smooth, about 4 minutes.

SPRAY a small (8" by 8") casserole dish lightly with nonstick cooking spray, spread the polenta about ½ inch thick, and allow it to cool to room temperature. As it cools, the polenta will set up and become firm (about 25 to 30 minutes).

NOTE: For even better results, use traditional polenta, following the directions on the package. This will increase the cooking time by approximately 20 minutes.

CALORIES: 290; TOTAL FAT: 5 G; CARBOHYDRATE: 50 G; DIETARY FIBER: 4 G; PROTEIN: 13 G

DARK CHOCOLATE, CHERRY, AND ORANGE RISOTTO

MAKES 3 CUPS

3¾ c. Vegetable Stock (page 24) or canned vegetable stock

½ tsp. Miraval Oil Blend (page 19) or vegetable oil

2 Tbsp. finely chopped red onion

1 c. carnaroli or arborio rice

⅓ c. plus 1 Tbsp. unsweetened dark cocoa

⅓ c. plus 1 Tbsp. dried Bing cherries

2 Tbsp. orange juice

¼ c. semisweet chocolate pieces

PLACE the vegetable stock in a small saucepan and bring to a simmer over medium-high heat. Remove from the heat and cover to keep warm until ready to use.

HEAT a large saucepan over medium-high heat. Add the oil and onions and cook, stirring until the onions are fragrant and starting to soften, 30 to 45 seconds. Add the rice and cook, stirring until the grains are toasted and glossy, 3 to 5 minutes. Add the cocoa and stir well to coat the grains. Add 1¼ cups of the hot stock to the pan, lower the heat to medium-low, and cook, stirring constantly to remove any lumps of cocoa and until the liquid is absorbed, 4 minutes. Add the cherries, orange juice, and ½ cup of the hot stock, and cook, stirring until the liquid is absorbed, 4 minutes. Add 1 cup of the hot stock and cook, stirring until the liquid is absorbed, 5 to 6 minutes. Add 1 cup of the hot stock and cook, stirring until the liquid is absorbed, 4 minutes. Add the chocolate pieces and stir until completely melted.

REMOVE from the heat and serve by itself or as an accompaniment to Grilled Ahi Tuna with Roasted Pineapple Salsa.

CALORIES: 250; TOTAL FAT: 5 G; CARBOHYDRATE: 48 G; DIETARY FIBER: 4 G; PROTEIN: 5 G

GRILLED VEGETABLES

¼ c. extra-virgin olive oil

1 Tbsp. fresh basil, chiffonaded

2 tsp. fresh oregano, chopped

1 tsp. fresh rosemary, minced

1 tsp. fresh thyme, minced

1 Tbsp. fresh garlic, minced

1 tsp. kosher salt

½ tsp. freshly ground black pepper

Pinch of crushed red pepper flakes (optional)

1 eight-ounce yellow squash, trimmed and sliced lengthwise ¼-inch thick

1 eight-ounce zucchini, trimmed and sliced lengthwise ¼-inch thick

1 four-ounce red bell pepper, stemmed, cored, seeded, and quartered

1 medium tomato, about 5 ounces, stemmed, cored, and quartered

1 two-ounce portobello mushroom, wiped clean, stemmed, ribs removed, and quartered

1 Tbsp. Roasted Garlic (page 22), chopped

2 tsp. Roasted Shallots (page 22), chopped

PREHEAT a grill to high.

TO make the marinade, stir together the oil, minced fresh garlic, herbs, crushed red pepper flakes, salt, and pepper in a large mixing bowl. Adjust seasoning to your taste, and remember that as with all marinades, it is best to exaggerate the flavors a bit, because they will be somewhat muted as they are absorbed into whatever you are marinating. Add the vegetables to the marinade and toss to combine, taking care to coat evenly. Let the vegetables marinate for 5 to 7 minutes. Drain well, making sure to reserve the marinade if you are planning on making a grilled vegetable salad (the marinade will double as a dressing). To avoid over-saturating the vegetables, do not marinate for more than 15 minutes.

PLACE the squash, zucchini, bell pepper, and portobello on the hottest part of the grill and the tomato quarters skin-side down on the cooler part of the grill. Cook, turning until the tomatoes are slightly charred, 1 to 2 minutes, and the other vegetables are marked on both sides and tender, 1 to 2 minutes per side. Remove the vegetables to a baking sheet or other dish, and lay them out on a single layer to allow quick cooling. When the grilled vegetables are cool, slice or dice, and return to the mixing bowl along with the roasted garlic and shallots and toss to combine all the ingredients.

(ALTERNATIVELY, preheat the oven to 400° F, place the vegetables on a single layer on a baking sheet or casserole dish, and roast, stirring occasionally, until tender, about 15 to 20 minutes.)

ADD the vegetables to the marinade and toss to combine. Let the vegetables marinate for at least 30 minutes and up to 2 hours. The vegetables will keep refrigerated in an airtight container for up to two days.

CALORIES: 120; TOTAL FAT: 4 G; CARBOHYDRATE: 16 G; DIETARY FIBER: 3 G; PROTEIN: 4 G

ROASTED GARLIC AND BASIL MASHED POTATOES

The power of garlic is a constant source of inspiration in our kitchen, and this side is a perennial favorite at Miraval. We pair these flavorful, low-fat potatoes with our Beef Fillets, but they're also a fitting companion to chicken and fish entrées.

MAKES 1½ CUPS; SERVING SIZE: ½ CUP

2 c. peeled and sliced russet potatoes (about 2 medium potatoes)

2 tsp. extra-virgin olive oil

⅛ tsp. kosher salt

⅛ tsp. freshly ground black pepper

1 Tbsp. pureed or mashed Roasted Garlic (page 22)

2 Tbsp. chopped fresh basil

PLACE the potatoes in a medium saucepan with enough cold water to cover by one inch, and bring to a boil over high heat. Reduce the heat and cook at a low boil until the potatoes are fork tender but not falling apart, 17 to 20 minutes.

DRAIN the potatoes well, place in a medium bowl, and mash with a potato masher. (Alternatively, turn the potatoes through a ricer into a bowl.) Stir in the oil, salt, and pepper and mix well. Add the garlic, mix well, and then add the basil, stirring to incorporate.

SERVE immediately.

CALORIES: 80; TOTAL FAT: 1.5 G; CARBOHYDRATE: 13 G; DIETARY FIBER: 2 G; PROTEIN: 2 G

ROASTED RED BELL PEPPER MASHED POTATOES

MAKES 2 CUPS; SERVING SIZE: ½ CUP

1 c. Roasted Red Bell Pepper, page 18 (about 1 large)

1 pound russet potatoes, peeled and sliced crosswise half-inch thick

¾ tsp. extra-virgin olive oil

½ tsp. salt

Pinch freshly ground black pepper

PUREE the roasted bell pepper in a food processor on high speed. Transfer to a bowl and set aside.

PLACE the potatoes in a medium saucepan with enough cold water to cover by one inch, and bring to a boil over high heat. Reduce the heat and cook at a low boil until the potatoes are fork tender but not falling apart, 17 to 20 minutes.

DRAIN the potatoes well, place in a medium bowl, and mash with a potato masher. (Alternatively, turn the potatoes through a ricer into a bowl.) Stir in the pureed peppers, oil, salt, and pepper and mix well.

SERVE immediately.

CALORIES: 130; TOTAL FAT: 1 G; CARBOHYDRATE: 27 G; DIETARY FIBER: 3 G; PROTEIN: 3 G

WASABI POTATO CAKES

MAKES 4 SERVINGS

4 oz. russet potato, peeled and grated

1 Tbsp. finely chopped yellow onion

1 Tbsp. chopped green onions

1 large egg white

½ c. wasabi powder

1 Tbsp. all-purpose or wheat flour

⅛ tsp. baking powder

⅛ tsp. kosher salt

½ tsp. Miraval Oil Blend
(page 19) or canola oil

PREHEAT the oven to 375° F.

COMBINE the potato, yellow and green onions, and egg white in a medium bowl and stir well to combine.

SIFT together the remaining ingredients except the oil, and stir into the potato mixture. Using a quarter-cup measure, shape the mixture into small cakes, squeezing each one as you form them so the ingredients will stick together.

HEAT a medium sauté pan over medium-high heat. Add the oil to the pan and when hot, add the cakes and cook until golden brown, turning once, 1 minute per side. Transfer the cakes to a baking sheet and bake in the oven until cooked through and hot, about 6 minutes. Serve hot.

CALORIES: 46; TOTAL FAT: TRACE; CARBOHYDRATE: 8 G; DIETARY FIBER: 1 G; PROTEIN: 21 G

ENTRÉES

BEEF FILLETS WITH ROASTED GARLIC AND BASIL MASHED POTATOES, BALSAMIC REDUCTION, AND TOMATO-SHALLOT SALAD WITH PEPPERED GOAT CHEESE

MAKES 4 SERVINGS

2 tsp. Miraval Oil Blend
(page 19) or canola oil

4 four-ounce beef fillets, trimmed

⅛ tsp. kosher salt

⅛ tsp. freshly ground black pepper

1 c. Roasted Garlic and Basil
Mashed Potatoes (page 141)

1 recipe Tomato-Shallot Salad with
Peppered Goat Cheese (recipe follows)

1 recipe Balsamic Reduction (page 14)

PREHEAT the oven to 375°F.

LIGHTLY season both sides of each fillet with salt and pepper.

HEAT a large heavy skillet over high heat. When the pan is hot, add the oil and the beef and cook until well seared, 1½ minutes. Turn the meat and sear on the second side, about 1 minute.

PLACE the pan in the oven and cook to medium rare (4 minutes), or to desired doneness. Remove the meat from the pan and let rest on a platter while assembling the plates.

TO serve, place ¼ cup of the Roasted Garlic and Basil Mashed Potatoes in the center of each of four plates. Arrange one fillet on each serving of potatoes and top with Tomato-Shallot Salad and one piece of Peppered Goat Cheese. Drizzle each plate with 1 tsp. of the Balsamic Reduction and serve immediately.

CALORIES: 380; TOTAL FAT: 13 G; CARBOHYDRATE: 26 G; DIETARY FIBER: 2 G; PROTEIN: 36 G

TOMATO-SHALLOT SALAD WITH PEPPERED GOAT CHEESE

We only use the meaty outer part of the tomato to make this salad—not the pulpy center or seeds—hence the ingredient name "tomato meat." To obtain the meaty pieces, trim the tomato as you would a bell pepper by cutting off the top and bottom, then roll the cut tomato onto its sides as you cut away the thicker, juicier parts. Reserve the remaining tomato pieces for other recipes, such as gazpacho, vegetable stock, or pico de gallo.

MAKES 1 CUP

1 c. julienned tomato meat

¼ c. thinly sliced shallots

4 tsp. Balsamic Reduction (page 14)

¼ c. chiffonade fresh basil

2 tsp. goat cheese, softened

¼ tsp. cracked black pepper

MIX together the tomato, shallots, and balsamic reduction in a small bowl. Add the basil and mix well.

FORM the goat cheese into four half-teaspoon-sized portions and roll each into a small ball. Press a pinch of pepper onto each ball.

SERVE as an accompaniment to the Beef Fillets, or divide the tomato salad among four plates and top each serving with one piece of peppered goat cheese.

BEEF FILLETS WITH BALSAMIC RED ONIONS, CREAMED SPINACH, AND BABY CARROTS

A lovely recipe for a family get-together on a cool autumn evening, this entrée is the very definition of mouthwatering. We source grass-fed beef, as it is leaner and more flavorful with less saturated fat, and contains heart-healthy omega-3 fatty acids. Keep in mind that grass-fed beef cooks faster than grain-fed beef, so adjust your cooking time accordingly. For a velvety accompaniment, top the steaks with Red Wine Demi-Glace (page 130).

MAKES 4 SERVINGS

4 four-ounce beef fillets, trimmed of all fat

⅛ tsp. kosher salt

⅛ tsp. freshly ground black pepper

1 recipe Balsamic Red Onions (recipe is on the next page)

1 recipe Creamed Spinach (recipe is on the next page)

1 recipe Blanched Carrots (recipe is on page 149)

ABOUT 15 minutes before grilling, remove the steaks from the refrigerator and bring to room temperature.

PREHEAT a grill or grill pan to high heat. (Alternatively, a large heavy skillet can be used.)

LIGHTLY season both sides of the fillets with salt and pepper.

PLACE the meat on the grill and cook for 1½ minutes. To make grill marks, turn the fillets one-quarter turn and continue cooking on the first side for 1½ minutes. Turn the fillets and cook on the second side for 1½ minutes. Turn the fillets one-quarter turn and cook for 3 minutes, for a total cooking time of 8 minutes for medium rare (140° F on an instant-read thermometer).

TRANSFER the fillets to a platter and let rest while assembling the plates, at least 4 minutes.

CALORIES: 440; TOTAL FAT: 14 G; CARBOHYDRATE: 41 G; DIETARY FIBER: 7 G; PROTEIN: 38 G

BALSAMIC RED ONIONS

MAKES 4 SERVINGS

¼ tsp. Miraval Oil Blend
(page 19) or canola oil

1 large red onion, ends removed,
peeled, and cut in half lengthwise

1½ c. balsamic vinegar

HEAT the oil in a large saucepan over high heat. Add the onions and cook until starting to color, 2 to 3 minutes. Turn and cook on the second side until starting to brown, 2 to 3 minutes.

ADD the balsamic vinegar and bring to a high simmer, about 1 minute. Reduce the heat and simmer for 15 minutes, turning the onions every 5 minutes. Lower the heat as the liquid reduces, and cook, stirring occasionally until the onions are tender and fall apart, 15 to 20 minutes.

REMOVE from the heat and serve immediately. (The balsamic syrup will continue to thicken as it cools.)

CREAMED SPINACH

MAKES 4 SERVINGS

⅓ c. low-fat cream cheese or
Neufchâtel, softened

1 Tbsp. rice milk

¼ tsp. Miraval Oil Blend
(page 19) or canola oil

2 Tbsp. thinly sliced garlic

5 c. fresh baby spinach, rinsed

¼ c. Vegetable Stock (page 24)

COMBINE the cream cheese and milk in a small bowl and whisk until very smooth and the milk is completely incorporated into the cream cheese.

HEAT a large skillet over high heat. When the skillet is hot, add the oil and the garlic and cook, stirring until the garlic starts to brown, about 45 seconds. Add half of the spinach and cook, stirring until nearly completely wilted, about 1 minute. Add the remaining spinach and the vegetable stock and cook, stirring until the spinach is completely wilted, 1½ to 2 minutes. Add the cream-cheese sauce, stir well, and cook for 20 seconds.

REMOVE from the heat and serve.

BLANCHED CARROTS

MAKES 4 SERVINGS

8 baby carrots, peeled and trimmed

¼ tsp. Miraval Oil Blend
(page 19) or canola oil

Pinch kosher salt

Pinch freshly ground black pepper

BRING a small pot of water to a boil. Add the carrots and cook until just tender, 4 minutes.

DRAIN well. Place the carrots in a bowl, toss with the oil and salt and pepper, and serve immediately.

BLACKENED SIRLOIN TACOS WITH SMOKY CHIPOTLE AIOLI AND BLACK BEANS CHARRO-STYLE

Zesty, smoky, and ever-so satisfying, these tacos are one of our most requested dishes at Miraval. If you are unable to obtain blue-corn tortillas in your area, use yellow-corn or flour tortillas to make your tacos. But if you do so, remember that the texture and the nutritional counts will vary.

MAKES 4 SERVINGS

1 tsp. chopped fresh basil

1 tsp. chopped fresh cilantro

1 tsp. chopped fresh oregano

½ tsp. ancho chili powder

½ tsp. minced fresh garlic

¼ tsp. kosher salt

1 lb. beef sirloin, trimmed of fat and sinew

½ tsp. Miraval Oil Blend (page 19)

4 six-inch corn tortillas

4 six-inch blue-corn tortillas

1 recipe Black Beans Charro-Style

1 recipe Chipotle-Cilantro Aioli (page 125)

½ c. Edamame Guacamole (page 219)

½ c. Tomato Pico de Gallo (page 227)

4 lime wedges, for garnish

PLACE the herbs, ancho powder, and garlic in a bowl and stir with a fork to combine. Add the meat to the bowl several pieces at a time, turning to coat on both sides. Lightly season the meat with the salt.

HEAT a large skillet or sauté pan over medium-high heat. Add the oil and when hot, add the meat; cook until blackened on the outside and medium rare, 3 to 4 minutes per side, depending upon the thickness. Transfer the meat to a cutting board to rest for 5 minutes, and then thinly slice.

IN a large, clean skillet heat the tortillas one at a time, 30 to 40 seconds each, turning once. Place on a plate and cover with a clean kitchen cloth to keep warm.

TO serve, divide the beans among four large plates. Lay one blue-corn and one yellow-corn tortilla on each plate and fill with the sirloin. Drizzle 1 tsp. of the aioli over the meat on each tortilla, and top with 2 tsp. each of the guacamole and pico de gallo. Garnish each plate with a lime wedge and serve immediately.

CALORIES: 240; TOTAL FAT: 11 G; CARBOHYDRATE: 7 G; DIETARY FIBER: 1 G; PROTEIN: 33 G

PISTACHIO-CRUSTED BEEF TENDERLOIN WITH RED WINE REDUCTION, CARAMELIZED-ONION ORZO CAKE, AND ROASTED VEGETABLES

MAKES 4 SERVINGS

4 four-ounce beef tenderloin fillets

½ tsp. kosher salt

¼ tsp. freshly ground black pepper

⅓ c. raw unsalted pistachios, chopped

1 recipe Caramelized-Onion
Orzo Cakes (page 136)

1 recipe Roasted Vegetables
(recipe follows)

1 recipe Red Wine Reduction (page 130)

PREHEAT the grill to high heat, and preheat the oven to 375° F.

LIGHTLY season both sides of the fillets with the salt and pepper.

WIPE the grill with a clean dishcloth or paper towel sprayed with canola oil. Place the fillets on the grill and cook for 1 minute. To make grill marks, turn the meat one-quarter turn and grill on the same side for 1 minute. Turn the meat and cook on the second side for 1 minute, and then turn one-quarter turn and grill on the same side for 1 minute.

PLACE the fillets on a baking sheet and roast for 8 to 9 minutes for medium rare (140° F on an instant-read thermometer). Remove from the oven and let rest for 5 minutes.

PLACE the pistachios in a shallow dish and roll each fillet in the nuts to lightly coat all sides.

TO serve, place one orzo cake in the center of each of four plates and arrange the vegetables around the orzo. Place one fillet on each orzo cake and drizzle 1 tsp. of the wine reduction around the meat. Serve immediately.

CALORIES: 530; TOTAL FAT: 15 G; CARBOHYDRATE: 51 G; DIETARY FIBER: 4 G; PROTEIN: 43 G

ROASTED VEGETABLES

MAKES 4 SERVINGS

We partially cook these vegetables on top of the stove to speed the cooking process. The roasting adds additional flavor.

8 oz. baby carrots, scrubbed clean, stems trimmed

4 oz. broccolini

½ tsp. Miraval Oil Blend (page 19)

⅛ tsp. kosher salt

⅛ tsp. freshly ground black pepper

PREHEAT the oven to 375° F.

BRING a pot of water to a boil. Add the carrots and cook until they start to become tender, 4 minutes. Add the broccolini and cook for 1 minute.

TRANSFER the vegetables to a baking dish and toss with the oil, salt, and pepper. Place in the oven and roast until tender and starting to brown, 8 minutes.

SERVE immediately.

BUFFALO FILET MIGNON WITH BACON, MUSHROOM, AND TOMATO FRICASSEE AND RED WINE DEMI-GLACE

MAKES 4 SERVINGS

4 four-ounce buffalo filet mignon, wiped dry (beef tenderloin can be substituted)

⅛ tsp. kosher salt

⅛ tsp. freshly ground black pepper

2 tsp. Miraval Oil Blend (page 19) or canola oil

1 c. Basic Mashed Potatoes (page 15)

1 recipe Red Wine Demi-Glace (page 130)

1 recipe Bacon, Mushroom, and Tomato Fricassee (recipe follows)

PREHEAT the oven to 375° F.

LIGHTLY season both sides of each filet with the salt and pepper.

HEAT a large heavy skillet over high heat. Add the oil; when hot, add the meat, and cook until seared, turning the pan to evenly distribute the oil around the pan so that the filets do not stick as they cook, about 2 minutes. Turn and sear the filets on the second side, 1 minute.

PLACE the pan in the oven and cook to desired doneness, about 5 minutes for medium rare. Remove the meat from the pan and let rest on a platter while assembling the plates.

SPOON ¼ cup of the mashed potatoes into the center of each of four plates and arrange the filets on top. Spoon 1 Tbsp. of the demi-glace over the meat and arrange the fricassee on top.

CALORIES: 410; TOTAL FAT: 18 G; CARBOHYDRATE: 24 G; DIETARY FIBER: 3 G; PROTEIN: 38 G

BACON, MUSHROOM, AND TOMATO FRICASSEE

MAKES 1 CUP

½ c. chopped bacon (2 oz.)

1 c. shiitake or crimini mushrooms

1 c. julienned tomatoes

2 Tbsp. chives, cut into 1-inch slices

HEAT a medium skillet over high heat. When the pan is hot, add the bacon and cook, stirring until the bacon starts to brown around the edges, 1½ minutes. Reduce the heat to medium and cook until the bacon is just browned and the fat is rendered, about 1 minute. Add the mushrooms and cook, stirring until the mushrooms absorb the fat, 1 minute. Add the tomatoes and cook, stirring until the mushrooms are wilted, 1 minute. Add the chives, stir well, and remove from the heat.

SERVE immediately.

BUFFALO TENDERLOINS WITH CORN-SAGE SAUCE AND TOASTED CORN BARLEY

MAKES 4 SERVINGS

4 four-ounce buffalo tenderloin steaks, patted dry (beef tenderloin can be substituted)

½ tsp. kosher salt

¼ tsp. freshly ground black pepper

1 tsp. canola oil or vegetable oil

5 oz. fresh baby carrots, trimmed and cut in half lengthwise

4 oz. trimmed broccoli florets (about 2 c.)

6 c. Corn Stock (recipe follows)

1 recipe Toasted Corn Barley (recipe follows)

1 c. Corn-Sage Sauce (recipe follows)

PREHEAT the oven to 350° F.

PREHEAT a large skillet over high heat. Add the oil and the steaks, season with salt and pepper, and cook until a crust forms, 1 minute. Turn the steaks and cook on the second side for 1 minute. Transfer the skillet to the oven and cook the steaks to desired doneness, about 5 minutes for medium rare. Transfer the steaks to a plate to rest.

MEANWHILE, place the corn stock in a medium saucepan and bring to a boil over high heat. Add the carrots and broccoli, reduce the heat to a simmer, and cook until just tender, about 4 minutes. Drain the vegetables in a colander.

TO serve, arrange ½ cup of the Toasted Corn Barley into the center of each of 4 large plates. Place a quarter of the vegetables to the side of the barley and spoon ¼ cup of the Corn-Sage Sauce to the other side of the plate. Place the steaks on the sauce, slightly atop the barley, and serve immediately.

CALORIES: 330; TOTAL FAT: 12 G; CARBOHYDRATE: 27 G; DIETARY FIBER: 6 G; PROTEIN: 30 G

CORN STOCK

MAKES ABOUT 10 CUPS

9 ears fresh corn, shucked and silk removed

3 qt. water

¼ tsp. kosher salt

CUT kernels from the corn and reserve for another use.

PLACE the corncobs in a large pot with the water and salt and bring to a boil over high heat. Reduce the heat to medium and simmer for 45 minutes.

STRAIN the broth through a fine mesh strainer or a cheesecloth-lined colander into a clean container and reserve until ready to use. (The stock can be kept refrigerated in an airtight container for up to five days, and frozen for up to one month.)

TOASTED CORN BARLEY

MAKES 2½ QUARTS

2 c. pearl barley

1 Tbsp. canola or vegetable oil

2 c. fresh corn kernels or frozen corn, thawed

1 c. chopped yellow onions

1 c. chopped red bell peppers

2 tsp. minced garlic

2 c. dry white wine

3 c. Corn Stock (page 155)

1½ tsp. kosher salt

½ tsp. freshly ground black pepper

IT is important that the saucepan be very hot before adding the barley in order to toast the kernels and release their nutty fragrance.

PREHEAT a large saucepan for several minutes over high heat until very hot. Add the barley and cook, stirring occasionally, until fragrant and starting to brown, 4 to 5 minutes.

REDUCE the heat to medium-high, add the oil, and stir to coat the barley. Add the corn, onions, bell peppers, and garlic; cook, stirring until the vegetables are soft, about 3 minutes. Add the white wine, stir well, and cook for 30 seconds. Add the corn stock, salt, and pepper. Stir well and bring to a boil. Lower the heat, cover, and simmer, stirring occasionally until the barley is tender but retains a slight crunch and the liquid is absorbed, 36 to 40 minutes.

CORN-SAGE SAUCE

MAKES 3 CUPS

2 tsp. canola or vegetable oil

1 c. chopped yellow onions

4 tsp. minced garlic

3 c. fresh corn kernels

1 c. peeled and diced
Yukon Gold potatoes

1 c. dry white wine

1 c. Corn Stock (page 155)

1 c. rice milk

1 Tbsp. chopped fresh sage,
or 1 tsp. dried sage

1½ tsp. kosher salt

½ tsp. freshly ground black pepper

HEAT a large saucepan over high heat. Add the oil, onions, and garlic; cook, stirring to combine. Add the potatoes and cook, stirring for 30 seconds. Add the corn and cook, stirring for 90 seconds. Add the wine and cook until nearly completely evaporated, 3 to 4 minutes. Add the corn stock and stir to combine. Add the rice milk, sage, salt, and pepper; stir well, and return to a boil. Reduce the heat to medium-low and simmer until the potatoes are fork tender and the liquid is reduced by a quarter in volume, about 20 minutes.

TRANSFER the contents of the pot to a blender and process on high speed until completely smooth, 1 to 2 minutes.

POUR through a fine mesh strainer into a clean container and cover to keep warm until ready to serve. (The sauce can be made up to one day in advance and kept refrigerated in an airtight container.)

RACK OF LAMB WITH CINNAMON-PEPPERCORN SAUCE

MAKES 4 SERVINGS

4 six-ounce New Zealand lamb racks (4 to 5 bones each), trimmed and frenched

¼ tsp. kosher salt

⅛ tsp. freshly ground black pepper

2 tsp. Miraval Oil Blend (page 19) or canola oil

1 recipe Butternut Squash–Pancetta Ravioli (page 135)

1 recipe Cinnamon-Peppercorn Sauce (recipe follows)

PREHEAT the oven to 375° F.

LIGHTLY season the lamb on all sides with the salt and pepper.

HEAT a large skillet or sauté pan over high heat. Add the oil and when hot, add the lamb in and cook, turning until well browned, 3 to 4 minutes on meaty side, then 1 minute on bony side.

TRANSFER the pan into your preheated oven and roast to desired temperature, 12 to 15 minutes for medium rare.

PLACE the racks on a large cutting board and let rest for 1 to 2 minutes. Use a knife to cut the racks into two 2-bone chops each and divide among four plates. Spoon the sauce over the meat and arrange two ravioli on each plate. Serve immediately.

CALORIES: 455; TOTAL FAT: 22 G; CARBOHYDRATE: 23 G; DIETARY FIBER: 9 G; PROTEIN: 39 G

CINNAMON-PEPPERCORN SAUCE

MAKES ⅓ CUP

¼ tsp. Miraval Oil Blend (page 19) or canola oil

½ c. thinly sliced yellow onion

¼ c. cleaned chopped portobellos

½ tsp. whole black peppercorns

1 tsp. fresh thyme

½ bay leaf

¼ c. brandy

1 c. good quality dry red wine, such as Cabernet Sauvignon or Merlot

1 cinnamon stick

1½ c. Red Wine Demi-Glace (page 130)

HEAT a medium saucepot over high heat. Add the oil; when hot, add the onions, mushrooms, peppercorns, thyme, and bay leaf; cook, stirring until the onions and mushrooms are soft, 3 minutes.

REMOVE the pot from the heat, add the brandy, and very carefully ignite with a match. Once the flame subsides, return the pot to medium-high heat. Add the wine and cinnamon, and bring to a simmer. Cook until the liquid is reduced by half, about 5 minutes, then add the demi-glace and reduce for 20 minutes at medium heat. The sauce will start to thicken, and that's when you're close to being done. Strain sauce through a fine mesh strainer and reserve for plating.

SKILLET-SEARED ELK WITH ROASTED SHALLOT, AGAVE, AND BLACKBERRY SAGE COMPOTE

Elk has a rich, distinct flavor. It is not gamey—it is absolutely delicious. Like venison, it is a very lean meat and easy to overcook. It's also similar to venison in both taste and appearance, and may be substituted for any recipe calling for venison. We advise you not to cook your medallions beyond medium-rare, as this will make the meat dry and tough.

MAKES 4 SERVINGS

1 baked potato or Basic Roasted Sweet Potatoes (page 19), peeled and sliced ½" thick

4 four-ounce elk medallions (see Source Guide)

2 tsp. molasses

2 tsp. Sedona Spice Rub (page 23)

1 recipe Roasted Shallot, Agave, and Blackberry Sage Compote (recipe follows)

2 tsp. Maytag or Stilton blue cheese, crumbled

2 tsp. Miraval Oil Blend (page 19)

FOR best results, place the elk medallions between two sheets of wax paper or plastic wrap and lightly pound with a meat mallet or other heavy, flat object (such as a small heavy skillet) to slightly flatten and tenderize the meat. The medallions should be about half as thick as they were before pounding.

PREHEAT a cast-iron skillet or sauté pan over high heat.

LIGHTLY brush or otherwise coat each side of the medallions with ¼ tsp. of the molasses, and then season with ¼ tsp. of the spice rub.

PLACE the medallions in the hot skillet with 1 tsp. of oil and sear on both sides to desired doneness, about 1 minute per side. The spice coating should be toasted but not burned.

REMOVE the elk from the pan and set aside. Lightly season potato slices with kosher salt and pepper, and place in skillet with remaining oil, searing on both sides until crusty and brown, about 1½ minutes per side. Use a spatula to turn the potatoes so they don't crumble.

PLACE two potato slices on each of four large plates, and top with one medallion each. Spoon 2 Tbsp. of the shallot-blackberry compote over the top of each medallion and crumble ½ tsp. of the cheese over the top. Serve immediately.

CALORIES: 190; TOTAL FAT: 2 G; CARBOHYDRATE: 9 G; DIETARY FIBER: 1 G; PROTEIN: 27 G

ROASTED SHALLOT, AGAVE, AND BLACKBERRY SAGE COMPOTE

MAKES ½ CUP

½ c. shallots, quartered

¾ tsp. Miraval Oil Blend (page 19)

½ c. frozen blackberries

3 Tbsp. blackberry or other berry-flavored liqueur

3 Tbsp. agave syrup (see Source Guide) or honey

1 Tbsp. chopped fresh sage

PREHEAT oven to 400° F.

PLACE the shallots in a small baking dish and toss with ½ tsp. of the oil to lightly coat. Roast until lightly browned and soft, 7 to 10 minutes.

HEAT a small saucepan over high heat. Add the shallots and remaining ¼ tsp. of oil blend, and sauté for one minute. Add the blackberry liqueur and reduce to a thick syrup, about 30 seconds, stirring often. Do not let the liqueur evaporate completely! Add agave syrup and cook until mixture returns to simmer, 30 to 45 seconds. Stir in the frozen blackberries and sage, and cook for 1 minute. Remove from heat.

COVER to keep warm until ready to serve.

SKILLET-SEARED RACK OF NEW ZEALAND LAMB WITH SUN-DRIED TOMATO JUS AND GOAT-CHEESE POLENTA

MAKES 4 SERVINGS

¼ c. Dijon mustard

1 tsp. fresh basil leaves

1 tsp. fresh oregano leaves

1 tsp. fresh thyme leaves

¼ tsp. fresh rosemary

¼ tsp. fresh tarragon leaves

4 six-ounce New Zealand lamb racks (4 to 5 bones each), trimmed and frenched

¼ tsp. kosher salt

⅛ tsp. freshly ground black pepper

2 tsp. Miraval Oil Blend (page 19) or canola oil

1 recipe Goat Cheese Polenta (recipe follows)

1 recipe Sun-Dried Tomato Jus (recipe follows)

PREHEAT the oven to 375° F.

COMBINE the mustard and herbs in the bowl of a food processor and process on high speed until the mixture is smooth and the mustard turns a bright green color, 1½ minutes.

LIGHTLY season the lamb on all sides with the salt and pepper.

HEAT a large skillet or sauté pan over high heat. Add the oil and when hot, add the lamb and cook, turning until well browned, 3 to 4 minutes on meaty side, then 1 minute on bony side. Remove pan from heat.

TRANSFER the meat to a plate or baking sheet. Brush each rack with 1 Tbsp. of the herb mustard, coating the entire rack except for the bones; return to sauté pan; and roast to desired temperature, 12 to 15 minutes for medium rare.

PLACE the racks on a large cutting board and let rest for 1 to 2 minutes. Using a sharp knife, cut the racks into two 2-bone chops each and fan over the polenta. Spoon the Sun-Dried Tomato Jus over the meat and serve immediately.

CALORIES: 470; TOTAL FAT: 14 G; CARBOHYDRATE: 51 G; DIETARY FIBER: 4 G; PROTEIN: 32 G

SUN-DRIED TOMATO JUS

MAKES ½ CUP

½ tsp. Miraval Oil Blend (page 19)

2 Tbsp. thinly sliced shallot

2 Tbsp. chopped sun-dried tomato

1 tsp. chopped fresh sage leaves

1 tsp. fresh thyme

1 whole black peppercorn

1½ c. Veal Stock (page 25) or store-bought beef stock

½ c. Cabernet Sauvignon or Merlot

PREHEAT a small saucepot on medium-high heat. Sauté shallots, herbs, sun-dried tomato, and black peppercorn with the oil until aromatic, about 1 minute and 15 seconds. Add the wine into the pan and reduce by half, about 1 minute. Reduce heat to medium, add veal/beef stock, and simmer until sauce reduces by a third and just begins to thicken, about 17 minutes. Strain to remove peppercorn. Hold warm until ready to serve.

GOAT-CHEESE POLENTA

MAKES 1½ CUPS

2½ c. skim milk, rice milk, or
Vegetable Stock (page 24)

½ c. polenta

2 Tbsp. (1 oz.) fresh goat cheese

½ tsp. kosher salt

¼ tsp. freshly ground black pepper

¼ tsp. fresh rosemary, minced

BRING liquid to simmer over medium-high heat in a small saucepot. Add polenta, reduce heat to medium-low, and stir until thick, about 5 minutes. Fold in the remaining ingredients and season to taste. Remove from flame and keep warm.

163

PAN-SEARED CERVENA VENISON WITH KILN-DRIED CHERRIES, WALNUTS, AND PORT-WINE JUS

Cervena venison is a New Zealand farm-raised/free-range deer, raised without added hormones or antibiotics. It is full flavored, tender, and delicious, with none of the gaminess often associated with venison. We use black walnuts in this recipe at Miraval; however, you can substitute the more readily available English walnuts.

MAKES 4 SERVINGS

4 four-ounce venison medallions cut from the short loin, tenderloin, or Denver leg cut (see Source Guide)

2 tsp. Miraval Oil Blend (page 19)

Pinch kosher salt

Pinch freshly ground black pepper

2 tsp. minced shallots

¼ c. kiln-dried cherries

3 Tbsp. chopped black walnuts

½ c. Ruby Port

8 oz. Red Wine Demi-Glace (page 130) or store-bought low-sodium beef stock

1 c. Basic Mashed Potatoes (page 15)

LIGHTLY season the meat on both sides with the salt and pepper.

HEAT a large skillet or sauté pan over high heat. Add the oil and when very hot—but not quite smoking—add the venison and sear until browned, about 1 minute per side.

JUST prior to turning the meat over in the pan, add the shallots, cherries, and walnuts to the pan with the meat and cook, stirring until the shallots are soft, about 1 minute. Remove the meat to a clean plate.

ADD the port to the pan and cook, stirring to deglaze the pan and until the liquid is reduced by three-quarters in volume, about 45 seconds. Do not allow the wine to completely evaporate! Add the demi-glace or stock, and cook until the mixture is reduced by about half and thick enough to coat the back of a spoon, 3 to 4 minutes.

PLACE ¼ cup mashed potatoes, or other starch, onto each of four plates along with half a cup of fresh steamed vegetables of your choice. Arrange the medallions around the potatoes and spoon 2 Tbsp. of the sauce, walnuts, and cherries over the meat. Serve immediately.

CALORIES: 300; TOTAL FAT: 10 G; CARBOHYDRATE: 12 G; DIETARY FIBER: 1 G; PROTEIN: 28 G

ACHIOTE-ORANGE GRILLED CHICKEN WITH WILLCOX PEACH RELISH

MAKES 4 SERVINGS

4 four-ounce boneless, skinless chicken breasts

1 c. Achiote-Orange Marinade (page 122)

1 c. Willcox Peach Relish (recipe follows)

1 c. Basic Jasmine Rice (page 15)

IN a small mixing bowl or casserole dish, combine the raw chicken breasts and 1 cup of the Achiote-Orange Marinade. Mix well to completely coat each breast evenly. Allow to marinate refrigerated for 1 hour.

PREHEAT grill on high heat for 15 minutes. Preheat the oven to 375° F.

DRAIN excess marinade from the chicken breasts and place on the hot grill. Allow to cook for 2 minutes per side, or until well marked. Place on a lightly oiled baking sheet and bake in the oven until the chicken is cooked through and reaches an internal temperature of 165° F, about 10 minutes.

SPOON ¼ cup of warm jasmine rice into the center of four large plates and place one chicken breast on each serving of rice. Spoon ¼ cup of peach relish over the top of each chicken breast. Serve immediately.

CALORIES: 200; TOTAL FAT:1.5 G; CARBOHYDRATE: 16 G; DIETARY FIBER: 2 G; PROTEIN: 28 G

WILLCOX PEACH RELISH

MAKES 2 CUPS

Many of the fruits and vegetables that we use at Miraval are harvested in the Sulphur Springs Valley, which runs north and south of Willcox, Arizona, about 100 miles east of Tucson. This fertile valley produces a bounty of fresh fruits and vegetables, including peaches, pears, tomatoes, and several varieties of apples. The peaches are especially tasty. However, if you don't have access to fresh peaches, frozen peaches are a suitable substitution. This recipe is equally good with chicken, duck, or pork; or with fish such as halibut, yellowfin tuna, or salmon; or as an accompaniment to corn tortilla chips.

1 c. yellow freestone peaches, medium diced

½ c. Basic Black Beans (page 14)

½ c. red bell pepper, medium diced

¼ c. red onion, small diced

2 Tbsp. cilantro, rinsed and chopped

1½ tsp. raspberry vinegar

1½ tsp. agave syrup (see Source Guide)

COMBINE all ingredients in a medium mixing bowl and refrigerate until ready to use. This relish can be served hot or cold.

OVEN-ROASTED BALSAMIC CHICKEN

MAKES 4 SERVINGS

4 four-ounce boneless,
skinless chicken breasts

⅛ tsp. kosher salt

⅛ tsp. freshly ground black pepper

½ tsp. Miraval Oil Blend
(page 19) or canola oil

2 c. Chicken Stock (page 20) or
canned low-sodium chicken broth

2 Tbsp. Balsamic Reduction (page 14)

¼ c. freshly cut corn kernels

12 grape or cherry tomatoes

1⅓ Tbsp. chopped green onions

1 c. Basic Mashed Potatoes (page 15)

PREHEAT the oven to 375° F.

LIGHTLY season the chicken breasts on both sides with the salt and pepper.

HEAT a large skillet or sauté pan over medium-high heat. Add the oil to the pan and when hot, add the chicken and cook until golden brown, about 2 minutes. Turn the breasts and cook for 2 minutes. Add the chicken stock and 1 Tbsp. of the balsamic reduction, stir well to deglaze the pan, and cook for 30 seconds. Add the corn, tomatoes, and green onions; stir well, and bake in the oven until the chicken is cooked through and reaches an internal temperature of 165° F, 7 to 9 minutes.

SPOON ¼ cup of the mashed potatoes into the center of four large plates, and place one chicken breast on each serving of potatoes. Spoon the pan sauce and vegetables over the chicken, and drizzle each serving with ¾ tsp. of the remaining balsamic reduction. Serve immediately.

CALORIES: 130; TOTAL FAT: 2.5 G; CARBOHYDRATE: 8 G; DIETARY FIBER: 1 G; PROTEIN: 19 G

CHICKEN RELLENO

4 four-ounce boneless,
skinless chicken breasts

1 c. all-purpose flour (you will have
some left over; discard after use)

1½ c. Spicy Cream Cheese
Filling (recipe follows)

1 recipe Relleno Batter (recipe follows)

2 c. Black Beans (recipe follows)

1 c. Mole Verde Sauce
(recipe on page 170)

Pinch of kosher salt

Pinch freshly ground black pepper

1 Tbsp. canola oil

PREHEAT oven to 400° F.

USE a paring knife to make an opening in the thicker end of each chicken breast to create a cavity for the Spicy Cream Cheese Filling: insert the knife and carefully wiggle it back and forth to make a pocket in the breast, being careful not to cut all the way through to the outside of the meat. Use a pastry bag to pipe the cream cheese filling into each breast until mixture is evenly distributed among each breast (about 3 Tbsp. per breast).

LIGHTLY season each breast with salt and pepper, and then dust them with flour, gently shaking to remove excess flour. Place in the Relleno Batter, turning to coat evenly.

PREHEAT a medium sauté pan over medium-high heat, and add 1 Tbsp. of canola oil to the pan.

CAREFULLY place each battered breast into the heated oil and sauté until brown on each side (about 45 seconds per side). Use a spatula to turn, as tongs may tear the batter off.

REMOVE the chicken from sauté pan and place on baking sheet. Bake in the oven until the filling has reached a temperature of 165° F, about 12 to 14 minutes.

TO PLATE: ladle ½ cup black beans into each bowl, top with the chicken and ¼ cup of the Mole Verde Sauce.

CALORIES: 310; TOTAL FAT: 12 G; CARBOHYDRATE: 17 G; DIETARY FIBER: 5 G; PROTEIN: 33 G

SPICY CREAM CHEESE FILLING

¾ c. low-fat Neufchâtel cheese,
allowed to warm to room
temperature to soften slightly

6 Tbsp. Anaheim green chili peppers,
roasted, peeled, and diced

4 Tbsp. jalapeños, roasted,
peeled, and diced

IN a medium mixing bowl, combine cream cheese and roasted peppers. Use a rubber spatula to mix all ingredients well, about one minute.

SPOON mixture into pastry bag.

RELLENO BATTER

MAKES 4 SERVINGS

4 large egg whites, ¾ cup
1 tsp. dark chili powder

1 tsp. cumin seed, ground

COMBINE all ingredients in a mixing bowl and whip with an electric mixer over medium speed until a loose meringue (soft peak) is formed, about 3 minutes.

BLACK BEANS

MAKES 3 CUPS

1 Tbsp. dried oregano
1 Tbsp. dried thyme
1 Tbsp. cumin seed, ground
1 Tbsp. coriander seed, ground
1 Tbsp. kosher salt

1 Tbsp. granulated garlic
1 c. black beans raw, picked through to remove any broken beans or stones
1 gallon (16 c.) water

ADD beans and seasonings into a pot with 3 quarts (12 cups) of water.

BOIL for about 1.5 hours or until tender. Check periodically to see if more water needs to be added.

MOLE VERDE SAUCE

MAKES 2 CUPS; SERVING SIZE: ¼ CUP

1 c. yellow onion, peeled and diced

4 Tbsp. garlic, chopped

3 c. tomatillos, peeled, rinsed, and quartered

4 Tbsp. jalapeños, rough chopped with seeds

½ c. green onion, chopped

1 c. cilantro, chopped

1 c. raw pumpkin seeds (pepitas)

6 cinnamon sticks

1 Tbsp. ground clove

1 Tbsp. kosher salt

1 tsp. freshly ground black pepper

1 Tbsp. canola oil

3 c. Chicken Stock (page 20)

¼ c. honey

1 c. raw spinach

2 Tbsp. lime juice and zest (1 average-sized lime)

PREHEAT a medium sauté pan over medium-high heat, and add 1 tablespoon of canola oil to the pan. Let oil heat for about 20 seconds.

ADD yellow and green onions, garlic, tomatillos, jalapeño, cilantro, pumpkin seeds, cinnamon, clove, salt, and pepper to the pan and sauté until aromatic, about 1½ minutes.

ADD 3 cups of chicken stock to the pan to deglaze, and stir to remove anything that may be stuck to the bottom of the pan. Simmer over medium heat for 30 minutes, stirring occasionally.

REMOVE from heat, allow to cool, and remove cinnamon sticks. Pour cooled sauce into a blender. Add honey, lime juice and zest, and spinach. Blend for 20 seconds or until smooth. The raw spinach will help to brighten the color of the sauce.

BLUE CORN–CRUSTED CHICKEN SCALLOPINI WITH ROASTED GARLIC JUS AND ASPARAGUS, RED BELL PEPPER, AND MUSHROOM RISOTTO

MAKES 4 SERVINGS

Four 4-ounce boneless, skinless chicken breasts

½ c. blue cornmeal

¾ tsp. kosher salt

½ tsp. ground coriander

½ tsp. garlic powder

½ tsp. dried oregano

¼ tsp. freshly ground pepper

¾ tsp. Miraval Oil Blend (page 19) or canola oil

One recipe Asparagus, Red Bell Pepper, and Mushroom Risotto (page 133)

Roasted Garlic Jus (recipe follows)

PREHEAT the oven to 425° F. Place each chicken breast between two sheets of plastic wrap and pound with a meat mallet to ½-inch thickness. (Alternatively, pound the chicken using the bottom of a heavy medium skillet.)

MIX together the cornmeal, coriander, garlic, oregano, and ½ tsp. of the salt in a shallow dish. Lightly season both sides of the chicken with a pinch of the remaining ¼ tsp. salt and black pepper.

ONE at a time, dredge the chicken on both sides in the seasoned cornmeal, shaking to remove any excess breading. Place the coated chicken on a clean dish until ready to cook.

PREHEAT a large ovenproof skillet over medium-high heat. Add the oil; when hot, add the chicken and cook for 1 minute. Turn the chicken, transfer to the oven, and bake until cooked through, 6 minutes. Remove from the oven.

TO SERVE, spoon a half cup of the risotto into the center of each of 4 plates. Arrange one chicken breast on each serving of risotto and spoon 2 Tbsp. of the Roasted Garlic Jus over each and decoratively around the plate. Serve immediately.

CALORIES: 340; TOTAL FAT: 5 G; CARBOHYDRATE: 39 G; DIETARY FIBER: 4 G; PROTEIN: 28 G

ROASTED GARLIC JUS

MAKES ½ CUP

1 recipe (¼ c.) Roasted Garlic (page 22)

½ c. Cabernet Sauvignon

1 c. Red Wine Demi-Glace (page 130)

HEAT a medium saucepan over medium-high heat. Add the garlic and cook until heated through, 20 seconds. Add the wine, bring to a simmer, and cook until reduced by half in volume, 2 minutes. Add the demi-glace and cook until thick enough to coat the back of a spoon and reduced to about a half cup in volume, 5 to 7 minutes.

STRAIN the sauce into a small clean bowl and cover to keep warm until ready to serve.

CILANTRO-CRUSTED SCALLOPS WITH CUMIN-SCENTED BLACK-BEAN CAKES, CORN SALSA, AND SMOKED RED PEPPER COULIS

MAKES 4 SERVINGS

1 tsp. Miraval Oil Blend (page 19)

4 large fresh scallops, about
2 oz. each, wiped dry

Pinch kosher salt

Pinch freshly ground black pepper

4 tsp. chopped cilantro

1 recipe Cumin-Scented Black Bean
Cakes (recipe on the next page)

1 recipe Corn Salsa (recipe on page 175)

½ recipe Smoked Red Pepper
Coulis (recipe on page 176)

SEASON the scallops lightly on both sides with the salt and pepper. Place the cilantro on a plate and turn each scallop on the cilantro to lightly coat with the herb on both sides. Heat a medium skillet over high heat until very hot. Add the oil and swirl to coat the bottom of the pan. Add the scallops and cook until well seared, 1½ to 2 minutes. Turn the scallops and cook until seared and nearly cooked through, 1½ to 2 minutes.

PLACE one black bean cake on each of four plates and top each with one scallop. Spoon about 1 tsp. of the corn salsa on top of each scallop and an additional 2 Tbsp. of the salsa around the sides. Drizzle the coulis around the edges of the plates and serve immediately.

CALORIES: 130; TOTAL FAT: 2 G; CARBOHYDRATE: 18 G; DIETARY FIBER: 3 G; PROTEIN: 12 G

CUMIN-SCENTED BLACK BEAN CAKES

MAKES 4 SERVINGS

1½ c. Basic Black Beans (page 14) or canned black beans, rinsed and drained well

1 large egg white

¾ tsp. ground cumin

2 Tbsp. finely chopped red bell pepper

2 Tbsp. finely chopped yellow onion

Pinch kosher salt

Pinch freshly ground black pepper

½ tsp. Miraval Oil Blend (page 19) or canola oil

PREHEAT the oven to 350° F.

PLACE 1 cup of the black beans, egg white, and cumin in the bowl of a food processor and process to a paste.

TRANSFER the blended ingredients to a bowl and add the remaining ½ cup black beans, onion, bell pepper, salt, and pepper; mix well with a rubber spatula.

PORTION out the mixture with a 2-ounce ice-cream scoop or ¼-cup measuring cup, and press into patties ½-inch thick.

HEAT a medium heavy skillet over high heat. Add the oil, lower the heat to medium-high, and cook the patties until golden brown, 1 to 1½ minutes. Turn and cook until golden brown on the second side, 1 to 1½ minutes.

TRANSFER to the oven and bake until cooked through, 10 to 12 minutes. Serve immediately.

CORN SALSA

MAKES ⅓ CUP

This is one of our favorite concoctions with corn—so simple, yet so succulent. We roast the corn for a nutty flavor prior to putting the black bean cakes in the oven. In lieu of roasting, you may cut the kernels from the ear and either pan sauté or blanch them in boiling water for 2 minutes and drain well. Use the remaining one-quarter cup kernels for welcomed texture in a salad or other recipe.

1 ear fresh corn

2 Tbsp. finely chopped red bell pepper

2 tsp. finely sliced green onions

½ tsp. rice wine vinegar

¼ tsp. Miraval Oil Blend (page 19) or canola oil

Pinch kosher salt

Pinch freshly ground black pepper

PREHEAT the oven to 350° F.

PLACE the unshucked ear of corn on the middle rack of the oven and roast until tender, 15 to 18 minutes. Let sit until cool enough to handle.

SHUCK the corn, remove the silk, and cut the kernels from the cob.

COMBINE ¼ cup of the corn kernels and the remaining ingredients in a small bowl. Stir well to combine, cover, and refrigerate until ready to use.

SMOKED RED PEPPER COULIS

MAKES ½ CUP

Our culinary team created this recipe with lazy summer afternoons in mind. Simply char the peppers over an open stove-top burner or outdoor grill, turning carefully with tongs as they cook. There will be more sauce than needed for the scallops. Savor every drop by drizzling the leftover sauce on grilled or baked seafood or chicken.

1 large red bell pepper

⅛ tsp. Miraval Oil Blend

2 Tbsp. chopped yellow onion

¼ tsp. chopped garlic

⅓ c. Vegetable Stock (page 24) or canned vegetable broth

⅛ tsp. kosher salt

Pinch freshly ground black pepper

USING the stove top or an outdoor smoker, smoke the bell pepper so that the skin can easily be removed and the pepper has a smoky aroma. (Alternatively, the pepper can be placed in a perforated pan or steamer set over a skillet containing ½ cup mesquite wood chips. Tightly cover and cook over low heat for 20 minutes.)

TRANSFER the pepper to a plastic bag for 5 minutes. Carefully peel away the skin, core, seed, and roughly chop the pepper.

HEAT a medium heavy skillet over medium-high heat. Add the oil, onion, and garlic and cook, stirring until the onion starts to soften and turn brown, 45 seconds to 1 minute. Add the bell pepper and cook, stirring for 20 seconds. Add the stock, salt, and pepper, and cook until the pepper is softened and heated through, 45 seconds.

TRANSFER the mixture to a blender and process until smooth.

THE coulis can be made in advance and kept refrigerated in an airtight container for up to four days.

GRILLED MAHIMAHI WITH CITRUS VINAIGRETTE, ROASTED RED BELL PEPPER MASHED POTATOES, AND WILTED SPINACH

MAKES 4 SERVINGS

4 four-ounce mahimahi fillets
½ tsp. extra-virgin olive oil
¼ tsp. salt
¼ tsp. freshly ground black pepper
1 recipe Roasted Red Bell Pepper Mashed Potatoes (page 141)
1 recipe Wilted Spinach (recipe follows)
1 recipe Citrus Vinaigrette (page 118)

PREHEAT a grill to high heat. Preheat the oven to 450° F.

PLACE the fish on a large dish and season on both sides with the salt and pepper. Drizzle the oil over fillets and turn to lightly coat.

GRILL the fish for 1 minute, turn one-quarter turn, and grill for 1 minute. Turn the fish and cook for 1 minute, turn one-quarter turn, and grill for 1 minute. (Alternatively, the fish can be seared for 2 minutes per side in ½ tsp. of oil in a large skillet over high heat.)

PLACE the fillets on a baking sheet and roast until tender and just cooked through, 10 minutes, checking the fish after 8 minutes. Remove from the oven and let rest for 5 minutes.

TO serve, spoon the mashed potatoes into the center of 4 large plates and arrange the spinach to the side. Place the fish on the potatoes and spoon the vinaigrette on and along the side of the potatoes. Serve immediately.

CALORIES: 270; TOTAL FAT: 2.5 G; CARBOHYDRATE: 36 G; DIETARY FIBER: 4 G; PROTEIN: 25 G

WILTED SPINACH

MAKES 4 SERVINGS

½ tsp. Miraval Oil Blend (page 19) or vegetable oil

4 oz. fresh baby spinach, rinsed and spun dry (about 4 c.)
2 Tbsp. water

HEAT a large skillet over high heat. Add the oil to the pan and swirl to evenly coat the bottom. Add the spinach and cook, stirring until lightly wilted, 45 seconds. Add the water and cook until the spinach is completely wilted and the water is evaporated, about 1½ minutes.

REMOVE from the heat and cover to keep warm until ready to serve.

GRILLED AHI TUNA WITH ROASTED PINEAPPLE SALSA

Ahi tuna, paired with our Roasted Pineapple Salsa, is a smart, protein-packed choice for an alfresco lunch. If fresh ahi isn't available, substitute any firm, mild-flavored fish, such as mahimahi.

MAKES 4 SERVINGS

4 four-ounce ahi tuna fillets

4 tsp. Sedona Spice Rub (page 23)

1½ tsp. Miraval Oil Blend (page 19) or canola oil

1 recipe Roasted Pineapple Salsa (recipe follows)

1 c. Dark Chocolate, Cherry, and Orange Risotto (page 138) or Basic Jasmine Rice (page 15)

LIGHTLY coat each fillet on both sides with 1 tsp. of the spice rub.

PREHEAT a large skillet over high heat. Add the oil and when hot, add the fish, shaking to prevent it from sticking to the bottom of the pan. Cook until golden brown, about 1 to 1½ minutes. Turn and cook until the fish is just done but still rare, 2 to 3 minutes, depending upon the thickness.

SPOON ¼ cup of risotto or jasmine rice onto the center of each plate. Remove the fish from the pan and place on the rice. Spoon the salsa onto each plate and serve immediately.

CALORIES: 233; TOTAL FAT: 5 G; CARBOHYDRATE: 25 G; DIETARY FIBER: 2 G; PROTEIN: 24 G

ROASTED PINEAPPLE SALSA

MAKES 1 CUP

1 c. fresh pineapple, peeled and cut into ½-inch cubes

¼ c. fresh orange juice

2 Tbsp. red bell pepper, finely chopped

1 Tbsp. red onion, finely chopped

1 Tbsp. fresh mint or basil, finely chopped

PREHEAT a heavy thick-bottomed medium skillet over high heat. Add the pineapple and cook undisturbed until caramelized, 30 to 40 seconds. (The pineapple will make a little "shriek" as it hits the pan.) Cook, stirring until the pineapple is charred on the outside, 1 to 1½ minutes. Add the juice, and cook, stirring until the liquid is almost evaporated and a thick syrup forms in the pan.

REMOVE the pan from the heat and pour the pineapple and syrup into a small bowl.

ADD the remaining ingredients to the bowl, stir to combine, and let rest until ready to serve.

THE CACTUS FLOWER RESTAURANT & COYOTE MOON · ENTRÉES

GRILLED SALMON WITH CHIPOTLE VINAIGRETTE

4 four-ounce skinless salmon fillets

⅛ tsp. kosher salt

⅛ tsp. freshly ground black pepper

4 c. mesclun salad mix

1 c. peeled and thinly sliced jicama

1 pear, cored and sliced thin

½ recipe Chipotle Vinaigrette (page 118)

2 Tbsp. fresh lemon juice

1 tsp. chopped chives

PREHEAT the grill to medium-high.

SEASON the salmon fillets with salt and pepper. Place the salmon on the hottest part of the grill and cook for 2 minutes. Turn the salmon and cook until medium rare, 1 to 2 minutes.

REMOVE the salmon to a clean plate and let rest for 2 minutes.

TO serve, toss the salad mix, pear, jicama, and lemon juice with ½ tsp. of water. Divide the salad among four large plates.

TOP each portion of salad with one salmon fillet and chives; drizzle with ¼ cup of the chipotle vinaigrette. Serve immediately.

CALORIES: 200; TOTAL FAT: 7 G; CARBOHYDRATE: 8 G; DIETARY FIBER: 3 G; PROTEIN: 23 G

MISO-GLAZED SEA BASS WITH JASMINE RICE AND SUGAR SNAP PEAS

MAKES 4 SERVINGS

1 Tbsp. extra-virgin olive oil

¼ c. chopped lemongrass

1 Tbsp. chopped ginger

1 c. peeled and diced Yukon Gold potato, about 4 oz.

6 Tbsp. red miso paste

2 c. Vegetable Stock (page 24) or canned vegetable broth

1 Tbsp. minced fresh cilantro

4 four-ounce sea bass fillets

⅛ tsp. kosher salt

⅛ freshly ground black pepper

1 recipe Jasmine Rice (recipe follows)

1 recipe Sugar Snap Peas (recipe follows)

PREHEAT the oven to 425° F.

TO make the glaze, heat the oil in a medium heavy skillet over medium-high heat. Add the lemongrass and ginger and cook, stirring until fragrant, 1 minute. Add the potato and cook, stirring for 1 minute. Add the miso, stir well to break up the paste, and cook for 30 seconds. Add the stock and bring the mixture to a boil. Reduce the heat to a low boil and cook, stirring occasionally until the potatoes are tender, 8 to 9 minutes.

TRANSFER the mixture to the bowl of a blender and process on high speed until smooth.

STRAIN into a clean container, stir in the cilantro, and set aside until ready to use.

SEASON both sides of each fillet with a pinch each of the salt and pepper.

HEAT the oil in a large ovenproof skillet over medium-high heat. Add the seasoned fish and sear for 1 minute. Turn and transfer the skillet to the oven and cook for 5 minutes.

REMOVE the pan from the oven, turn each fillet and let rest in the pan on top of the stove while assembling the remaining components.

TO serve, spoon ¼ cup of the rice on each of four large plates and angle the fillets on top of the rice. Place the peas to the side of the rice and drizzle the fish with the glaze. Serve immediately.

CALORIES: 370; TOTAL FAT: 8 G; CARBOHYDRATE: 46 G; DIETARY FIBER: 6 G; PROTEIN: 30 G

JASMINE RICE

MAKES 4 SERVINGS

½ tsp. Miraval Oil Blend
(page 19) or canola oil

¼ c. finely chopped carrots

2 c. Basic Jasmine Rice (page 15)

¼ c. Vegetable Stock (page 24)
or canned vegetable broth

⅛ tsp. kosher salt

⅛ tsp. freshly ground black pepper

HEAT the oil in a medium saucepan over medium heat. Add the carrots and cook, stirring until soft, 2 minutes. Add the rice, stir well, and cook for 15 seconds. Add the stock, salt, and pepper; cook, stirring until the rice is hot and the liquid is evaporated, 1½ to 2 minutes.

REMOVE from the heat and cover to keep warm until ready to serve.

SUGAR SNAP PEAS

MAKES 4 SERVINGS

¼ tsp. Miraval Oil Blend
(page 19) or canola oil

2 c. sugar snap peas

Pinch kosher salt

Pinch freshly ground black pepper

½ c. Vegetable Stock (page 24)
or canned vegetable broth

HEAT the oil in a large heavy skillet over medium-high heat. Add the peas, salt, and pepper and cook, stirring for 1 minute. Add the stock and cook, stirring until the peas are just tender and retain a crunch, 2 to 2½ minutes.

REMOVE from the heat and serve immediately.

PAN-SEARED BLACK COD WITH SAFFRON-INFUSED SAUCE, PARSNIP PUREE, AND WILTED SPINACH

Nutritional note from Junelle Lupiani: "Black cod, or sablefish, is one of the richest sources of essential omega-3 fatty acids—over one gram per four-ounce portion. I often recommend it for people who don't have a palate for oily fish since it has a nice light, buttery flavor."

MAKES 4 SERVINGS

4 four-ounce black cod fillets

½ tsp. kosher salt

¼ tsp. freshly black pepper

½ tsp. Miraval Oil Blend (page 19) or vegetable oil

1 recipe Parsnip Puree (recipe follows)

1 recipe Wilted Spinach (page 177)

½ recipe Saffron-Infused Sauce (recipe is on page 186)

1 recipe Oven-Roasted Beet Jewels (recipe is on page 186)

SEASON the fish on both sides with the salt and pepper.

PREHEAT a large skillet over medium-high heat. Add the oil to the pan and swirl to evenly coat the bottom. Slowly lay the fish into the pan, one at a time, giving the pan a small shake to keep each fillet from sticking. Cook until lightly golden brown, 3 minutes. Turn the fish and cook until golden brown, 4 minutes.

REMOVE the fish from the oven and place on a clean dish while assembling the plates.

TO serve, spoon the parsnip puree in the center of four large plates and place the spinach on the side. Arrange the fish on the parsnip puree, drizzle with the sauce, and top each serving with three beet balls. Serve immediately.

CALORIES: 160; TOTAL FAT: 7 G; CARBOHYDRATE: 1 G; DIETARY FIBER: 0 G; PROTEIN: 22 G

PARSNIP PUREE

MAKES 1¼ CUPS

Note: The length of time the parsnips take to cook depends upon how large they have been chopped.

1 lb. parsnips, peeled, stems trimmed, and roughly chopped

1 Tbsp. extra-virgin olive oil

⅛ kosher salt

Pinch freshly ground black pepper

PLACE the parsnips in a medium pot of water and bring to a boil. Reduce the heat to low and cook until completely tender, 30 to 40 minutes.

TRANSFER the parsnips to a food processor. Add the oil, salt, and pepper; and process on high speed until smooth, scraping down the sides of the machine as needed.

SERVE immediately.

SAFFRON-INFUSED SAUCE

MAKES 1½ CUPS

½ tsp. Miraval Oil Blend
(page 19) or canola oil

1 c. chopped shallots

1 tsp. chopped garlic

1 c. dry white wine

1 tsp. saffron threads

¾ c. peeled and finely chopped
Yukon Gold potato

1 whole vanilla bean

3 c. water

½ tsp. kosher salt

HEAT a medium saucepan over high heat. Add the oil and when hot, add the shallots and cook, stirring until soft, 1½ to 2 minutes. Add the garlic and cook, stirring until fragrant, 30 seconds. Add the wine, stir, and cook until reduced by half, about 1 minute. Add the saffron and stir well. Add the potato and vanilla bean and cook, stirring occasionally until the wine is nearly completely reduced, 2½ to 3 minutes. Add the water, cover, and bring to a boil. Uncover, lower the heat, and simmer until the potatoes are tender, about 30 minutes. Add the salt and cook for an additional minute.

REMOVE the pan from the heat and remove the vanilla bean. Cut the vanilla bean in half lengthwise and scrape out the seeds using the tip of a paring knife. Scrape the seeds into the blender with the remaining ingredients and puree to a sauce consistency.

COVER to keep warm until ready to serve.

OVEN-ROASTED BEET JEWELS

MAKES 4 SERVINGS

1 medium-sized beet

¼ tsp. Miraval Oil Blend
(page 19) or canola oil

PREHEAT the oven to 350° F.

USING a small melon baller, scoop 12 balls from the beet.

PLACE the balls in a small baking dish, toss with the oil, and bake until tender, about 10 minutes.

REMOVE from the oven and set aside until ready to serve as a topping.

PAN-SEARED ARCTIC CHAR
WITH GAZPACHO, QUINOA, AND
GRILLED VEGETABLES

Ranging from pale pink to bright red, arctic char is widely available and high in omega-3 fatty acids. Depending on your taste, salmon, halibut, and sea bass make welcome substitutes.

MAKES 4 SERVINGS

4 four-ounce arctic char fillets
¼ tsp. kosher salt
⅛ tsp. freshly ground black pepper
½ tsp. Miraval Oil Blend
(page 19) or canola oil
1 recipe Basic Quinoa (page 18)
½ recipe Grilled Vegetables, zucchini and squash only (page 140)
1 recipe Gazpacho (page 80)
Finely grated fresh lemon or lime zest

LIGHTLY season the fish fillets on both sides with the salt and pepper.

HEAT the oil in a large skillet over medium-high heat. Add the fish and sear on the first side, 1 minute. Turn, cover, and cook until firm and almost medium rare, 3 minutes.

TRANSFER the fish to a large plate to rest.

ARRANGE one strip of grilled zucchini in the middle of each of four plates and place one strip of squash on top to form an X shape. Spoon the quinoa over the vegetables and place the char on the top. Spoon the Gazpacho sauce around the fish, top with zest, and serve immediately.

CALORIES: 200; TOTAL FAT: 8 G; CARBOHYDRATE: 9 G; DIETARY FIBER: 1 G; PROTEIN: 23 G

PAN-SEARED WILD SALMON WITH RATATOUILLE SAUCE AND BROWN RICE

MAKES 4 SERVINGS

1⅔ c. Vegetable Stock (page 24) or water

1 c. brown rice

¼ tsp. kosher salt

16 spears medium asparagus, woody ends trimmed

½ recipe Ratatouille Sauce (page 129)

4 ½-inch thick slices from an average-sized yellow squash or zucchini

4 ½-inch by 3-inch strips red bell pepper, raw

4 four-ounce boneless, skinless salmon fillets

⅛ tsp. freshly ground black pepper

½ tsp. Miraval Oil Blend (page 19) or canola oil

PLACE the stock, brown rice, and ⅛ tsp. salt in a medium saucepan and bring to a simmer over medium heat. Cook uncovered until the rice is just tender and the liquid is absorbed, about 30 minutes. Remove the rice from the heat and let sit undisturbed.

BRING a medium pot of water to a boil. Add the asparagus and cook until just past raw, about 1½ minutes. Drain the asparagus and shock by plunging it into ice water to stop the cooking process. Allow to cool completely, about 3 minutes. Drain well and set aside.

CUT four ½-inch thick slices on the bias (at an angle so that each squash chip is oval shaped) from the squash, and using an apple corer, cut a circle out of the center of each squash round. Insert four or five cooked and chilled asparagus spears and one raw bell pepper strip in the center of each uncooked squash disk and set aside. The asparagus and pepper strip should be a tight fit in the squash ring to keep all the ingredients together. It's also very important that the squash and bell pepper be kept raw until the bundles are assembled and cooked just prior to plating, so that as the asparagus is being reheated, the squash and pepper strip will be cooked to just the right consistency.

LIGHTLY season the salmon fillets on both sides with the remaining ⅛ tsp. salt and the pepper.

HEAT a large skillet or sauté pan over high heat until very hot, about 3 minutes. Add the oil to the pan; when hot, add the fish, lower the heat to medium-high and cook, turning once, until golden brown on both sides and medium rare, about 2 minutes per side.

REMOVE the pan from the heat and let the fish rest for 1 minute.

MEANWHILE, bring a large pan of water to a boil. Place the asparagus bundles in a colander or steamer and place over the boiling water until the bundles just begin to steam, about 1 minute.

TO serve, divide the rice among four large plates and top each serving with one salmon fillet. Spoon the ratatouille sauce over the fish, and place one asparagus bundle on the side. Serve immediately.

CALORIES: 360; TOTAL FAT: 9 G; CARBOHYDRATE: 40 G; DIETARY FIBER: 5 G; PROTEIN: 28 G

PORCINI-CRUSTED BLACK COD WITH TRUFFLE OIL AND GARLIC SPINACH

MAKES 4 SERVINGS

2 Tbsp. dried porcini mushrooms

4 four-ounce skinless black cod fillets

¼ tsp. kosher salt

⅛ tsp. freshly ground black pepper

1½ tsp. Miraval Oil Blend
(page 19) or canola oil

1 recipe Garlic Wilted Spinach
(recipe follows)

1 tsp. white truffle oil

PREHEAT the oven to 350° F.

USING a coffee grinder, grind the dried mushrooms into a fine powder. Transfer the powder to a plate.

LIGHTLY season both sides of each fillet with the salt and pepper, and then dredge into the mushroom powder, lightly coating on both sides. Shake to remove any excess.

PREHEAT a large skillet over high heat. Add the oil and when hot, add the fish, shaking to prevent them from sticking to the bottom of the pan. Cook the fish until golden on the first side, about 30 seconds. Turn the fillets, transfer the pan to the oven, and bake until the fish is just cooked through, 6 to 7 minutes. Remove the fish from the oven.

DIVIDE the spinach between four large plates and arrange the fillets on the spinach. Drizzle each serving with ¼ tsp. of the truffle oil and serve immediately.

CALORIES: 200; TOTAL FAT: 10 G; CARBOHYDRATE: 2 G; DIETARY FIBER: 1 G; PROTEIN: 23 G

GARLIC WILTED SPINACH

MAKES 4 SERVINGS

1¾ tsp. Miraval Oil Blend
(page 19) or canola oil

4 tsp. minced garlic

1 lb. fresh baby spinach, washed

Pinch kosher salt

Pinch freshly ground black pepper

HEAT 1 tsp. of the oil in a large skillet over medium-high heat. Add the garlic and cook, stirring until fragrant and turning golden brown, 1 to 1½ minutes. Add one-quarter of the spinach to the pan and cook, stirring until starting to wilt, 1 to 2 minutes. Add the remaining oil, stir well, and add the remaining spinach, one-quarter at a time, ensuring that the previous amount has wilted before adding the next.

ADD the salt and pepper, stir well, and remove the pan from the heat. Serve immediately.

SONORAN SHRIMP SCAMPI PASTA

MAKES 4 SERVINGS

2 Tbsp. thinly sliced sun-dried tomato

6 oz. farfalle (bowtie) pasta

12 oz. peeled, fresh large
(21/25 count) shrimp

⅛ tsp. kosher salt

Pinch freshly ground black pepper

2 Tbsp. plus ¼ tsp. extra-virgin olive oil

¼ c. roasted, peeled, and chopped fresh
poblano chili; or canned chili,
rinsed and drained

1 Tbsp. minced garlic

1 Tbsp. minced cilantro

¼ c. tequila

2 Tbsp. fresh lime juice

1 recipe Scampi Sauce (recipe follows)

PLACE the sun-dried tomatoes in a small bowl and cover with warm water. Let sit until plump, about 1 hour. Drain well and set aside.

BRING a medium pot of lightly salted water to a boil. Add the pasta and cook until al dente, 10 to 12 minutes. Drain, rinse under cold running water, and drain well. Toss the pasta with ¼ tsp. of the oil to prevent it from sticking and set aside.

HEAT the remaining 2 Tbsp. oil in a large heavy skillet over medium-high heat. Add the shrimp and sear, 1 to 1½ minutes. Turn the shrimp and cook for 30 seconds. Add the poblano and garlic and cook, stirring, for 45 seconds. Add the tomatoes and cilantro, stir well, and cook for 45 seconds. Add the tequila and lime juice, and cook, stirring until the liquid is reduced by half, 1 minute. Add the Scampi Sauce, stir well to incorporate, and cook for 30 seconds. Add the drained pasta and cook, stirring until heated through and evenly coated with the sauce, 1½ to 2 minutes.

DIVIDE the shrimp scampi pasta among four pasta bowls and serve immediately.

CALORIES: 450; TOTAL FAT: 6 G; CARBOHYDRATE: 59 G; DIETARY FIBER: 5 G; PROTEIN: 30 G

SCAMPI SAUCE

MAKES 1¼ CUPS

¼ tsp. extra-virgin olive oil

2 Tbsp. minced yellow onion

1 Tbsp. minced jalapeño

2 tsp. minced garlic

2 Tbsp. fresh lime juice

2 tsp. tequila

2 c. rice milk

½ c. peeled and chopped russet potato

¼ c. chopped firm tofu

¼ c. Neufchâtel cheese or
low-fat cream cheese

2 Tbsp. low-fat sour cream

½ tsp. kosher salt

Pinch freshly ground black pepper

HEAT the oil in a medium heavy skillet over medium-high heat. Reduce the heat to medium; add the onion, jalapeño, and garlic; and cook, stirring until the onion has slightly browned, 1 to 1½ minutes. Add the lime juice and tequila and stir to deglaze the pan, 30 seconds. Add the remaining ingredients except the salt and pepper, cover, and cook until the potato pieces are tender and the liquid is reduced, 18 to 20 minutes.

TRANSFER the mixture to the bowl of a blender, add the salt and pepper, and process on high speed until smooth. Use immediately.

DUCK WITH CRANBERRY BARBECUE SAUCE AND WASABI POTATO CAKES

MAKES 4 SERVINGS

4 four-ounce duck breasts, trimmed of all fat and sinew

⅛ tsp. kosher salt

⅛ tsp. freshly ground black pepper

¼ tsp. Miraval Oil Blend (page 19) or canola oil

¼ c. Cranberry Barbecue Sauce (recipe follows)

1 recipe Wasabi Potato Cakes (page 142)

PREHEAT the oven to 425° F.

LIGHTLY season the duck breasts on both sides with the salt and pepper.

HEAT the oil in a large ovenproof skillet over medium-high heat. Add the duck and sear on both sides for 2½ minutes then turn over and transfer the skillet to the oven and roast until nearly medium rare, about 5 minutes. Remove the duck from the oven and let rest in the pan for 1 minute. Slice each breast into three pieces (slicing across the breast).

TO serve, spoon 1 Tbsp. of the barbecue sauce into the center of four large plates and place one potato cake on top of the sauce. Arrange one duck breast over the top of each potato cake.

CALORIES: 220; TOTAL FAT: 4.5 G; CARBOHYDRATE: 25 G; DIETARY FIBER: 1 G; PROTEIN: 20 G

CRANBERRY BARBECUE SAUCE

MAKES 1 CUP

This tangy take on a backyard classic sauce is delicious and goes well with duck, chicken, pork, baked tofu, and so on. Use as you would any barbecue sauce. It will keep for up to five days refrigerated.

1 c. ketchup or pureed fresh tomato

1 c. cranberry juice cocktail (sweetened)

½ c. dried cranberries

½ c. apple cider vinegar

¼ c. Blackening Spice Blend (page 19)

¼ c. agave syrup (see Source Guide) or honey

¼ c. molasses

COMBINE all the ingredients in a heavy medium saucepan and bring to a simmer over medium heat. Cook the sauce, stirring occasionally, until the cranberries are plump and the liquid begins to thicken, about 12 minutes.

TRANSFER the mixture to a blender and process on high speed until smooth, 45 seconds.

SERVE warm, or allow to cool.

PRICKLY PEAR MARINATED DUCK BREASTS WITH ANCHO CHILI–MANGO SALSA

MAKES 4 SERVINGS

4 four-ounce duck breasts,
trimmed of all fat and sinew

1 recipe Prickly Pear Marinade (page 128)

¼ tsp. Miraval Oil Blend (page 19)

1 recipe Ancho Chili, Dried Cherry
and Mango Salsa (page 124)

PREHEAT the oven to 400° F.

PLACE the duck breasts in a shallow baking dish and cover with the marinade. Cover with plastic wrap and refrigerate for at least 1 hour and no more than 2 hours.

REMOVE the duck from the marinade and pat dry.

HEAT the oil in a large ovenproof skillet over medium-high heat. Add the duck and sear on both sides for 1½ minutes each, turning once. Transfer the skillet to the oven and roast for 4 minutes. Remove the pan from the oven, turn the duck breasts, and return to the oven. Roast until nearly medium rare, 4 minutes.

REMOVE the duck from the oven and let rest for five minutes.

TO serve, place one duck breast on each of four large plates. Spoon the salsa over the duck.

CALORIES: 190; TOTAL FAT: 5 G; CARBOHYDRATE: 10 G; DIETARY FIBER: 1 G; PROTEIN: 25 G

PRICKLY PEAR MARINATED DUCK BREASTS WITH CRANBERRY-ORANGE CHUTNEY

MAKES 4 SERVINGS

4 four-ounce duck breasts, trimmed of all fat and sinew

1 recipe Prickly Pear Marinade (page 128)

¼ tsp. Miraval Oil Blend (page 19)

1 recipe Cranberry-Orange Chutney (recipe follows)

PREHEAT the oven to 400° F.

PLACE the duck breasts in a shallow baking dish and cover with the marinade. Cover with plastic wrap, refrigerate, and marinate for 2 hours.

REMOVE the duck from the marinade and pat dry.

HEAT the oil in a large ovenproof skillet over medium-high heat. Add the duck and sear on both sides for 1½ minutes each, turning once. Transfer the skillet to the oven and roast until nearly medium rare, about 8 minutes.

REMOVE the duck from the oven and let rest in the pan for 2 minutes.

PLACE one duck breast on each of four large plates, and spoon the chutney to the side. Serve immediately.

CALORIES: 180; TOTAL FAT: 5 G; CARBOHYDRATE: 11 G; DIETARY FIBER: 1 G; PROTEIN: 23 G

CRANBERRY-ORANGE CHUTNEY

MAKES ABOUT 2 CUPS

This chutney is delicious hot or cold and also goes great with breakfast scones, pancakes, chicken, pork, and wild game.

1½ c. fresh orange juice

1 c. dried cranberries

½ c. orange segments

½ c. pomegranate juice, unsweetened

4½ tsp. freshly grated orange zest

½ tsp. freshly grated lime zest

½ tsp. fresh lime juice

3 cinnamon sticks

COMBINE all the ingredients in a heavy medium saucepan and bring to a simmer over medium heat. Cook the sauce, stirring occasionally, until the cranberries are plump and the liquid begins to thicken, about 10 minutes. Remove the pan from the heat and let rest until ready to serve.

CARAMELIZED THREE-ONION POLENTA "LASAGNA" WITH WILTED BABY ARUGULA, GOAT CHEESE, AND RATATOUILLE SAUCE

MAKES 4 SERVINGS

1 recipe Caramelized Three-Onion Polenta (page 137)

2 c. Ratatouille Sauce (page 129)

¼ c. Goat-Cheese Tofu Spread (recipe follows)

2 c. baby arugula or spinach

PREHEAT oven to 375° F.

WHEN the polenta has set up in the casserole dish, coat the top evenly with the goat-cheese spread using a rubber spatula or other utensil. Place the dish in the oven and bake until the spread begins to brown lightly and the polenta is hot, about 10 to 12 minutes. Remove from oven and cut into four equal portions.

USING a spatula, transfer each portion to a separate plate and top with ¼ cup of arugula (or spinach). Ladle a half cup of ratatouille sauce over the top of each polenta square. The heat of the sauce will wilt the greens.

CALORIES: 220; TOTAL FAT: 2.5 G; CARBOHYDRATE: 42 G; DIETARY FIBER: 6 G; PROTEIN: 7 G

GOAT-CHEESE TOFU SPREAD

MAKES A GENEROUS ¼ CUP

2 Tbsp. (packed) chopped soft (silken) tofu

2½ Tbsp. fresh goat cheese (chèvre)

1½ tsp. low-fat cottage cheese

Pinch kosher salt

Pinch freshly ground black pepper

COMBINE the goat cheese, tofu, cottage cheese, salt, and pepper in the bowl of a food processor and process until smooth, scraping down the sides of the bowl as needed.

NOTE: Ricotta cheese can be substituted for the goat cheese and/or the tofu in this recipe.

PORTOBELLO-TOFU STIR-FRY

MAKES 4 SERVINGS

2 Tbsp. plus 1 tsp. sesame oil

2 tsp. low-sodium soy sauce,
plus more to taste

2 tsp. balsamic vinegar

2 Tbsp. plus 1 tsp. minced,
peeled gingerroot

Pinch crushed red pepper

4 portobello mushrooms, wiped clean,
stems and gills removed, julienne

½ c. thinly sliced strips of firm
tofu or baked bean curd

2 tsp. minced garlic

8 ears baby corn (canned or fresh)

2 Tbsp. bamboo shoots,
sliced (canned or fresh)

2 Tbsp. small broccoli florets

2 Tbsp. chopped red bell pepper

2 Tbsp. thinly sliced water
chestnuts (canned or fresh)

2 tsp. thin strips carrot

¼ c. bean sprouts

TO MAKE THE MARINADE, whisk together 2 Tbsp. of the sesame oil, 2 tsp. of the soy sauce, the balsamic vinegar, 1 tsp. of the ginger, and the red pepper in a medium bowl. Pour half of the mixture into a second bowl.

PLACE the mushrooms in one bowl of the marinade, and the tofu in second bowl of the marinade; let marinate at room temperature for 15 to 30 minutes.

DRAIN the vegetables and tofu and set aside. Discard the marinade.

HEAT the remaining 1 tsp. sesame oil in a wok or large heavy skillet over high heat. When the oil begins to smoke, add the remaining 2 Tbsp. ginger and cook, stirring until it begins to brown, about 45 seconds. Add the garlic and cook, stirring until it begins to brown, 45 seconds to 1 minute. Add the corn, bamboo shoots, broccoli, bell pepper, water chestnuts, and carrot; cook, stirring until the broccoli and carrots are tender, about 4 minutes. Add the mushrooms and tofu, and cook, stirring until the mushrooms begin to soften, about 2 minutes. Add the bean sprouts and stir to combine, and remove the pan from the heat.

ADJUST the seasoning to taste as desired with soy sauce, and serve immediately.

CALORIES: 150; TOTAL FAT: 8 G; CARBOHYDRATE: 16 G; DIETARY FIBER: 2 G; PROTEIN: 6 G

FIRE-GRILLED VEGETABLE RISOTTO WITH QUINOA

MAKES 3 CUPS; SERVING SIZE: ¾ CUP

½ c. yellow onion, diced medium

2 tsp. garlic, chopped

⅛ tsp. saffron threads

1½ tsp. Miraval Oil Blend (page 19)

¾ c. arborio rice

¼ c. Chardonnay

3¼ c. Vegetable Stock (page 24), hot

2 Tbsp. Parmesan cheese

½ c. Grilled Vegetables (page 140)

2 Tbsp. packed shiitake mushrooms, julienned

½ c. packed baby spinach

¼ c. red bell pepper, diced

¼ c. edamame beans

¼ c Basic Quinoa (page 18)

2 tsp. white truffle oil

½ tsp. kosher salt

¼ tsp. freshly ground black pepper

PREHEAT medium pot over medium-high heat.

SAUTÉ onions and garlic in oil with saffron until translucent, about 3 minutes. Stir often, using wooden spoon or a high-temperature rubber spatula.

ADD arborio rice and continue to sauté until the rice is lightly browned, about 2 minutes.

DEGLAZE the pan with Chardonnay and continue cooking until the liquid is almost evaporated, about 30 seconds.

ADD the heated vegetable stock, a half cup at a time, stirring often and allowing each batch of liquid to almost evaporate before adding the next batch, until the rice is cooked, about 25 minutes.

STIR in the Parmesan cheese.

ADD in the remaining ingredients except the white truffle oil. Stir until all ingredients are fully incorporated and the mushrooms are cooked, about 2 minutes.

SERVE hot with a small drizzle of white truffle oil.

CALORIES: 310; TOTAL FAT: 6 G; CARBOHYDRATE: 50 G; DIETARY FIBER: 4 G; PROTEIN: 10 G

SONORAN RISOTTO WITH QUINOA

MAKES 3 CUPS; SERVING SIZE: ¾ CUP

½ c. yellow onion, diced medium

2 tsp. chopped garlic

1½ tsp. Miraval Oil Blend (page 19)

¾ c. arborio rice

¼ c. Chardonnay

3¼ c. Vegetable Stock, hot

2 Tbsp. Cotija cheese

½ c. fresh corn kernels

1½ Tbsp. fresh tomatillos

1½ tsp. fresh chopped cilantro

5 Tbsp. red bell pepper, diced

2½ Tbsp. poblano chilies, minced

¼ c. Basic Quinoa (page 18)

4 Tbsp. Cumin-Scented Corn
Tortilla Strips (page 218)

½ tsp. kosher salt

¼ tsp. freshly ground black pepper

PREHEAT medium pot over medium high heat.

SAUTÉ onions and garlic in oil until translucent, about 3 minutes. Stir often, using wooden spoon or a high temperature rubber spatula.

ADD arborio rice and continue to sauté until the rice is lightly browned, about 2 minutes.

DEGLAZE the pan with Chardonnay and continue cooking until the liquid is almost evaporated, about 30 seconds.

ADD the heated vegetable stock, a half cup at a time, stirring often and allowing each batch of liquid to almost evaporate before adding the next batch, until the rice is cooked, about 25 minutes.

STIR in the Cotija cheese. Add the salt and pepper, quinoa, and remaining vegetables except for the cilantro. Stir until they are fully incorporated, about 1 minute.

SERVE hot with a small pinch of tortilla strips and cilantro for garnish.

CALORIES: 200; TOTAL FAT: 2 G; CARBOHYDRATE: 38 G; DIETARY FIBER: 2 G; PROTEIN: 4 G

TEMPEH SCALLOPINI WITH FETTUCCINE

A high source of protein that is easily digestible, tempeh is a whole soybean product formed into cakes by a controlled fermentation process. Tempeh has a meaty, almost nutty flavor that our chefs rely on throughout the year. This recipe is a perfect introduction to using one of Miraval's favorite ingredients.

MAKES 4 SERVINGS

1 c. low-sodium soy sauce

1 c. fresh orange juice

2 Tbsp. roughly chopped fresh rosemary

1 tsp. chopped garlic

4 pieces five-grain tempeh (4 oz.)

1 tsp. Miraval Oil Blend
(page 19) or canola oil

¼ tsp. freshly ground black pepper

4 oz. fettuccine

1 c. finely sliced carrots

1 c. finely sliced zucchini

1 c. finely sliced shiitake mushrooms

2 tsp. capers with their brining liquid

PREHEAT the oven to 425° F.

PLACE the soy sauce, orange juice, rosemary, and garlic in a shallow baking dish and stir to combine. Add the tempeh and marinate at room temperature for 1 hour.

BRING a pot of lightly salted water to a boil over high heat. Add the pasta and cook until al dente, 10 minutes. Drain well, spray with ¼ tsp. of the oil, and set aside.

REMOVE the tempeh from the marinade, reserving the marinade. Lightly season the tempeh on both sides with a pinch of the pepper.

HEAT ½ tsp. of the oil in a large ovenproof skillet over medium-high heat. Add the tempeh and sear on each side for 45 seconds. Transfer the skillet to the oven and cook until completely warmed through and slightly browned, 7 to 8 minutes. Remove from the oven and let rest in the skillet.

HEAT the remaining ¼ tsp. of the oil in a large skillet over medium-high heat. Add the vegetables and cook, stirring until they begin to soften, 3 to 4 minutes. Add the capers and their liquid and the remaining marinade, stir well, and cook until the liquid is reduced by half, 1½ minutes. Add the cooked pasta, toss to evenly coat with the liquid, and cook until warmed through, 1 to 2 minutes.

DIVIDE the pasta between 4 large pasta bowls and place one piece of tempeh on each serving. Serve immediately.

CALORIES: 355; TOTAL FAT: 7 G; CARBOHYDRATE: 58 G; DIETARY FIBER: 3 G; PROTEIN: 17 G

THE PALM COURT

A casual hub for quick, healthy snacks and smoothies amidst the daily buzz at Miraval, the Palm Court is also where we post sign-up sheets for an inspiring variety of Miraval activities. Naturally, conversations begin over shared interests, like the ever-popular early morning hike or our signature Equine Experience.

The beverages at the Palm Court satiate every mood throughout the day, from organic coffees, espressos, and lattes to energy-packed vegetable and fruit smoothies, infusions, and freshly squeezed juices. Freshly baked miniature goodies are always on hand; our chocolate-chip cookies are a satisfying reward after The Challenge course, an invigorating tennis match, or a desert trail bike ride.

FRESH FRUIT DRINKS AND SMOOTHIES

AMBROSIA

For a morning boost, reenergize with Miraval's signature fresh fruit drink that's packed with vital nutrients. A heavy-duty juicer will process the entire fruit, including skins. While we leave the lemon rind on for added zest, you may wish to remove it.

MAKES 12 OUNCES

1 c. pineapple
½ c. red grapes
1 four-ounce lemon, with rind on and quartered
1 ten-ounce orange, skin removed

COMBINE all the ingredients in the bowl of a heavy-duty juicer or blender, and process on high speed until smooth and frothy.

POUR into a tall glass and serve immediately.

CALORIES: 290; TOTAL FAT: 1 G; CARBOHYDRATE: 76 G; DIETARY FIBER: 10 G; PROTEIN: 4 G

BERRY BERRY

MAKES 14 OUNCES

1 c. soy milk
½ banana
¼ c. fresh or frozen blueberries
¼ c. fresh or frozen raspberries
¼ c. fresh or frozen strawberries
1 Tbsp. agave syrup (see Source Guide) or honey
½ c. crushed ice

COMBINE all the ingredients in the bowl of a blender, and process on high speed until smooth and frothy.

POUR into a tall glass and serve immediately.

CALORIES: 300; TOTAL FAT: 5 G; CARBOHYDRATE: 57 G; DIETARY FIBER: 7 G; PROTEIN: 10 G

CLEAR, AGELESS SKIN SMOOTHIE

Nutritional note from Junelle Lupiani: "Smoothies are a great, quick energy option any time of day. Just remember that many have a similar calorie count to a plated meal when using them as a substitute."

MAKES 12 OUNCES

2 c. cucumber, with skin on

1 c. Granny Smith apple, stemmed and seeded

1 c. celery hearts

1 heart of romaine lettuce, about 6 oz.

⅓ c. fresh pineapple

COMBINE all the ingredients in the bowl of a heavy juicer or blender, and process on high speed until smooth and frothy.

POUR into a tall glass and serve immediately.

CALORIES: 170; TOTAL FAT: 0 G; CARBOHYDRATE: 44 G; DIETARY FIBER: 7 G; PROTEIN: 2 G

FROZEN MINT LEMONADE

MAKES 8 OUNCES

1 c. Miraval Lemonade (page 211)

½ c. crushed ice

10 mint leaves

COMBINE the ingredients in the bowl of a blender, and blend on high speed until frothy.

POUR into a tall glass and serve immediately.

CALORIES: 70; TOTAL FAT: 0 G; CARBOHYDRATE: 21 G; DIETARY FIBER: 0 G; PROTEIN: 0 G

Frozen Mint Lemonade

GINGER JUICE

2 c. fresh gingerroot,
peeled and chopped

PUT chopped fresh ginger into juicer to extract the maximum amount of juice.

CALORIES: 10; TOTAL FAT: 0 G; CARBOHYDRATE: 2 G; DIETARY FIBER: 0 G; PROTEIN: TRACE

IRON BOOST

MAKES 12 OUNCES

2 c. packed baby spinach,
washed and spun dry

1 c. crushed ice

½ banana, peeled

¼ c. fresh or frozen strawberries,
washed and stems removed

1 Tbsp. water

2 tsp. agave syrup (see
Source Guide) or honey

COMBINE all the ingredients in the bowl of a blender, and process on high speed
until frothy and well combined.

POUR into a tall glass and serve immediately.

CALORIES: 120; TOTAL FAT: 0.5 G; CARBOHYDRATE: 30 G; DIETARY FIBER: 4 G; PROTEIN: 3 G

MIRAVAL LEMONADE

MAKES 6 CUPS; SERVING SIZE:
8 OUNCES

¾ to 1 c. cane sugar, depending
on desired sweetness

1 c. water

1 c. fresh-squeezed lemon juice
(4 to 6 average-sized lemons)

2 c. cold water (to dilute)

2 c. ice (to dilute)

HEAT the sugar and one cup of water together in a small saucepan over medium heat, stirring occasionally, until the sugar is dissolved completely, about 5 minutes.

JUICE 4 to 6 lemons using a juicer or handheld citrus reamer, enough for one cup of juice. Strain out the seeds.

ADD the lemon juice and the sugar water to a pitcher. Add the remaining 2 cups of cold water and ice. Use more or less depending on how strong you like your lemonade. Refrigerate until completely cooled, 30 to 40 minutes, or just pour over ice. If the lemonade is too sweet for your taste, add a little more lemon juice to it.

SERVE with additional ice, as desired.

CALORIES: 70; TOTAL FAT: 0 G; CARBOHYDRATE: 21 G; DIETARY FIBER: 0 G; PROTEIN: 0 G

MIRAVAL GINGER TEA

MAKES 10 OUNCES

½ c. Ginger Juice (page 210) or
2 c. fresh gingerroot, peeled and sliced

⅓ c. honey

2 Tbsp. fresh-squeezed lemon juice
(half of an average-sized lemon)

5 c. bottled water

COMBINE the ingredients (after squeezing the juice out of the lemon, toss the lemon into the water). Bring to a boil and simmer for 15 to 20 minutes. Remove lemon and serve. If you used the slices of ginger, strain the tea before drinking.

CALORIES: 70; TOTAL FAT: 0 G; CARBOHYDRATE: 20 G; DIETARY FIBER: 0 G; PROTEIN: 0 G

MIRA-VITALITY

MAKES 8 OUNCES

9 oz. fresh carrots, washed

2 c. packed baby spinach, washed and spun dry

6 oz. fresh beets (raw), stemmed and peeled

5 oz. cucumbers, skin on

1 tsp. Ginger Juice (page 210)

COMBINE all the ingredients in the bowl of a heavy-duty juicer or blender, and process on high speed until smooth and frothy.

POUR into a tall glass and serve immediately.

CALORIES: 80; TOTAL FAT: 0 G; CARBOHYDRATE: 16 G; DIETARY FIBER: 1 G; PROTEIN: 4 G

PROTEIN PLUS

MAKES 14 OUNCES

½ c. soy milk

½ banana, peeled

¼ c. whey protein powder (or other protein powder)

¼ c. fresh or frozen blueberries

2 Tbsp. açai juice

1 Tbsp. agave syrup (see Source Guide), or honey

1 tsp. ground flaxseed

½ c. crushed ice

COMBINE all the ingredients in the bowl of a blender, and process on high speed until smooth and frothy.

POUR into a tall glass and serve immediately.

CALORIES: 290; TOTAL FAT: 4.5 G; CARBOHYDRATE: 44 G; DIETARY FIBER: 4 G; PROTEIN: 21 G

THE BRAVE BILL LOUNGE
& THE OASIS

Just as the Palm Court is Miraval's daytime hub, the Brave Bill Lounge is the cozy gathering place for evening activity. More than a lounge, the Brave Bill is an intimate spot to unwind and reflect. Here, our guests sit back and enjoy an assortment of hors d'oeuvres and crudités. After settling in overstuffed sofas, the most common request is for our signature Blueberry Margarita.

Since mindfulness is about inspiration, not deprivation, cocktails, wines, liqueurs, and nightcaps are available in the Brave Bill Lounge.

The Oasis is a tranquil snack and beverage bar located at Miraval's Life in Balance Spa, with its three sparkling outdoor pools. The full bar includes nonalcoholic smoothies and fresh juices, as well as cocktails and wines. Guests also enjoy freshly made complimentary snacks throughout the day, such as chips and guacamole and crudités and hummus.

DIPS AND SNACKS

ASIAN SALSA

MAKES 2 CUPS; SERVING SIZE: 2 TBSP.

¾ c. tomato, diced

¾ c. green bell pepper, diced

2 Tbsp. green onions, sliced

¾ tsp. garlic, minced

¾ tsp. shallots, minced

3 Tbsp. fish sauce

2 Tbsp. fresh lime juice

¾ tsp. lemongrass, minced

½ c. fresh cilantro, chopped

1½ tsp. pure cane sugar

1½ tsp. Thai red-curry paste

1 Tbsp. gingerroot, minced

COMBINE all the ingredients in a large bowl and mix well.

REFRIGERATE, tightly covered, for 30 minutes and up to 4 hours before serving.

CALORIES: 10; TOTAL FAT: 0 G; CARBOHYDRATE: 2 G; DIETARY FIBER: 0 G; PROTEIN: 0 G

CANDIED PINE NUTS

MAKES 1 CUP; SERVING SIZE: 4 TBSP.

2 Tbsp. Blackening Spice Blend (page 19)

4 tsp. agave syrup (see Source guide)

1 c. pine nuts

PREHEAT the oven to 375° F. Cover a small baking sheet with a silicone mat or parchment paper and set aside.

COMBINE the spices and syrup in a medium bowl and stir well. Add the pine nuts and stir to coat. Spread the nuts on the prepared baking sheet and roast until golden brown and fragrant, 7 to 8 minutes.

BREAK apart the nuts with a fork, and let cool before serving.

CALORIES: 250; TOTAL FAT: 23 G; CARBOHYDRATE: 11 G; DIETARY FIBER: 2 G; PROTEIN: 5 G

BLACK-BEAN CHIPOTLE HUMMUS

MAKES 2 CUPS; SERVING SIZE: ¼ CUP

1½ Tbsp. adobo sauce from
canned chipotle chilies (chilies
reserved for another use)

1 Tbsp. cilantro, chopped

1½ tsp. garlic, minced

¾ tsp. extra-virgin olive oil

½ tsp. ground cumin

½ tsp. chili powder

½ tsp. kosher salt

1½ c. Basic Black Beans (page 14) or
canned black beans, rinsed and drained

Toasted Tortilla Chips (page 227), Toasted
Pita Chips (page 222), or crudités,
as optional accompaniments

PLACE all the ingredients except the beans in the bowl of a food processor, and blend on high speed for 10 seconds. Add the beans and mix until smooth, scraping down the sides of the bowl as needed.

TRANSFER the hummus to an airtight container and refrigerate until well chilled before serving with accompaniment of choice. (The hummus will keep refrigerated for up to five days.)

CALORIES: 120; TOTAL FAT: 2.5 G; CARBOHYDRATE: 17 G; DIETARY FIBER: 6 G; PROTEIN: 6 G

CUMIN-SCENTED CORN TORTILLA STRIPS

MAKES 4 SERVINGS

1 6-inch corn tortilla, cut
into ½-inch strips

½ tsp. Miraval Oil Blend
(page 19) or canola oil

Pinch ground cumin

Pinch kosher salt

Pinch freshly ground black pepper

PREHEAT the oven to 400° F. Lightly coat a small baking sheet with nonstick cooking spray.

PLACE the strips on the prepared baking sheet and toss with the oil and the seasonings. Bake until crisp and fragrant, 5 minutes.

REMOVE from the oven and let cool on the baking sheet. Serve warm or at room temperature.

CALORIES: 13; TOTAL FAT: 1 G; CARBOHYDRATE: 3 G; DIETARY FIBER: 0 G; PROTEIN: 0 G

EDAMAME GUACAMOLE

MAKES 2 CUPS; SERVING SIZE: 2 TBSP

1 c. frozen edamame beans, thawed

1 c. fresh broccoli florets

1 c. avocado, chopped

1 Tbsp. plus 1 tsp. fresh lime juice

½ tsp. garlic, minced

¼ tsp. jalapeño, minced

2 Tbsp. tomato, chopped and seeded

1 Tbsp. red onion, minced

1 Tbsp. green onions, thinly sliced

1½ tsp. fresh cilantro, chopped

½ tsp. kosher salt

Pinch freshly ground black pepper

BRING a medium pot of water to a boil. Prepare an ice bath and set aside.

COOK the edamame beans at a rolling boil until tender, 10 to 11 minutes. Drain the beans into a strainer and shock in the ice bath. Drain well.

PUREE the avocado, lime juice, garlic, and jalapeño in a food processor at high speed. Add the edamame beans and process on high speed.

MEANWHILE, cook the broccoli at a rolling boil until tender, 7 to 8 minutes. Drain the broccoli and shock in the ice bath. Drain well and pat dry.

ADD the broccoli to the edamame mixture and process on high speed until very smooth, scraping down the sides of the bowl as needed to incorporate all the ingredients.

TRANSFER the mixture to a medium bowl and fold in the remaining ingredients, mixing with a rubber spatula until well incorporated.

TRANSFER the guacamole to an airtight container and refrigerate until well chilled, about 1 hour, before serving with accompaniment of choice. (The guacamole will keep in the refrigerator for up to two days.)

CALORIES: 25; TOTAL FAT: 2 G; CARBOHYDRATE: 1 G; DIETARY FIBER: 1 G; PROTEIN: 1 G

MIRAVAL SALSA

MAKES 2 CUPS; SERVING SIZE: 2 TBSP.

3 vine-ripened tomatoes, cored
(approximately one lb.)

¼ tsp. Miraval Oil Blend (page 19)

½ c. canned diced tomatoes

¼ c. small diced red onion

1 Tbsp. fresh cilantro,
rinsed and chopped

1 Tbsp. fresh oregano, chopped

2 Tbsp. fresh garlic, minced

1 Tbsp. jalapeño, finely chopped

¼ tsp. freshly ground black pepper

1½ Tbsp. lime juice, fresh squeezed
(about one average-sized lime)

PREHEAT grill on high heat. Remove cores from tomatoes, using a paring knife or a tomato shark. Combine the tomatoes and oil together in a medium mixing bowl, and then transfer the tomatoes to the grill to blacken the skin. Using a pair of kitchen tongs, turn the tomatoes regularly to ensure even roasting. Alternate method for roasting tomatoes: preheat oven to 450° F, place the oil-coated tomatoes on a baking sheet or other oven-safe dish, and roast until the skins begin to split, about 12 minutes.

REMOVE the tomatoes from the heat and place in a medium mixing bowl. Allow to cool to room temperature (about 20 minutes). Reserve all juices. Peel the blackened skin from the tomatoes (don't worry about leaving a little bit on—it will improve the look and flavor of your salsa). Rough chop the tomatoes and puree in a blender or food processor with the canned diced tomatoes. Combine with the remaining ingredients in medium mixing bowl.

TO create a smoky chipotle salsa, add 2 tsp. canned chipotle in adobo sauce to the blender when pureeing the tomatoes. Alternately, a small amount of chipotle powder may be stirred into the salsa.

CALORIES: 18; TOTAL FAT 0 G; CARBOHYDRATE: 4 G; DIETARY FIBER: 0 G; PROTEIN: 0 G

HERB PESTO

MAKES 1 CUP; SERVING SIZE: 1 TSP.

1 c. fresh basil, packed

2 Tbsp. fresh oregano

1 Tbsp. Roasted Garlic (page 22)

2 Tbsp. pumpkin seeds (pepitas), roasted

2 Tbsp. extra-virgin olive oil

½ c. Thickened Vegetable Stock (page 24)

⅛ tsp. kosher salt

⅛ tsp. freshly ground black pepper

PLACE all ingredients into a food processor or blender. Puree until smooth.

CALORIES 20; TOTAL FAT 2 G; CARBOHYDRATES 1 G; DIETARY FIBER 1 G; PROTEIN 0 G

LEMON-GARLIC HUMMUS WITH TOASTED PITA CHIPS

MAKES 2¼ CUPS; SERVING SIZE: ¼ CUP

3 c. canned garbanzo beans, rinsed and drained well

6 Tbsp. fresh lemon juice (3 to 4 average-sized lemons)

½ tsp. minced garlic

8 tsp. extra-virgin olive oil

Toasted Pita Chips (recipe below), as accompaniment

PLACE all the ingredients in the bowl of a food processor and blend on high speed until smooth, scraping down the sides of the bowl as needed. Adjust the flavor to your liking with additional lemon juice or garlic as needed.

TRANSFER the hummus to an airtight container and refrigerate until well chilled before serving with Toasted Pita Chips. This hummus also goes well with our Toasted Tortilla Chips (page 227). (The hummus will keep, refrigerated, for up to five days.)

CALORIES: 130; TOTAL FAT: 6 G; CARBOHYDRATE: 16 G; DIETARY FIBER: 4 G; PROTEIN: 5 G

TOASTED PITA CHIPS

MAKES 4 TO 8 SERVINGS; SERVING SIZE: ½ CUP

2 seven-inch whole-wheat pita breads

½ tsp. Miraval Oil Blend (page 19) or vegetable cooking spray

PREHEAT the oven to 400° F. Stack the pita bread and cut in half with a sharp knife. Stack the slices again and cut into eighths.

TOSS the bread in a medium bowl with the oil to lightly coat. (Alternatively, lay the pita triangles on the baking sheet and spray lightly on one side with vegetable cooking spray.)

BAKE the bread until fragrant and starting to crisp, 7 to 8 minutes. Remove from the oven and cool slightly on the baking sheet before serving. (The pita chips will continue to crisp as they cool.)

SERVE warm or at room temperature.

CALORIES: 45; TOTAL FAT: 0.5 G; CARBOHYDRATE: 9 G; DIETARY FIBER: 1 G; PROTEIN: 2 G

RED BELL PEPPER HUMMUS

Our chefs favor this hummus for its versatility and bright flavor. Enjoy it as a sandwich spread—it's such a nice addition—or as a nutritious dip for vegetables or pita chips. If you're going to use it as a spread, be sure to thin the consistency slightly with extra vegetable stock.

MAKES 2 CUPS; SERVING SIZE: ¼ CUP

¼ tsp. extra-virgin olive oil

2 Tbsp. red onion, chopped

1 tsp. garlic, minced

1¼ c. Roasted Red Bell Peppers, chopped, about 2 large peppers (page 18)

1 c. cooked garbanzo beans

1 Tbsp. fresh cilantro, chopped

½ tsp. ground cumin

¼ tsp. ground coriander

¼ tsp. kosher salt

Pinch freshly ground black pepper

½ c. Vegetable Stock (page 24) or canned vegetable broth

Toasted Tortilla Chips (page 227), Toasted Pita Chips (page 222), or crudités, as optional accompaniments

HEAT the oil in a medium pot over medium-high heat. Add the onion and garlic and cook, stirring until soft, 1 minute. Add the bell peppers, beans, cilantro, cumin, coriander, salt, and pepper; and cook, stirring for 1 minute. Add the vegetable stock and cook for 10 seconds. Remove from the heat.

TRANSFER the mixture to the bowl of a food processor and process on high speed until smooth, scraping down the sides of the bowl as needed. Adjust seasoning to taste and let cool slightly.

TRANSFER the hummus to an airtight container and refrigerate until well chilled before serving with accompaniment of choice. (The hummus will keep, refrigerated, for up to five days.)

CALORIES: 45; TOTAL FAT: 1 G; CARBOHYDRATE: 8 G; DIETARY FIBER: 2 G; PROTEIN: 2 G

ROASTED TOMATO-HERB PESTO

MAKES 2 CUPS; SERVING SIZE: 1 TSP.

4 vine-ripened tomatoes,
average size (about 1½ lbs.)

½ tsp. extra-virgin olive oil

4 tsp. fresh garlic, minced

4 tsp. cilantro, chopped

4 tsp. basil, chiffonade

2 Tbsp. Parmigiano-Reggiano

4 tsp. walnuts, chopped

Kosher salt, to taste

PREHEAT a grill to high heat. Place the tomatoes on the grill and cook, turning until charred and soft, about 5 minutes. Remove the tomatoes from the grill, and place in a mixing bowl or baking sheet; when cool, peel and core. Reserve the juices that will drip out of the grilled tomatoes as they cool, and mix it in with the other ingredients.

PLACE the tomatoes and the remaining ingredients in the bowl of a blender, and process on high speed to a smooth sauce, about 1 minute.

PLACE the sauce in an airtight container and refrigerate until ready to use. (The sauce will keep refrigerated for up to seven days.)

CALORIES: 5; TOTAL FAT: 0 G; CARBOHYDRATE: 0 G; DIETARY FIBER: 0 G; PROTEIN: 0 G

SPICY SOY NUT–PRETZEL MIX

Whether you're preparing for a casual dinner party or snacks for the office, our Spicy Soy Nut–Pretzel Mix can be made in advance and kept covered with plastic wrap for up to a day. Truth be told, we don't think it will last that long at your house—this addictive snack tends to disappear quickly!

MAKES 5 CUPS; SERVING SIZE: ½ CUP

2½ c. salted, small pretzel sticks

2½ c. unsalted soy nuts (or any other raw nuts or combination of raw nuts, if desired)

¼ c. agave syrup (see Source Guide) or honey

2½ Tbsp. Blackening Spice Blend (page 19)

PREHEAT the oven to 375° F. Lightly coat a baking sheet with vegetable cooking spray.

COMBINE all the ingredients in a large bowl and toss to coat evenly with the spices. Bake the mix until deep brown in color, 30 to 34 minutes. Remove from the oven and let cool on the baking sheet. (The mixture will also crisp as it cools.)

TRANSFER the mix to a decorative bowl and serve at room temperature.

CALORIES: 230; TOTAL FAT: 6 G; CARBOHYDRATE: 30 G; DIETARY FIBER: 8 G; PROTEIN: 16 G

SHRIMP PICO DE GALLO SALAD

As far as flavor goes, the simplicity of this trusted recipe belies its deliciousness. Season after season, it continues to be one of Miraval's most requested dishes. Our chefs are certain you'll receive the same rave reviews when served chilled and fresh at your next patio party.

MAKES 4 SERVINGS

1½ c. chopped boiled shrimp

1 c. chopped tomatoes

2 Tbsp. minced red onion

2 Tbsp. minced cilantro

1½ tsp. minced jalapeño

6 Tbsp. sour cream

1½ tsp. fresh lime juice

1½ tsp. minced garlic

¼ tsp. kosher salt

Pinch freshly ground black pepper

8 leaves romaine lettuce

Cumin-Scented Corn Tortilla Strips (page 218), as optional accompaniment

COMBINE the shrimp, tomatoes, red onion, cilantro, and jalapeño in a medium bowl and stir well.

TO make the dressing, combine the remaining ingredients except romaine and tortilla strips, if using, in a small bowl and mix well.

ADD the dressing to the shrimp mixture and toss to evenly coat.

TO serve, arrange 2 romaine leaves on each of four salad plates and divide the shrimp salad among the leaves. Garnish the top of each serving with the tortilla chips, as desired, and serve. Chef's note: Omit the sour cream for a delicious, dairy-free salsa.

CALORIES: 90; TOTAL FAT: 1 G; CARBOHYDRATE: 7 G; DIETARY FIBER: 1 G; PROTEIN: 13 G

TOASTED TORTILLA CHIPS

MAKES 8 LARGE CHIPS
TWO CHIPS PER SERVING

One 12-inch flour tortilla (or spinach or roasted red-pepper wrap)

¼ tsp. Miraval Oil Blend (page 19) or canola oil

PREHEAT the oven to 425° F, and preheat a grill to high heat.

PLACE the tortilla on the grill and cook to make grill marks, 30 to 40 seconds per side.

REMOVE from the grill and lightly coat one side of the tortilla with the oil. Cut into eighths, place on a small baking sheet, and bake until crisp and the edges start to brown, 4 to 5 minutes.

REMOVE from the oven and serve hot or at room temperature.

CALORIES: 200; TOTAL FAT: 4.5 G; CARBOHYDRATE: 33 G; DIETARY FIBER: 2 G; PROTEIN: 5 G

TOMATO PICO DE GALLO

MAKES 1 CUP; SERVING SIZE: ¼ CUP

¾ c. diced ripe tomatoes

¼ c. chopped red onions

1 Tbsp. fresh lime juice (1 to 2 average-sized limes)

1½ tsp. chopped fresh cilantro

1 tsp. jalapeño, minced and seeded

⅛ tsp. chili powder

⅛ tsp. ground cumin

⅛ tsp. kosher salt

Toasted Pita Chips (page 222) or Toasted Tortilla Chips (page 227), as accompaniment

MIX all the ingredients in a medium bowl and stir well to combine. Cover and refrigerate until well chilled, 1 to 2 hours, before serving.

SERVE with chips.

CALORIES: 15; TOTAL FAT: 0 G; CARBOHYDRATE: 4 G; DIETARY FIBER: 1 G; PROTEIN: 1 G

TOMATILLO SALSA

Nutritional note from Junelle Lupiani: "Salsas are a great way enjoy more vegetables and add flavorful interest to many meals and snacks. Feel free to experiment with seasonal vegetables for a new twist on our classic recipes. Salsa can be stored in the refrigerator for up to five days, so prepare it ahead of time for a quick flavor burst to add to any dish served during a busy week."

MAKES 1⅓ CUPS; SERVING SIZE: ¼ CUP

½ tsp. canola oil

2 c. fresh tomatillos, peeled and quartered

¼ c. red onions, chopped

¼ c. cilantro, chopped

1½ tsp. jalapeño, minced

¼ tsp. garlic, minced

½ c. water

½ tsp. cane sugar

½ c. tomatillos, chopped

⅓ c. avocado, chopped

¼ c. red bell pepper, chopped

½ tsp. kosher salt

Toasted Pita Chips (page 222) or Toasted Tortilla Chips (page 227), as accompaniment

HEAT the oil in medium-heavy skillet over high heat. Add the quartered tomatillos and cook, stirring until they begin to turn golden brown, 2 to 2½ minutes. Add the onions, 3 Tbsp. of the cilantro, jalapeño, and the garlic; cook, stirring until the onions start to soften, 45 seconds. Add the water and sugar, and cook until the tomatillos are soft and the liquid is reduced by half, 3 to 4 minutes.

TRANSFER the mixture to a blender and process until smooth.

POUR the puree into a bowl, add the remaining ingredients, and stir well to combine. Cover and refrigerate until well chilled, 1 to 2 hours, before serving.

SERVE chilled or at room temperature.

CALORIES: 40; TOTAL FAT: 1.5 G; CARBOHYDRATE: 7 G; DIETARY FIBER: 2 G; PROTEIN: 1 G

FLATBREADS

BASIC FLATBREAD DOUGH

Nutritional note from Junelle Lupiani: "A common thread among many Miraval guests is the desire for easy recipes for single servings that can be prepared ahead of time. Our flatbread recipe is the perfect answer: make the dough on a Sunday afternoon, place the individual balls of dough in small freezer bags, and freeze. During the week, remove one bag of dough from the freezer in the morning, and let it defrost in the refrigerator throughout the day. A delicious flatbread can then be easily made for dinner with minimal effort."

Our basic dough is the perfect canvas for your creativity. Choose your favorite toppings—marinara sauce, cream cheese, pesto, grilled chicken, or fresh summer vegetables—and enjoy!

MAKES 12 SERVINGS

1 c. warm water, not above 110° F

1 Tbsp. active dry yeast

¼ c. extra-virgin olive oil, plus
1 tsp. to grease the bowl

¼ c. honey or agave syrup
(see Source Guide)

2 c. whole-wheat flour

1½ c. semolina flour

1 tsp. kosher salt

COMBINE the water, yeast, ¼ cup of the oil, and the honey in the bowl of an electric mixer fitted with a dough hook, and let the mixture sit until foamy, 5 to 10 minutes.

STIR together the flour, semolina, and salt in a medium bowl.

WITH the machine on low speed, slowly add the flour mixture one-half cup at a time to the yeast mixture. After all the dry ingredients have been added, continue to mix the dough on low speed for 5 minutes.

LIGHTLY oil a large bowl with 1 tsp. oil and place the dough inside. Cover the dough with plastic wrap, and let sit until almost double in size, about 1 hour.

TURN out the dough onto a lightly floured work surface, and divide into 12 equal portions. One at a time, roll out each portion to ¼" in thickness.

USE as directed in the recipe.

CALORIES: 170; TOTAL FAT: 4 G; CARBOHYDRATE: 29 G; DIETARY FIBER: 3 G; PROTEIN: 5 G

CHICKEN CAESAR FLATBREAD

MAKES 2 SERVINGS

⅙ recipe (2 servings) Basic
Flatbread Dough (page 230)

¼ c. grated Parmigiano-Reggiano

1 c. shredded romaine lettuce

1 Tbsp. Miraval Chipotle-
Caesar Dressing (page 119)

4 oz. Basic Grilled Chicken (page 15)
or cooked chicken, thinly sliced

PREHEAT the oven to 400° F.

PLACE two flatbread dough rounds on a work surface. Evenly cover each round with the cheese, place on a baking sheet, and bake until the dough is crisp and the cheese is melted, 7 minutes.

MEANWHILE, place the lettuce and chicken in a medium bowl and toss with the dressing.

TRANSFER the flatbreads to a cutting board, cut into four wedges, and top with the salad mixture. Serve immediately.

CALORIES: 280; TOTAL FAT: 8 G; CARBOHYDRATE: 37 G; DIETARY FIBER: 3 G; PROTEIN: 18 G

CHICKEN, HERB, AND PESTO FLATBREAD

MAKES 1 SERVING

1⁄12 recipe (1 serving) Basic
Flatbread Dough (page 230)

1 Tbsp. Marinara Sauce (page 126)

1 tsp. Herb Pesto (page 221)

2 oz. Basic Grilled Chicken (page 15)
or cooked chicken breast, thinly sliced

4 baby zucchini, ends trimmed
and halved lengthwise

3 thin slices Roma tomato

1 Tbsp. crumbled goat cheese

PREHEAT the oven to 400° F.

PLACE one flatbread dough round on a work surface. Spoon the marinara and pesto sauces over the dough, spreading to coat evenly, and layer with the remaining ingredients. Place the flatbread on a baking sheet or pizza stone, and bake until the dough is crisp and the cheese is melted, 10 to 15 minutes.

TRANSFER the flatbread to a cutting board, cut into four wedges, and serve immediately.

CALORIES: 280; TOTAL FAT: 9 G; CARBOHYDRATE: 36 G; DIETARY FIBER: 4 G; PROTEIN: 16 G

GOUDA AND SHRIMP FLATBREAD

½ recipe (1 serving) Basic
Flatbread Dough (page 230)

2 Tbsp. Marinara Sauce (page 126)

¼ c. fresh spinach

2 large cooked shrimp, cut
into ½-inch pieces

2 Tbsp. grated Gouda cheese

PREHEAT the oven to 400° F.

PLACE one flatbread dough round on a work surface. Spoon the sauce over the dough, spreading to coat evenly, and layer with the remaining ingredients. Place the flatbread on a baking sheet and bake until the dough is crisp and the cheese is melted, about 10 minutes.

TRANSFER the flatbread to a cutting board, cut into four wedges, and serve immediately.

CALORIES: 260; TOTAL FAT: 10 G; CARBOHYDRATE: 32 G; DIETARY FIBER: 3 G; PROTEIN: 12 G

GRILLED-VEGETABLE FLATBREAD WITH SUN-DRIED TOMATO AND GREEK-OLIVE TAPENADE

3 tsp. sun-dried tomatoes
(rehydrate in hot water first if
they are not tender to the bite)

1½ tsp. pitted kalamata olives

½ recipe (1 serving) Basic
Flatbread Dough (page 230)

3 Tbsp. baby spinach leaves

4 thin slices Roma tomato (about half
of an average-sized Roma tomato)

3 Tbsp. diced Grilled
Vegetables (page 140)

1½ tsp. crumbled Cotija cheese

1 tsp. Parmigiano-Reggiano,
microplaned or grated

PREHEAT the oven to 400° F.

TO make the tapenade, finely dice the sun-dried tomatoes and olives, and combine in a small bowl, mashing together with a fork until they become a chunky paste.

PLACE flatbread dough round on a work surface. Spread the tapenade evenly across the dough using a rubber spatula. Place the spinach on the dough next, and then top with the tomato slices, vegetables, and cheeses. Place the flatbread on a baking sheet and bake until the dough is crisp and the cheese is melted, about 10 minutes.

TRANSFER the flatbread to a cutting board, cut into four wedges, and serve immediately.

CALORIES: 185; TOTAL FAT: 7 G; CARBOHYDRATE: 24 G; DIETARY FIBER: 5 G; PROTEIN: 9 G

HAWAIIAN FLATBREAD

MAKES 1 SERVING

½ recipe (1 serving) Basic
Flatbread Dough (page 230)

1 tsp. Roasted Tomato-
Herb Pesto (page 225)

1 Tbsp. Marinara Sauce (page 126)

2 oz. prosciutto, thinly sliced

4 thin slices fresh pineapple

1 Tbsp. crumbled goat cheese

PREHEAT the oven to 400° F.

PLACE one flatbread dough round on a work surface. Spoon the pesto and marinara sauces over the dough, spreading to coat evenly, and layer with the remaining ingredients. Place the flatbread on a baking sheet and bake until the dough is crisp and the cheese is melted, about 10 minutes.

TRANSFER the flatbread to a cutting board, cut into four wedges, and serve immediately.

CALORIES: 320; TOTAL FAT: 13 G; CARBOHYDRATE: 37 G; DIETARY FIBER: 3 G; PROTEIN: 18 G

HUMMUS AND BAKED TOFU FLATBREAD

MAKES 1 SERVING

½ recipe (1 serving) Basic
Flatbread Dough (page 230)

2 Tbsp. Lemon-Garlic
Hummus (page 222)

4 thin slices Roma tomato (about
half of an average-sized Roma)

2 canned artichoke hearts, quartered

2 Tbsp. baked tofu, thinly sliced

2 Tbsp. Red Wine Reduction (page 130)

PREHEAT oven to 400° F.

PLACE one flatbread dough round on a work surface. Spoon the hummus over the dough, spreading to coat evenly, and layer with the remaining ingredients. Place the flatbread on a baking sheet or pizza stone, and bake until the dough is crisp and the tofu is melted, about 10 minutes.

TRANSFER the flatbread to a cutting board, cut into four wedges, and serve immediately.

CALORIES: 290; TOTAL FAT: 6 G; CARBOHYDRATE: 43 G; DIETARY FIBER: 7 G; PROTEIN: 14 G

MEDITERRANEAN CHICKEN FLATBREAD

MAKES 1 SERVING

½ recipe (1 serving) Basic
Flatbread Dough (page 230)

¼ c. Marinara Sauce (page 126)

2 oz. Basic Grilled Chicken (page 15) or
cooked chicken breast, thinly sliced

2 Tbsp. thinly sliced mozzarella cheese

1 tsp. thinly sliced, pitted kalamata olives

PREHEAT the oven to 400° F.

PLACE one flatbread dough round on a work surface. Spoon the sauce over the dough, spreading to coat evenly, and layer with the remaining ingredients. Place the flatbread on a baking sheet and bake until the dough is crisp and the cheese is melted, about 10 minutes.

TRANSFER the flatbread to a cutting board, cut into four wedges, and serve immediately.

CALORIES: 250; TOTAL FAT: 10 G; CARBOHYDRATE: 32 G; DIETARY FIBER: 4 G; PROTEIN: 8 G

MOZZARELLA AND TOMATO-BASIL CAPRESE FLATBREAD

MAKES 1 SERVING

½ recipe (1 serving) Basic
Flatbread Dough (page 230)

1 Tbsp. Herb Pesto (page 221)

4 thin slices Roma tomato (about half
of an average-sized Roma tomato)

2 Tbsp. thinly sliced mozzarella cheese

3 fresh basil leaves, thinly sliced

PREHEAT the oven to 400° F.

PLACE one flatbread dough round on a work surface. Spoon the pesto sauce over the dough, spreading to coat evenly, and layer with the remaining ingredients. Place the flatbread on a baking sheet and bake until the dough is crisp and the cheese is melted, about 10 minutes.

TRANSFER the flatbread to a cutting board, cut into four wedges, and serve immediately.

CALORIES: 250; TOTAL FAT: 10 G; CARBOHYDRATE: 32 G; DIETARY FIBER: 4 G; PROTEIN: 8 G

Mozzarella and Tomato-Basil
Caprese Flatbread

WHITE BEAN AND MUSHROOM FLATBREAD

MAKES 1 SERVING

½ recipe (1 serving) Basic Flatbread Dough (page 230)

2 Tbsp. White Bean Spread (recipe follows)

2 Tbsp. chopped shiitake mushrooms, sautéed

2 canned artichoke hearts, quartered

2 Tbsp. Roasted Red Bell Peppers (page 18)

1 Tbsp. shredded mozzarella cheese

PREHEAT the oven to 400° F.

PLACE one flatbread dough round on a work surface. Spoon white bean spread over the dough, spreading to coat evenly, and layer with the remaining ingredients. Place the flatbread on a baking sheet or a pizza stone, and bake until the dough is crisp and the cheese is melted, about 10 minutes.

TRANSFER the flatbread to a cutting board, cut into four wedges, and serve immediately.

CALORIES: 260; TOTAL FAT: 8 G; CARBOHYDRATE: 38 G; DIETARY FIBER: 6 G; PROTEIN: 11 G

WHITE BEAN SPREAD

MAKES 1 CUP; SERVING SIZE: ¼ CUP

½ c. Basic White Beans (page 17)

½ c. extra-firm tofu

¼ tsp. fresh garlic, minced

⅓ c. spinach, packed

2 tsp. rice wine vinegar

Pinch of kosher salt

Pinch of freshly ground black pepper

COMBINE all the ingredients in a food processor and puree until smooth.

CALORIES: 60; TOTAL FAT: 1.5 G; CARBOHYDRATE: 7 G; DIETARY FIBER: 2 G; PROTEIN: 5 G

COCKTAILS

BLUEBERRY MARGARITA

MAKES 2 COCKTAILS

3 oz. premium tequila

½ c. fresh blueberries

2 tsp. agave syrup (see Source Guide)

½ c. margarita mix/Miraval Lemonade (page 221)

Splash of fresh lime juice

8 fresh blueberries, for garnish

PLACE everything in a pitcher and stir. Add ice or fill two glasses with ice and pour over.

CALORIES: 170; TOTAL FAT: 0 G; CARBOHYDRATE: 13 G; DIETARY FIBER: 0 G; PROTEIN: 0 G

MINDFUL MARTINI

MAKES 2 COCKTAILS

3 oz. premium vodka

2 oz. triple sec

1 oz. pomegranate juice

½ oz. açai juice

2 fresh blackberries, for garnish

COMBINE the ingredients in a cocktail shaker filled with ice and shake vigorously.

STRAIN into two tall martini glasses, garnish with a blackberry, and serve immediately.

CALORIES: 185; TOTAL FAT: 0 G; CARBOHYDRATE: 22 G; DIETARY FIBER: 0 G; PROTEIN: 0 G

Mindful Martini

GINGER FUSION MARTINI

MAKES 2 COCKTAILS

4 oz. premium vodka

1 ounce triple sec

½ ounce sweet-and-sour mix

2 tsp. grenadine syrup

½ ounce Miraval Ginger Tea (page 211)

COMBINE the ingredients in a cocktail shaker filled with ice and shake vigorously.

STRAIN into two tall martini glasses and serve immediately.

CALORIES: 180; TOTAL FAT: 0 G; CARBOHYDRATE: 13 G; DIETARY FIBER: 0 G; PROTEIN: 0 G

POMEGRANATE MARGARITA

MAKES 2 COCKTAILS

1 Tbsp. margarita salt, optional

2 lime wedges

3 oz. premium tequila

4 oz. pomegranate juice

2 oz. margarita mix

1 oz. triple sec

4 tsp. fresh lime juice

PLACE the margarita salt on a plate. Wet the rim of each margarita or martini glass with a lime wedge and dip into the salt, pressing slightly to adhere. Reserve the lime wedges for garnish.

COMBINE the remaining ingredients in a cocktail shaker filled with ice and shake vigorously until well chilled.

STRAIN the cocktail into the prepared glasses, garnish the rims with the reserved lime wedges, and serve immediately.

CALORIES: 220; TOTAL FAT: 0 G; CARBOHYDRATE: 32 G; DIETARY FIBER: 0 G; PROTEIN: 0 G

PRICKLY PEAR LEMON DROP

MAKES 2 COCKTAILS

4 oz. premium vodka

1 oz. fresh lemon juice

½ oz. prickly pear syrup
(see Source Guide)

COMBINE the ingredients in a cocktail shaker filled with ice and shake vigorously.

STRAIN into 2 tall martini glasses and serve immediately.

CALORIES: 155; TOTAL FAT: 0 G; CARBOHYDRATE: 6.5 G; DIETARY FIBER: 0 G; PROTEIN: 0 G

WATERMELON MOJITO

MAKES 2 COCKTAILS

16 fresh mint leaves

½ oz. fresh lime juice

3 oz. watermelon vodka

½ oz. agave syrup (see
Source Guide) or honey

6 drops grenadine syrup

Club soda

2 lime wedges, for garnish

IN two highball glasses, muddle together the mint leaves and lime juice. Add the vodka, agave, and grenadine; stir well. Add ice to come three-quarters of the way up the glass, then add enough club soda to fill. Stir well, garnish with the lime wedges, and serve.

CALORIES: 120; TOTAL FAT: 0 G; CARBOHYDRATE: 6 G; DIETARY FIBER: 0 G; PROTEIN: 0 G

DESSERTS

BASIC BUTTERSCOTCH SAUCE

MAKES 2½ CUPS; SERVING SIZE:
2 TABLESPOONS OR 1 FLUID OUNCE

2 c. light brown sugar

½ c. agave syrup (see Source Guide) or light corn syrup

8 Tbsp. (1 stick) unsalted butter

1 c. heavy cream

1½ tsp. pure vanilla extract

COMBINE the sugar, syrup, and butter in a heavy medium saucepan and cook over high heat, whisking occasionally until the mixture starts to bubble violently and pull away from the sides of the pan, 3 to 4 minutes. Turn off the heat, and very slowly add the cream, whisking until well incorporated and the mixture is smooth and deep brown in color. Whisk in the vanilla and set aside to cool to room temperature.

COVER tightly and refrigerate until ready to use. (The sauce will keep refrigerated for up to seven days.)

CALORIES: 190; TOTAL FAT: 9 G; CARBOHYDRATE: 28 G; DIETARY FIBER: 0 G; PROTEIN: 0 G

BASIC CHOCOLATE SAUCE

MAKES 2 CUPS; SERVING SIZE:
2 TABLESPOONS OR 1 FLUID OUNCE

¾ c. unsweetened cocoa powder

½ c. granulated sugar

½ c. boiling water

½ c. maple syrup

½ Tbsp. vanilla extract

IN a medium-sized bowl, combine cocoa powder and sugar. Slowly add the boiling water while whisking constantly. Add in maple syrup and vanilla extract, and whisk until smooth. Strain through a fine mesh strainer and transfer to a container. Refrigerate for at least 2 hours before serving. Keep refrigerated for up to two weeks or freeze for up to a month.

CALORIES: 50; TOTAL FAT: 0.5 G; CARBOHYDRATE: 11 G; DIETARY FIBER: 0 G; PROTEIN: 3 G

DARK-CHOCOLATE VEGAN CRÈME BRÛLÉE

Traditional crème brûlée custard-based recipes, made with eggs and heavy cream, can be placed under an oven broiler to "brûlée" or "burn" their sugar toppings. However, our vegan custard cannot be placed in the oven, as the mixture will break down. The sugar topping can only be accomplished with a kitchen torch, which has become an easy-to-find kitchen tool. We promise the result to be worthy of your efforts!

MAKES 2 CUPS; SERVING SIZE: ½ CUP

2 c. crumbled tofu (about 12 oz.)
10 Tbsp. unsweetened cocoa powder
1¼ c. sugar, plus 4 tsp. to brûlée the tops
4 tsp. soy milk
½ c. cubed avocado

COMBINE the tofu, cocoa, sugar, milk, and avocado in a blender and process on high speed until smooth.

SPOON the mixture into four six-ounce ramekins or decorative heatproof bowls, cover loosely with plastic wrap, and refrigerate at least 6 hours or overnight.

SPRINKLE the top of each custard with 1 tsp. of the sugar. Caramelize the sugar using a blowtorch. Place the ramekins on four dessert plates and serve immediately.

CALORIES: 240; TOTAL FAT: 5 G; CARBOHYDRATE: 56 G; DIETARY FIBER: 6 G; PROTEIN: 9 G

BRÛLÉED BANANA SPLIT

A simple yet delicious dessert, this recipe is perfect for summertime with refreshing sorbet and vanilla ice cream.

2 medium bananas

4 tsp. turbinado sugar

½ c. Nonfat Vanilla Ice Cream (recipe follows)

½ c. Mango Sorbet (recipe follows)

½ c. Raspberry Sorbet (recipe follows)

¼ c. Basic Chocolate Sauce (page 243), optional

¼ c. Basic Butterscotch Sauce (page 243), optional

¼ c. Raspberry Coulis (page 273), optional

Toasted nuts, optional

TO assemble, peel 2 bananas and cut lengthwise. Lay halves flat and cut again in half on a bias. Sprinkle ½ tsp. of sugar on the flat side of each piece of banana. Caramelize the sugar using a hand torch or place on a sheet pan in the oven under broiler for 10 minutes or until the sugar has melted and turned a light amber color. Serve two pieces of brûléed banana with a 1 oz. scoop each of vanilla ice cream and raspberry and mango sorbets. Top with chocolate sauce, butterscotch sauce, raspberry coulis, and/or toasted ground nuts if desired.

CALORIES: 230; TOTAL FAT: 1.5 G; CARBOHYDRATE: 60 G; DIETARY FIBER: 6 G; PROTEIN: 2 G

NONFAT VANILLA ICE CREAM

MAKES 1 QUART

3 c. nonfat milk

3 Tbsp. cornstarch

¾ c. granulated sugar

2 vanilla beans, cut lengthwise and scraped

COMBINE cornstarch, sugar, and ½ cup milk in a small bowl and whisk until smooth; set aside.

BRING the remaining 2½ cups milk and scraped vanilla beans to a boil in a medium saucepot. Add cornstarch mixture and continue to cook over medium heat, whisking constantly to prevent the cornstarch from clumping or scorching on the bottom of the pan. Bring to a boil, then remove from heat. Strain through a fine mesh strainer and cool to room temperature. Transfer to a container and refrigerate for 2 hours.

PROCESS mixture in an ice-cream machine according to manufacturer's directions. Serve immediately, or cover and freeze for up to two weeks.

MANGO SORBET

MAKES 1 QUART

¾ c. water

½ c. sugar

5 c. chopped fresh or
frozen peeled mango

3 Tbsp. fresh lime juice

COMBINE the water and sugar in a small saucepan and bring to a simmer over medium heat. Cook until the sugar is dissolved, about 3 minutes.

BLEND the hot syrup, mango, and lime juice in a blender in two batches. Transfer to a bowl, cover, and refrigerate until well chilled, 2 hours.

TRANSFER the mango mixture to an ice-cream machine, and process according to the manufacturer's directions.

SERVE immediately, or place in an airtight plastic container and freeze until ready to serve. (The sorbet will keep in the freezer for up to one month.)

CALORIES: 190; TOTAL FAT: 1 G; CARBOHYDRATE: 50 G; DIETARY FIBER: 3 G; PROTEIN: 2 G

RASPBERRY SORBET

MAKES 1 QUART

¾ c. water

½ c. sugar

4 c. fresh or frozen raspberries

3 Tbsp. fresh lemon juice

COMBINE the water and sugar in a small saucepan and bring to a simmer over medium heat. Cook until the sugar is dissolved, about 3 minutes.

BLEND the hot syrup, raspberry, and lemon juice in a blender in two batches. Transfer to a bowl, cover, and refrigerate until well chilled, 2 hours.

TRANSFER the raspberry mixture to an ice-cream machine, and process according to the manufacturer's directions.

SERVE immediately, or place in an airtight plastic container and freeze until ready to serve. (The sorbet will keep in the freezer for up to one month.)

CALORIES: 130; TOTAL FAT: 1 G; CARBOHYDRATE: 33 G; DIETARY FIBER: 8 G; PROTEIN: 2 G

COCONUT-LIME PUDDING WITH TROPICAL FRUIT SALSA

A sweet surprise for friends with food sensitivities, this pudding is gluten-free, dairy-free, and soy-free. A mindful choice is to use agave syrup or honey rather than refined sugar.

MAKES 4 SERVINGS

¾ c. rice milk, at room temperature

2½ Tbsp. cornstarch or arrowroot

¾ c. light coconut milk

⅓ c. agave syrup (see Source Guide) or honey

3 Tbsp. fresh lime juice

1 large egg

MIX together the cornstarch and ¼ cup of the rice milk in a medium bowl, whisking until smooth, to make a slurry.

COMBINE the coconut milk, agave syrup, and lime juice with the remaining ½ cup rice milk in a large saucepan; bring to a boil over medium-high heat, whisking occasionally. Add the cornstarch slurry to the pan, whisk to remove any lumps, and return to a boil, cooking for 1 minute. Remove from the heat.

BEAT the egg lightly in a small bowl. Add ¼ cup of the hot mixture to the egg, whisking constantly. Add the egg mixture to the pan and return to the heat; whisking constantly, return to a simmer.

REMOVE from the heat and divide equally among four 4-ounce ramekins, wine, or martini glasses for serving. Let cool to room temperature and refrigerate until well chilled before serving. (The puddings can be kept refrigerated, tightly covered, for up to two days.)

CALORIES: 170; TOTAL FAT: 5 G; CARBOHYDRATE: 30 G; DIETARY FIBER: 0 G; PROTEIN: 2 G

TROPICAL FRUIT SALSA

MAKES ½ CUP; SERVING SIZE: 2 TBSP.

2 Tbsp. pineapple, diced, peeled, and cored

2 Tbsp. strawberries, diced and hulled

2 Tbsp. fresh blueberries

2 Tbsp. kiwi, peeled and diced

¼ tsp. mint, chiffonaded

COMBINE all the ingredients in a small bowl and stir to combine.

SERVE immediately.

BUTTERSCOTCH-CHOCOLATE TIRAMISU

MAKES 4 SERVINGS

16 Ladyfingers (recipe follows)

1 large egg, separated

1 Tbsp. plus 1¼ tsp. sugar

2 Tbsp. mascarpone cheese

2 Tbsp. low-fat cream cheese, at room temperature

¼ c. heavy cream

2 Tbsp. nonfat milk

4 tsp. Basic Butterscotch Sauce (page 243), well chilled

4 tsp. brewed espresso or strong black coffee, well chilled

4 tsp. Basic Chocolate Sauce (page 243), well chilled

Sweetened cocoa powder, for dusting

PLACE the egg yolk and 1 Tbsp. of the sugar in the bowl of a standing mixer fitted with a whisk attachment, or with an electric mixer, and beat until frothy and pale yellow, 2 minutes. Add the mascarpone and cream cheese and whisk on high speed until smooth and ribbons form, 2 minutes. Transfer to a medium bowl.

IN a clean bowl, beat the heavy cream and milk with an electric mixer until soft peaks form. Fold into the egg-yolk mixture.

PLACE the egg white in a clean, dry bowl for a standing mixer fitted with the balloon attachment, or using an electric mixer, beat on medium speed to soft peaks. With the machine on high speed, add the remaining 1¼ tsp. of the sugar and beat to medium peaks. Gently fold meringue into the egg-yolk mixture.

TO assemble the desserts, place four martini glasses on a work surface. In the bottom of each glass, spoon ½ tsp. of the chocolate sauce and swirl to evenly coat the bottom and a ¼ inch up the sides. Spoon 1 Tbsp. of the mascarpone mixture over the chocolate sauce and top with 1 tsp. of the butterscotch sauce.

LAY 2 ladyfingers on the butterscotch and drizzle with ½ tsp. of the coffee.

CONTINUE layering with 1 Tbsp. of the mascarpone and 1 tsp. of the chocolate sauce. Top the chocolate sauce with 2 ladyfingers and drizzle with ½ tsp. of the coffee.

SPOON 1 Tbsp. of the mascarpone mixture on top and sprinkle lightly with cocoa powder.

COVER the glasses with plastic wrap and refrigerate at least 2 hours and for up to 24 hours before serving.

CALORIES: 270; TOTAL FAT: 18 G; CARBOHYDRATE: 21 G; DIETARY FIBER: 1 G; PROTEIN: 8 G

LADYFINGERS

MAKES 164 (1½-INCH) LADYFINGERS, 120 (2-INCH) LADYFINGERS, OR 60 (4-INCH) LADYFINGERS

Deeply creamy but not too sweet, our tiramisu is served elegantly in martini glasses. Chef Kim suggests making the ladyfingers smaller than the traditional size in order to layer four inside each glass. If you choose to stay with tradition, remember that the nutritional information and calorie count will change.

2 large eggs, separated

3 Tbsp. sugar

1 Tbsp. cornstarch

2 tsp. unsweetened cocoa powder

2 Tbsp. all-purpose flour

PREHEAT the oven to 350° F. Line two large baking sheets with parchment paper and lightly spray with nonstick cooking spray.

PLACE the egg yolks and 1 Tbsp. sugar in the bowl of an electric mixer fitted with a balloon attachment or with an electric mixer and beat until frothy and pale yellow, 3 minutes.

SIFT together the cornstarch and cocoa.

PLACE the egg whites in a clean, dry bowl for a standing mixer fitted with a balloon attachment, or using an electric mixer, and beat on medium speed to soft peaks. With the machine on high speed, add the remaining 2 Tbsp. of the sugar and the cornstarch mixture and beat until well incorporated and a shiny meringue, 3 minutes.

GENTLY fold the meringue into the beaten egg yolks. Sift the flour into the mixture, gently folding to incorporate.

TRANSFER the meringue mixture to a pastry bag fitted with a regular tip and pipe in 2-inch strips onto the prepared sheet pans. (Alternatively, spoon the meringue into a large plastic ziplock bag. Cut ½ inch from the bottom of the bag and pipe onto the sheet pan.)

BAKE 10 to 12 minutes or until set and lightly brown. Remove from the oven and let cool on the baking sheet for 1 hour before serving.

CHOCOLATE CARIBBEAN CREPES WITH VANILLA YOGURT SAUCE

MAKES 6 SERVINGS

½ c. plain nonfat yogurt

1 Tbsp. agave syrup (see Source Guide) or honey

½ tsp. pure vanilla extract

⅔ c. pineapple, peeled, cored, and chopped

4 strawberries, hulled and quartered

1 Tbsp. spiced rum, such as Captain Morgan

½ vanilla bean, cut in half lengthwise and seeds scraped out

1 tsp. mint, finely chopped

6 Chocolate Crepes (recipe follows)

TO make the vanilla yogurt sauce, combine the yogurt, agave syrup, and vanilla extract in a small bowl and stir to combine. Set aside, or cover and refrigerate until ready to use. (The sauce can be made in advance and kept up to three days, covered, in the refrigerator.)

TO make the fruit topping, lightly coat the bottom of a large skillet with cooking spray and heat over high heat.

ADD the pineapple, strawberries, and vanilla bean and seeds to the pan and cook, stirring for 1 minute. Remove the pan from the heat, add the rum, and carefully ignite with a match. Return the pan to the heat and cook, stirring until the liquid is reduced by half, about 1 minute. Remove from the heat and stir in the mint.

TO serve, spread 1½ Tbsp. of the sauce onto the bottom of each of six dessert plates. Roll the crepes into cylinders and arrange over the sauce on each plate. Divide the fruit topping among the plates and serve immediately.

CALORIES: 90; TOTAL FAT: 1.5 G; CARBOHYDRATE: 18 G; DIETARY FIBER: 1 G; PROTEIN: 2 G

CHOCOLATE CREPES

MAKES 6 SIX-INCH CREPES

We have two hints to unlock the secret to crepes, aside from incorporating chocolate in the recipe: First, let the batter rest for at least one hour before you start preparing the crepes, which allows the flour to absorb the liquid ingredients. Second, make sure your pan is nice and hot before you begin cooking.

⅓ c. all-purpose flour

6 Tbsp. 2 percent milk

2 Tbsp. sugar

1 Tbsp. water

1 Tbsp. unsweetened cocoa powder

1½ tsp. unsalted butter, melted

⅛ tsp. salt

COMBINE all the ingredients in a blender and process on high speed. Transfer to a measuring cup, cover, and let rest in the refrigerator for 1 hour and up to 24 hours.

LIGHTLY coat the bottom of a 6-inch nonstick skillet with cooking spray and heat over medium heat.

LADLE 2 Tbsp. of the crepe batter into the bottom of the pan and cook until just starting to set, about 30 seconds. Loosen the sides of the crepe with a rubber spatula and cook until completely set, 5 to 10 seconds. Flip the crepe, using the spatula, and cook until the second side is set, about 30 seconds. Turn the crepe out onto a large plate to rest, with aluminum foil to keep warm, and cook the remaining crepes.

CHOCOLATE-CRANBERRY COCONUT MACAROONS

You can change this recipe to suit your tastes—simply keep the proportion of dry ingredients the same. For instance, if you don't like coconut, add more cereal. Chef Kim uses celiac-friendly cereal at Miraval: gluten-free Organic Maple Buckwheat Flakes. Yet you can substitute any flake-type breakfast cereal, from Special K to Bran Flakes.

These refrigerate well should you live in a hot, humid climate. Store the macaroons in an airtight container in the refrigerator after 24 hours to prevent separation and "weeping."

MAKES 2 DOZEN

2 c. flake-type cereal, such as Organic Maple Buckwheat Flakes or Special K

½ c. sweetened or unsweetened coconut flakes

¼ c. dried cranberries

¼ c. mini semisweet chocolate chips

3 large egg whites

¾ c. sugar

½ tsp. pure vanilla extract

⅛ tsp. salt

PREHEAT the oven to 350° F.

LINE two large baking sheets with parchment paper and set aside.

COMBINE the cereal, coconut, cranberries, and chips in a large bowl.

IN a bowl fitted with an electric mixer, beat the egg whites on medium speed until frothy. Gradually add the sugar and whip until thick and glossy. Add the vanilla and salt, and continue to mix for another 10 seconds.

FOLD the meringue into the dry ingredients, being careful not to deflate the meringue.

USING a ¾-ounce scoop (1½ Tbsp.), portion the mixture onto the prepared baking sheets and bake for 8 minutes. Rotate the sheet pans and continue baking until golden brown and the cookies lift freely from the parchment, about 16 minutes.

LET cool on the baking sheets before serving, at least 30 minutes. Store in an airtight container for up to two days.

CALORIES: 50; TOTAL FAT: 1 G; CARBOHYDRATE: 10 G; DIETARY FIBER: 0 G; PROTEIN: 1 G

CRANBERRY, PECAN, AND WHITE-CHOCOLATE BREAD PUDDING

A greased 1-quart soufflé dish can be used to bake the pudding instead of the individual ramekins but will require a longer baking time. This recipe also doubles well.

MAKES 4 SERVINGS

2⅔ c. cubed crusty wheat bread
¼ c. dried cranberries
2 Tbsp. chopped pecans
2 Tbsp. chopped white chocolate
1 large egg
1 large egg white
½ c. evaporated milk
½ c. nonfat milk
¼ c. light brown sugar
½ tsp. ground cinnamon

COMBINE the bread, cranberries, pecans, and chocolate in a large bowl.

COMBINE the remaining ingredients in a medium bowl and whisk well to combine. Add to the dry ingredients, stir, and let sit until the liquid is absorbed into the bread, about 30 minutes.

PREHEAT the oven to 350° F. Lightly grease four 4-ounce ramekins.

DIVIDE the batter among the ramekins and bake until golden brown and the middle is just set, 28 to 30 minutes. (Alternatively, the pudding can be baked in a greased 1-quart soufflé dish for about 35 minutes.)

SERVE the pudding hot either in ramekins or turned out onto dessert plates.

CALORIES: 260; TOTAL FAT: 7 G; CARBOHYDRATE: 42 G; DIETARY FIBER: 2 G; PROTEIN: 8 G

HAZELNUT MOUSSE DOMES WITH CHOCOLATE GANACHE

MAKES 6 SERVINGS

¼ c. semisweet chocolate pieces

3 Tbsp. plain nonfat yogurt

2 Tbsp. low-fat buttermilk

2 Tbsp. sugar

¼ tsp. pure vanilla extract

1 Tbsp. water

1 tsp. powdered gelatin

1 Tbsp. nonfat milk

1 Tbsp. Frangelico or other hazelnut-flavored liqueur

2 large egg whites, at room temperature

1 recipe Chocolate Sponge Cake (recipe follows)

1 recipe Chocolate Ganache (recipe on page 259)

¼ c. toasted hazelnuts, ground

TO make the hazelnut mousse, melt the chocolate in a small glass dish or measuring cup in the microwave, stirring every 10 seconds.

WHISK together the yogurt, buttermilk, 1 Tbsp. of the sugar, and the vanilla extract in a medium bowl. Add the melted chocolate and whisk to combine.

PLACE the water in a small ramekin and sprinkle with the gelatin. Let sit for 1 minute.

PLACE the milk and Frangelico in a small skillet and bring to a simmer over low heat. Add the gelatin and stir over low heat until dissolved. Remove from the heat and whisk into the chocolate mixture.

PLACE the egg whites in a medium bowl and beat with an electric mixer on medium speed to soft peaks. Add the remaining 1 Tbsp. sugar and whip to medium peaks, about 2 minutes. Fold the beaten egg whites into the chocolate mixture, working the whites through the middle and around the sides to incorporate.

LIGHTLY coat the inside of a silicone mold containing six 2-ounce cups with cooking spray and set aside.

SPOON the mousse into the prepared silicone mold cups and level with a spatula. Cover the mold with plastic wrap and freeze until the mousse is firm, at least 1 hour. The mousses can be frozen for up to two days before being served. (Alternatively, transfer the mousse to a small stainless steel bowl and freeze until almost firm. Line a small baking sheet or baking dish with parchment paper. Portion the frozen mousse mixture using a 2-ounce ice-cream scoop, place on the prepared sheet, cover loosely, and refreeze until firm and ready to assemble the domes.)

USING a 2-inch cookie cutter, cut six disks from the cake. Turn out the mousse domes and press the cake rounds onto the bottoms.

PLACE the assembled domes on a wire rack and drizzle with the chocolate ganache to completely cover. Press toasted hazelnuts to the bottom edge of each dome. Place the chocolate-coated domes on a parchment-lined plate and refrigerate until the chocolate is set, 30 minutes.

PLACE one mousse dome onto each of six plates and serve immediately.

CALORIES: 340; TOTAL FAT: 17 G; CARBOHYDRATE: 41 G; DIETARY FIBER: 3 G; PROTEIN: 7 G

CHOCOLATE SPONGE CAKE

MAKES ONE 8-INCH ROUND CAKE, OR SIX 2-INCH ROUND CAKES

1 Tbsp. unsweetened cocoa powder

1 Tbsp. all-purpose flour

2 large egg whites, at room temperature

3 Tbsp. sugar

1 tsp. finely ground hazelnuts

PREHEAT the oven to 350° F.

LIGHTLY coat the inside of an 8-inch round cake pan with cooking spray. Cut an 8-inch round piece of parchment, place on the bottom of the pan, and lightly coat with cooking spray. Set aside.

SIFT together the cocoa and flour into a medium bowl.

PLACE the egg whites in a medium bowl and beat with an electric mixer on medium speed to soft peaks. Add the sugar and whip to medium peaks, about 2 minutes. Fold the beaten egg whites and hazelnuts into the chocolate mixture, working the whites through the middle and around the sides to incorporate.

SPREAD the batter evenly onto the bottom of the prepared pan and bake until the cake rises, pulls away from the sides of the pan, and springs back when lightly touched, 12 to 14 minutes.

REMOVE from the oven and let cool completely in the pan, about 30 minutes.

TRANSFER the cake to a cutting board and peel away the parchment paper. Use as directed in the Hazelnut Mousse Domes.

CHOCOLATE GANACHE

MAKES 1 HEAPING CUP

Once you have mastered ganache, you will look for recipes that call for this velvety, rich blanket of chocolate. Remember to keep it at room temperature for a pourable consistency, as needed to encase the Hazelnut Mousse Domes. We reach for this recipe for a variety of desserts, and especially love it as an ice-cream topping or drizzled over fresh strawberries.

¾ c. semisweet chocolate pieces

6 Tbsp. fat-free milk

¼ c. heavy cream

1 Tbsp. corn syrup

PLACE the chocolate in a small bowl and set aside.

COMBINE the milk, cream, and corn syrup in a small glass measuring cup and microwave until very hot. (Alternatively, bring the mixture to a simmer in a very small saucepan over medium heat.)

POUR the hot milk mixture into the chocolate and whisk until very smooth. Use immediately to coat the mousse domes.

HONEY BLOSSOM CRÈME BRÛLÉE

MAKES 6 SERVINGS

1⅓ c. 2 percent milk

⅔ c. nonfat powdered dry milk

⅓ c. nonfat milk

1 vanilla bean, cut lengthwise
and scraped

4 large egg yolks

¼ c. honey

3½ Tbsp. sugar

PREHEAT the oven to 325° F.

COMBINE the low-fat milk, dry milk, nonfat milk, and vanilla bean and seeds in a medium saucepan; bring to a simmer over medium heat, whisking to dissolve the dry milk powder. Remove from the heat. (The dry milk adds a thicker consistency to the finished custards, so the usual heavy cream is not necessary.)

BEAT the egg yolks, honey, and 1½ Tbsp. sugar in a large bowl until frothy. Slowly whisk 1 cup of the hot milk mixture into the egg mixture to combine. Continue to add the hot milk mixture, one ladle at a time, into the egg mixture and strain through a fine mesh strainer into a clean container.

DIVIDE the egg mixture into six 3-ounce ramekins. Place the ramekins inside a deep baking dish and pour enough hot water into the baking dish to come halfway up the sides of the ramekins. Cover the baking dish with aluminum foil and bake until the custards are set but still slightly loose in the center, 50 to 55 minutes.

REMOVE the baking dish from the oven, uncover, and let rest in the hot water for 10 minutes. Remove the ramekins from the water and let rest for 30 minutes. Refrigerate completely before serving, at least 4 hours. (If storing longer before serving, cover each ramekin tightly with plastic wrap before refrigerating.)

SPRINKLE the top of each custard with 1 tsp. of the sugar. Caramelize the sugar using a blowtorch. Place the ramekins on six dessert plates and serve immediately.

CALORIES: 160; TOTAL FAT: 4 G; CARBOHYDRATE: 24 G; DIETARY FIBER: 0 G; PROTEIN: 7 G

HONEY TUILE COOKIES

Thin, crisp, and delicate, this versatile cookie suits all occasions and can be formed into any shape by cutting templates from heavy paper or thin plastic sheets. We make sure they cool completely before removing from the baking sheet so they hold their shape.

Try these alongside the Vanilla Tapioca Pudding with Tropical Fruit Compote, or your favorite ice cream and fresh fruit.

MAKES 36 "SPOON" COOKIES

½ c. confectioners' sugar
4 Tbsp. unsalted butter, softened
2 Tbsp. honey
1 large egg white
½ c. all-purpose flour

PREHEAT the oven to 350° F. Line each of two large baking sheets with a silicone cooking mat.

IN the bowl of a standing mixer fitted with a paddle attachment or with an electric mixer, cream together the sugar and butter on low speed until starting to become fluffy, 1 minute. Increase the speed to medium and mix for an additional minute.

ADD the honey and mix on medium speed until well blended. Add the egg white and mix on medium speed for 30 seconds. (The mixture will separate and look curdled; this is fine.) Scrape down the sides of the bowl and add the flour. Blend on low speed to incorporate, scraping the sides as needed to incorporate all the ingredients. Blend on medium speed until well combined, 1 minute.

(THE batter can be refrigerated, tightly covered, for up to five days, and frozen for up to one month.)

TRACE the outline of a teaspoon onto a heavy sheet of paper or a plastic sleeve, using a felt-tip pen. Cut out the shape using a pair of scissors, and use this as a template for making the cookies.

SPOON the batter through the template onto the prepared baking sheets, 1 heaping teaspoon at a time in order to make 36 "spoons," each time spreading the batter to the edges of the template with a small offset spatula. Bake until just golden brown around the edges but still soft to the touch, 5 to 6 minutes. Allow the cookies to cool completely on the baking sheet.

CAREFULLY slide a very thin spatula under each cookie to remove the cookies to an airtight container until ready to serve.

CALORIES: 30; TOTAL FAT: 1.5 G; CARBOHYDRATE: 4 G; DIETARY FIBER: 0 G; PROTEIN: 0 G

IRISH CREAM ROULADE

Most pastry chefs will use cake flour for the finest sponge-cake texture, but Chef Kim purposefully created this recipe with the more common all-purpose flour to show that either ingredient results in a lovely, moist cake.

MAKES 18 SERVINGS

⅓ c. all-purpose flour

¼ c. unsweetened cocoa powder

10 large egg whites

1 c. granulated sugar

¼ tsp. cream of tartar, to add to egg whites, optional

½ recipe Bailey's Irish Cream Ice Cream (recipe follows)

1 recipe Basic Chocolate Sauce (page 243), optional

Confectioners' sugar, optional

PREHEAT the oven to 350° F.

TO make the sponge cake, sift together the flour and cocoa into a large bowl.

WHIP the egg whites in the bowl of an electric mixer until frothy and almost to soft peaks. Beat in cream of tartar, if desired, to help stabilize egg white foam. With the machine running, add ¾ cup of the sugar in three stages and whip to medium peaks.

USING a large rubber spatula, fold the whipped egg whites into the dry ingredients, turning the bowl to fully incorporate. (This process will take several minutes. The flour will clump initially, and there may be a few flecks of cocoa when you are finished; this is okay.)

SPRAY a half-sheet pan with nonstick spray. Top the pan with a sheet of parchment and spray with nonstick spray (or top with a silicone mat). Pour the batter onto the pan and bake until the cake rises, pulls away from the sides of the pan, and springs back when lightly touched, 22 to 24 minutes.

PLACE the pan on a wire rack and let the cake rest until cool, about 30 minutes. With a serrated knife, separate the cake from the edges of the pan. Let the cake rest in the pan on the wire rack until completely cool, 1 to 2 hours.

WITH the cake still in the pan, sprinkle the remaining ¼ cup sugar evenly over the surface. Shake the pan so the sugar is evenly distributed. Pour off the remaining sugar and discard.

PLACE a clean piece of parchment paper over the cake and top with a second large baking sheet. Turn the sheet pan over to release the cake from the baking pan and pull away the parchment paper.

SPOON 3 cups of the ice cream into the center of the cake. Using an offset spatula or a small rubber spatula, evenly spread the ice cream over the top of the cake, leaving ½-inch border on the long side closest to you, ¾-inch border on the opposite long side, and ½-inch each on either end. Starting at the long end closest to you and using the parchment paper, roll the roulade over the ice-cream filling, pressing down to make the cake adhere at the opposite edge.

FREEZE until firm, about 4 hours.

TO serve, slice the cake into 18 equal portions. Drizzle with chocolate sauce, if desired, or sprinkle with confectioners' sugar. Serve immediately.

CALORIES: 50; TOTAL FAT: 0.5 G; CARBOHYDRATE: 11 G; DIETARY FIBER: 0 G; PROTEIN: 3 G

BAILEY'S IRISH CREAM ICE CREAM

MAKES 1½ QUARTS

2 c. granulated sugar
½ c. cornstarch or arrowroot
8 c. nonfat milk
1½ tsp. pure vanilla extract

½ c. Bailey's Irish Cream or
other Irish Cream liqueur, or
2 Tbsp. coffee concentrate
1 c. mini semisweet chocolate chips

WHISK together the sugar and cornstarch in a large bowl to mix well. Set aside.

HEAT the milk in a large saucepan over medium-high heat and bring to a simmer. Remove from the heat.

ADD 1 cup of the hot milk to the sugar mixture and whisk to combine. Add the sugar/hot milk mixture to the hot milk, whisk well, and return to the heat. Bring to a boil, whisking constantly, and cook until frothy and thickened, 2 to 3 minutes. Remove from the heat and strain through a fine mesh strainer into a clean container. Add the vanilla and liqueur and stir well. Cover the mixture, pressing down the plastic against the surface to prevent a skin forming. Refrigerate until well chilled, at least 2 hours.

FREEZE mixture in an ice-cream machine according to the manufacturer's directions. While the mixture is still soft, fold in the chocolate chips. Transfer to an airtight plastic container and freeze for at least 2 hours, or until ready to serve. If using this ice cream in the Irish Cream Roulade, freeze for 20 to 30 minutes before assembling roulade. (The ice cream will keep frozen for up to one month.)

LEMON MERINGUE BAKED ALASKA

The chiffon-cake recipe used for the Baked Alaska is also a versatile dessert on its own: simply cut into circles with a cookie cutter and pair with fresh summer fruit for a simple, clean end to a meal. This recipe will make one 9-inch cake, or eight 2-inch cake rounds.

MAKES 8 SERVINGS

6 Tbsp. sugar
¼ c. water
3 Tbsp. canola oil or vegetable oil
2 large eggs, separated
1 tsp. pure vanilla extract
½ c. cake flour
1 tsp. baking powder
2 c. Lemon Sherbet (recipe follows)
Meringue (recipe on page 266)

PREHEAT the oven to 350° F.

TO make the chiffon cake, lightly coat the inside of a 9-inch round springform pan with cooking spray. Cut an 8-inch round piece of parchment, place on the bottom of the pan, and lightly coat with cooking spray. Set aside.

IN the bowl of an electric mixer with a whisk attachment, beat together the water, oil, egg yolks, vanilla, and 3 Tbsp. of the sugar on medium speed until smooth. Add the cake flour and baking powder and beat for 30 seconds on high speed until there are no lumps. Transfer to a medium bowl.

WASH the mixing bowl and attachment and dry completely with a clean cloth. Place the egg whites in the bowl and beat with an electric mixer on medium speed until soft peaks form. Add the remaining 3 Tbsp. sugar and whip to medium peaks, about 2 minutes. Fold the beaten egg whites into the vanilla mixture, working the whites through the middle and around the sides to incorporate, being careful not to deflate the whites.

SPREAD the batter evenly onto the bottom of the prepared pan and bake until the cake rises, pulls away from the sides of the pan, and springs back when lightly touched, 22 to 25 minutes.

REMOVE from the oven and let cool completely in the pan, about 30 minutes. Remove the sides from the springform pan and transfer the cake to a cutting board. Peel away the parchment paper.

USING a 2-inch cookie cutter, cut eight disks from the cake.

TURN out the eight sherbet domes and press the cake rounds onto the bottoms.

PLACE the assembled domes on a wire rack and spread with the meringue to completely cover. Working quickly and using a blowtorch, lightly brown the meringue.

PLACE one Baked Alaska on each of eight plates and serve immediately.

CALORIES: 250; TOTAL FAT: 7 G; CARBOHYDRATE: 47 G; DIETARY FIBER: 0 G; PROTEIN: 3 G

LEMON SHERBET

MAKES 1 QUART

You can substitute nonfat milk for the rice milk in this recipe. We use rice milk in our version, as this recipe was developed for our dairy-intolerant guests. It is important to immediately pipe the sherbet into the molds to make the Baked Alaska, as the low-fat content in this recipe makes the sherbet hard and then difficult to work with once it freezes.

1½ c. fresh lemon juice

2 tsp. finely grated lemon zest

2 c. Simple Syrup (page 23)

1 c. rice milk

STIR together all the ingredients in a medium bowl. Cover tightly and refrigerate until well chilled, at least 2 hours. (The mixture can be kept refrigerated, tightly covered, for up to three days.)

TRANSFER the lemon mixture to an ice-cream machine and process according to the manufacturer's directions.

PIPE the prepared sherbet immediately into eight 2-inch silicone mold cups.

(ALTERNATIVELY, scoop eight 2-ounce portions of sherbet onto a small sheet pan or baking dish cover, with parchment paper, and freeze until ready to assemble the desserts.)

ANY leftover sherbet should be placed in an airtight container and frozen.

MERINGUE

MAKES 8 SERVINGS

⅓ c. sugar

¼ c. corn syrup

4½ tsp. agave syrup (see Source Guide)

½ c. water

2 large egg whites

COMBINE the sugar, corn syrup, agave, and water in a medium saucepan and cook over medium heat to a thick syrup. Remove from the heat.

IN a bowl fitted with an electric mixer, or using a handheld mixer, beat the egg whites to soft peaks. With the machine running, drizzle in the hot syrup and continue beating until the meringue is glossy and reaches medium peaks.

COOL the mixture for 3 minutes and then transfer to a pastry bag to pipe meringues onto the Baked Alaskas.

MINDFUL CHOCOLATE-CHIP COOKIES

MAKES 30 COOKIES

2 Tbsp. unsalted butter, softened

2 Tbsp. mashed ripe banana

1 c. brown sugar

1 large egg

2 Tbsp. agave syrup (see Source Guide) or honey

1 tsp. pure vanilla extract

1½ c. all-purpose flour

1 tsp. baking soda

¼ tsp. kosher salt

¾ mini semisweet chocolate chips

PREHEAT the oven to 350° F.

COMBINE the butter and banana in a bowl fitted with an electric mixer and cream together with the machine on medium-high, 1 to 2 minutes. Add the sugar and mix well for 2 minutes. Add the egg, agave syrup, and vanilla extract; mix until well combined, 1 to 2 minutes.

SIFT together the flour and baking soda into a small bowl and add the salt. With the machine on low speed, add the dry ingredients to the wet ingredients and mix just until the dough comes together. Stir in the chocolate chips and mix only until incorporated, being careful not to overmix.

COVER two large baking sheets with parchment paper or cover with silicone cooking sheets. Scoop the dough 1 Tbsp. at a time, roll into a ball, and place on the baking sheet. Continue with the remaining dough, leaving about 2 inches between each cookie. Bake one sheet of cookies at a time until golden brown, 10 to 12 minutes.

TRANSFER the cookies with a spatula from the baking sheets to a wire rack to cool. Serve warm or at room temperature. (The cookies can be kept in an airtight container for up to three days.)

CALORIES: 70; TOTAL FAT: 2.5 G; CARBOHYDRATE: 13 G; DIETARY FIBER: 1 G; PROTEIN: 1 G

PAVLOVA WITH LEMON CURD, FRESH BERRIES, AND RASPBERRY COULIS

Fresh egg whites are important to the success of any meringue dessert. You'll also find that egg whites whip best at room temperature.

MAKES 1 DOZEN

1 c. sugar

1 Tbsp. cornstarch

3 egg whites

3 Tbsp. water

1 tsp. white vinegar

1 recipe Lemon Curd (recipe follows)

6 oz. assorted fresh berries

1 Tbsp. Grand Marnier, or other orange-flavored liqueur, such as Triple Sec

1 recipe Raspberry Coulis (page 273)

PREHEAT the oven to 300° F.

COMBINE the sugar and cornstarch in a small bowl and stir well to combine.

WHIP the egg whites in the bowl of an electric mixer on medium speed. Beat until soft peaks start to form, about 2 minutes. Lower the speed to medium-low and with the machine running, gradually add half of the sugar mixture. Then with the machine running, add the water 1 Tbsp. at a time, alternating with the remaining sugar mixture, beating well after each addition. Add the vinegar and beat well until a shiny meringue.

TRANSFER the meringue to a pastry bag with a regular tip and pipe the meringue in 3-inch circles onto the prepared sheet pan, going around 3 times so the sides are approximately 1-inch high. (Alternately, spoon the meringue into a large plastic ziplock bag. Cut ½ inch from the bottom of the bag and pipe onto the sheet pan.)

BAKE for 30 minutes. Open the oven door by two inches and continue to bake with the door open until the meringues are completely set, an additional 35 to 40 minutes. Remove from the oven and let cool on the baking sheet and let sit at room temperature for 1 hour before serving.

TOSS the berries with the Grand Marnier in a small bowl.

TO serve, spoon 1½ Tbsp. of the Raspberry Coulis onto each dessert plate. Set the meringues onto the coulis and spoon 2 Tbsp. of the Lemon Curd into the center of each.

DIVIDE the berries between the plates, arranging onto the lemon curd, and serve immediately.

CALORIES: 240; TOTAL FAT: 2.5 G; CARBOHYDRATE: 58 G; DIETARY FIBER: 7 G; PROTEIN: 3 G

LEMON CURD

MAKES 1½ CUPS

1½ c. sugar

6 Tbsp. cornstarch

1½ c. water

5 large egg yolks

½ c. plus 2 Tbsp. fresh lemon juice

COMBINE the sugar and cornstarch in a medium bowl and whisk to combine. Add the water and whisk to combine. Transfer the mixture to a large saucepan. Add the egg yolks and lemon juice and whisk well.

COOK the mixture over medium heat, whisking constantly, until thick and glossy, 3 minutes. Remove from the heat and strain through a fine mesh strainer into a clean container. Cover with plastic wrap, pressing the wrap against the surface to prevent a skin from forming. Refrigerate until completely chilled, 1 to 2 hours.

SERVE chilled.

PECAN-PIE EMPANADAS

MAKES 8 SERVINGS

6 Tbsp. pecans, chopped

¼ c. light brown sugar

¼ c. agave syrup (see Source Guide) or honey

1 large egg

1 Tbsp. bourbon, optional

2 tsp. butter, melted

½ tsp. orange zest, finely grated

¼ tsp. pure vanilla extract

Pinch kosher salt

6 sheets phyllo dough

1½ tsp. granulated sugar

⅛ tsp. ground cinnamon

1 recipe Sweetened Whipped Cream (page 23), Soy Caramel Swirl Ice Cream (page 274), or store-bought nonfat vanilla ice cream, optional

PREHEAT the oven to 350° F.

COMBINE the light brown sugar, agave syrup, egg, bourbon, butter, zest, vanilla, and salt in a medium bowl and whisk until well combined. Stir in the pecans and mix well. Pour into an ungreased deep 2-cup baking dish and bake uncovered until set but slightly soft to the touch, 18 to 21 minutes.

LET the pecan filling cool at room temperature for 30 minutes. Cover with plastic wrap and refrigerate until completely chilled, at least 4 hours. (The pecan filling can be kept tightly covered in the refrigerator for up to two days.)

COVER a large baking sheet with parchment paper and spray lightly with cooking spray. Set aside.

LAY one sheet of phyllo dough on a work surface and spray lightly with cooking spray. Lay a second sheet on top of the first and spray lightly with cooking spray. Cut the sheets lengthwise into thirds.

SPOON 2 Tbsp. of the pecan loaf onto the bottom corner of one strip of phyllo. Bring up the edge of the phyllo over the pecan loaf as though making a paper football and continue making triangular thirds, folding the phyllo over to make a triangular package enclosing the phyllo. Complete with the remaining ingredients, placing each on the prepared baking sheet. Spray the top of the empanadas with a little nonstick cooking spray.

STIR together the granulated sugar and cinnamon in a small dish and sprinkle ½ tsp. of the mixture over the top of each pecan empanada. Bake until golden brown, about 25 minutes.

REMOVE the empanadas from the oven and let rest for 10 minutes on the baking sheet.

PLACE one empanada on each of eight plates and place either 2 Tbsp. of whipped cream or a scoop of ice cream to the side. Serve immediately.

CALORIES: 360; TOTAL FAT: 21 G; CARBOHYDRATE: 39 G; DIETARY FIBER: 1 G; PROTEIN: 5 G

Prickly Pear Granita

PRICKLY PEAR GRANITA

You can use this recipe as a template to make your own flavor profiles—for example, melon and mint or cranberry-pomegranate juice. Just add a little water to your favorite juice combination and a little sugar, if needed. Adding a touch of citrus, such as the lime juice in this recipe, can give your granita a little "tang," which will help balance the sweetness.

MAKES 16 QUARTER-CUP SERVINGS

3½ c. prickly pear puree
½ c. water
¼ c. lime juice

WHISK all ingredients together in a small bowl. Transfer mixture to an 8" x 8" square pan. Freeze mixture for at least 12 hours. Once frozen, scrape surface of the granita with a fork, giving it a light, fluffy appearance. Once all the mixture is scraped, transfer granita to a smaller container, cover, and freeze until ready to serve.

CALORIES: 60; TOTAL FAT: 0.5 G; CARBOHYDRATE: 15 G; DIETARY FIBER: 5 G; PROTEIN: 1 G

RASPBERRY COULIS

MAKES 2½ CUPS

3 c. fresh raspberries, rinsed and patted dry; or frozen, unsweetened raspberries
½ c. water
¼ c. sugar

COMBINE all ingredients in a medium saucepan and cook over medium-low heat until the raspberries break down and mixture is thick, stirring occasionally, 8 to 10 minutes.

REMOVE from the heat and transfer to a blender. Blend on high speed until smooth. Strain through a fine mesh strainer into a clean container, cover tightly, and refrigerate until ready to use. (The coulis will keep refrigerated for up to five days, and can be frozen for up to two weeks.)

CALORIES: 80; TOTAL FAT: 0.5 G; CARBOHYDRATE: 20 G; DIETARY FIBER: 6 G; PROTEIN: 1 G

SOY CARAMEL SWIRL ICE-CREAM BALLS WITH PRALINE TOPPING AND BRANDY CARAMEL SYRUP

Somewhere between the velvety ice cream and the brandy caramel syrup, this dessert became unforgettable. You can prepare the ice-cream balls up to an hour ahead of time (the praline crunch can only be frozen for up to one hour; any longer and it will turn soggy). Simply roll each ball in the praline topping and place on a small baking sheet to freeze until ready to serve.

MAKES 8 SERVINGS

½ recipe Soy Caramel Swirl Ice Cream (recipe follows)

½ recipe Brandy Caramel Syrup (recipe on page 276)

¼ recipe Praline Topping (recipe on page 276)

LINE a small baking sheet with parchment paper.

TO assemble the desserts, scoop out eight 2-ounce (¼ cup) portions of the ice cream and roll each scoop into a ball. Place the balls on the parchment sheet to firm, about 10 minutes.

ROLL each scoop of ice cream in the praline crunch topping, pressing about 2 Tbsp. of the crumbs onto each ice-cream ball to completely coat. (If necessary, place the coated ice-cream balls back in the freezer while assembling the desserts.)

TO serve, spoon 1 tsp. of Brandy Caramel Syrup into a martini or parfait glass, swirling to coat the sides. Place one ice-cream ball in each glass and serve immediately.

CALORIES: 250; TOTAL FAT: 4 G; CARBOHYDRATE: 51 G; DIETARY FIBER: 0 G; PROTEIN: 1 G

SOY CARAMEL SWIRL ICE CREAM

MAKES 1 QUART

1 c. sugar

¼ c. cornstarch or arrowroot

4 c. soy milk

1 Tbsp. Amaretto or other almond-flavored liqueur, or ¼ tsp. almond extract

½ c. Dairy-Free Caramel Sauce (recipe follows)

WHISK together the sugar and cornstarch in a large bowl to mix well. Set aside.

HEAT the milk in a large saucepan over medium-high heat and bring to a simmer. Remove from the heat.

ADD 1 cup of the hot milk to the sugar mixture and whisk to combine. Add the sugar/hot milk mixture to the hot milk, whisk well, and return to the heat. Bring to a boil, whisking constantly, and cook until frothy and thickened, 2 to 3 minutes. Remove from the heat and strain through a fine mesh strainer into a clean container. Stir in the liqueur and refrigerate until well chilled, about 2 hours.

TRANSFER the mixture to an ice-cream machine and process according to the manufacturer's directions.

WHILE the mixture is still soft, swirl in the cooled caramel mixture. Place in an airtight plastic container and freeze until the mixture hardens and the swirls are set, about 1 hour, before serving. (The ice cream will keep in the freezer for up to one month.)

DAIRY-FREE CARAMEL SAUCE

MAKES ½ CUP

½ c. soy milk, at room temperature

9 Tbsp. sugar

3 Tbsp. water

¼ tsp. lemon juice

PLACE the soy milk in a very small saucepan or skillet and heat over medium heat. Remove from the heat and set aside.

COMBINE the sugar and water in a medium saucepan and stir to combine, being careful to not get any sugar on the sides of the pan. Cook over high heat for 1 minute. Reduce the heat and cook undisturbed over medium-low heat until the mixture starts to caramelize and reaches about 320° F on a candy thermometer, 2 minutes. Continue cooking until the sugar mixture becomes a medium amber color, about 1 minute. Remove from heat, add the warm soy milk to the pot, and cook, whisking constantly for 1 minute. (Note that when the milk is added to the pot, the mixture will bubble furiously; be careful not to burn yourself.)

LET cool completely before using in the ice-cream recipe. (Or, cover and keep warm until ready to serve as a topping to cakes and ice creams.)

BRANDY CARAMEL SYRUP

MAKES 18 TSP. (6 TBSP.)

½ c. light brown sugar
½ c. water

1 Tbsp. brandy

COMBINE the sugar and water in a small saucepan. Bring to a simmer over medium-high heat and cook undisturbed until golden brown and large bubbles form on the top, 3 to 4 minutes.

STIR in the brandy and transfer to a small container. Refrigerate until cooled, about 1 hour. (The syrup can be made in advance and kept refrigerated for up to one week in an airtight container.)

PRALINE TOPPING

MAKES ABOUT 3½ CUPS

Stir the sugar constantly with a heavy rubber spatula to get rid of the lumps. Most important, pay attention to the color of the sugar as it melts before you add the nuts; do not let it go darker than amber, as it can burn quickly.

This process requires mindful organization and speed. Have the pecans ready to add when the sugar reaches the desired color, and make sure your sheet pan is prepared, as the cooked pecan mixture will harden very quickly. Spread the cooked pecan mixture as thinly as possible on the baking sheet, as this helps with even chopping in your food processor.

2 c. chopped pecans
1¾ tsp. salt

2 c. sugar

COVER a baking sheet with a silicone cooking mat. (Alternatively, cover the sheet with parchment paper and coat lightly with vegetable cooking spray.)

COMBINE the pecans and salt in the bowl of a food processor and pulse until finely chopped.

PLACE the sugar in a medium saucepan over medium-low heat and cook, stirring constantly with a heavy rubber spatula to break up the lumps, until it turns a light amber color, about 6 minutes. Add the pecan pieces, stir to combine, and pour immediately onto the prepared baking sheet.

SPREAD the mixture with the spatula as thinly as possible.

LET cool at room temperature until hardened, at least 1 hour.

PLACE the praline sheet in a food processor and process into ½-inch pieces to serve. (The praline topping can be kept in an airtight container at room temperature for up to three days.)

TURTLE CAKE

MAKES 16 SERVINGS

1½ c. all-purpose flour

¾ c. cocoa powder

2 tsp. baking soda

½ c. whole-wheat flour

¼ c. oat bran

¼ tsp. kosher salt

1½ c. sugar

1 c. brewed regular coffee, cooled to room temperature

1 c. unsweetened applesauce

½ c. nonfat sour cream

2 large egg whites

2 tsp. vanilla extract

½ c. pecans, chopped

1 recipe Turtle Frosting (recipe follows)

1 recipe Caramel Sauce (recipe follows)

PREHEAT the oven to 325° F. Lightly coat a 9" x 12" cake pan with vegetable cooking spray.

SIFT the all-purpose flour, cocoa, and baking soda into a large bowl. Whisk in the wheat flour, oat bran, and salt.

WHISK together the sugar, coffee, applesauce, sour cream, egg whites, and vanilla in a medium bowl. Add the wet ingredients to the dry ingredients and whisk well, being careful not to overwork the batter.

POUR the batter into the prepared pan and bake until set and a toothpick comes out clean when inserted into the center of the cake, 52 to 55 minutes.

REMOVE the cake from the oven and set on a wire rack to cool in the pan for 30 minutes. Turn out onto the rack to finish cooling.

PLACE the pecans in a small baking dish and bake until fragrant and lightly golden, about 6 minutes. Let cool completely.

TO assemble the cake, spread the Turtle Frosting over the top of the cake, spreading to the edges and making decorative swirls with an offset spatula or butter knife. Drizzle the Caramel Sauce over the top of the cake and slightly down the sides, and sprinkle the pecans on top.

SLICE into 16 portions and divide among plates. Serve immediately.

CALORIES: 330; TOTAL FAT: 10 G; CARBOHYDRATE: 64 G; DIETARY FIBER: 3 G; PROTEIN: 4 G

TURTLE FROSTING

MAKES 1 CUP

2 Tbsp. unsalted butter, softened

¼ c. light brown sugar

3 Tbsp. skim milk

2 c. confectioners' sugar

1 tsp. pure vanilla extract

IN the bowl of a standing mixer fitted with a paddle attachment or with an electric mixer, combine the butter and brown sugar and beat on low speed until smooth. Add the milk and vanilla extract and mix for 30 seconds. Add the powdered sugar and mix on medium speed until smooth, 1 minute.

TRANSFER to a small bowl and cover until ready to use.

CARAMEL SAUCE

MAKES 1¾ CUPS

1 c. heavy cream

½ c. nonfat milk

1½ c. sugar

6 Tbsp. water

½ tsp. lemon juice

HEAT the cream and milk together in a small saucepan over medium heat and set aside.

COMBINE the sugar, water, and lemon juice in a small heavy saucepan and bring to a boil over high heat. Continue cooking but without stirring until amber in color and large bubbles form, 3 to 4 minutes. Remove from the heat, add the hot cream mixture, and whisk until smooth.

LET cool slightly and transfer to a clean container until ready to serve. (The sauce can be kept refrigerated in an airtight container for up to one week.)

VANILLA-BEAN FLAN WITH FRESH BERRIES AND SWEETENED WHIPPED CREAM

MAKES 6 SERVINGS

1 c. 2 percent milk

¾ c. heavy cream

¼ c. half-and-half

1 vanilla bean, cut in half, seeds scraped out

2 large eggs

2 large egg yolks

½ c. plus 5 Tbsp. sugar

3 Tbsp. water

⅛ tsp. fresh lemon juice

4 oz. fresh seasonal berries

1 Tbsp. Sweetened Whipped Cream (page 23)

PREHEAT the oven to 325° F.

PLACE six 4-ounce ramekins in a deep baking dish and set aside.

COMBINE the milk, cream, half-and-half, and vanilla bean and its seeds in a medium-heavy saucepan; bring to a simmer over medium heat. Remove from the heat.

BEAT the eggs, egg yolks, and 5 Tbsp. of the sugar in a large bowl until frothy. Whisk 1 cup of the hot milk mixture into the egg mixture to combine. Gradually whisk the remaining hot milk mixture into the egg mixture and strain through a fine mesh strainer into a clean container. Set aside.

TO make the caramel for the bottom of the ramekins, combine the water, lemon juice, and the remaining ½ cup sugar in a small saucepan, stirring to incorporate the water into the sugar, being careful not to get the sugar mixture onto the sides of the pan. Cook undisturbed over medium heat until a light amber color, about 3 minutes. Remove the pan from the heat and spoon 1 Tbsp. of the caramel into the bottom of each greased ramekin.

LADLE the egg mixture over the caramel in each ramekin, dividing evenly. Pour hot water into the baking dish to come halfway up the sides of the ramekins. Cover the baking dish tightly with aluminum foil and bake until the custards are set but still slightly loose in the center, 45 to 50 minutes.

REMOVE from the oven, uncover, and let the custards rest in the hot water for 10 minutes.

REMOVE the custards from the water and cool slightly before refrigerating. Chill completely before serving, at least 4 hours. (If storing longer before serving, cover each ramekin tightly with plastic wrap before refrigerating.)

REMOVE the flans from the refrigerator. Using an index finger, press around the outside edge of each flan to release from the ramekins.

INVERT each flan into a shallow dessert bowl or onto a dessert plate. Top each flan with fruit and ½ tsp. of Sweetened Whipped Cream. Serve immediately.

CALORIES: 260; TOTAL FAT: 17 G; CARBOHYDRATE: 22 G; DIETARY FIBER: 0 G; PROTEIN: 6 G

VANILLA TAPIOCA PUDDING WITH TROPICAL FRUIT COMPOTE AND HONEY TUILE COOKIES

½ c. plus 2 Tbsp. small or medium pearl tapioca

½ c. water

2½ c. skim milk

1 cinnamon stick

½ vanilla bean, split in half and seeds scraped out

¼ c. sugar

1 large egg

1 recipe Tropical Fruit Compote (recipe follows)

Ground cinnamon, for garnish

4 Honey Tuile Cookies (page 261)

TO make the pudding, in the top of a double boiler or in a heatproof bowl, combine the tapioca and water and let sit until the tapioca completely absorbs the water, 5 minutes.

ADD 2 cups of the milk, the cinnamon stick, vanilla bean and seeds, and sugar to the tapioca, whisk well, and place over a pot of simmering water. Cook over medium heat, stirring occasionally, until the mixture is starting to thicken and become glossy in appearance, 12 to 15 minutes. Remove from the heat.

WHISK together the egg and the remaining ½ cup milk in a small bowl. Whisking constantly, add the egg mixture to the hot tapioca mixture, 1 tablespoon at a time, making sure that the previous addition has been completely absorbed before adding more.

RETURN the tapioca to the double boiler and cook over simmering water until the pearls are translucent, 20 to 25 minutes.

TRANSFER the tapioca to a shallow pan and cover with plastic wrap, pressing the wrap against the surface to prevent a film from forming. Refrigerate until well chilled.

TO serve, spoon ¼ cup of the fruit compote into the bottom of each of four martini glasses or footed dessert cups. Spoon ¼ cup of the pudding over the compote in each glass and lightly sprinkle the top of each serving with cinnamon. Arrange one spoon-shaped cookie in each glass and serve immediately.

CALORIES: 240; TOTAL FAT: 1.5 G; CARBOHYDRATE: 52 G; DIETARY FIBER: 1 G; PROTEIN: 6 G

TROPICAL FRUIT COMPOTE

MAKES 4 QUARTER-CUP SERVINGS

2 Tbsp. fresh or unsweetened
orange juice

2 tsp. cornstarch

1 c. unsweetened pineapple juice

1 cinnamon stick

1 star anise

½ vanilla bean, split in half
and seeds scraped out

¼ c. fresh or frozen pineapple, chopped

½ c. fresh or frozen mango, chopped

1 large banana, peeled and cut
into 8 slices on the bias

TO make the cornstarch slurry, stir together 2 teaspoons of the orange juice and the cornstarch in a small ramekin and set aside.

COMBINE the pineapple juice, remaining orange juice, cinnamon stick, star anise, and vanilla bean and seeds in a medium skillet. Bring the mixture to a simmer over medium heat. Whisk in the cornstarch slurry, bring to a boil, and cook until the mixture is thick enough to coat the back of a spoon, 2 minutes. Add the pineapple and mango, stir well to combine, and cook until the sauce is slightly reduced, 2 minutes.

REMOVE from the heat and fold in the banana slices. Let cool slightly and transfer to a clean bowl. Cover and refrigerate until well chilled before serving, at least 2 hours.

DISCARD the cinnamon stick, star anise, and vanilla bean, and serve.

ZINFANDEL POACHED PEARS WITH DARK CHOCOLATE TOFU MOUSSE

⅔ c. crumbled tofu (about 4 oz.)

3 Tbsp. plus 1 tsp. unsweetened cocoa powder

6 Tbsp. plus 2 tsp. sugar

1½ tsp. soy milk or rice milk

1 recipe Zinfandel Poached Pears (recipe follows)

1 recipe Raspberry Coulis (page 273)

COMBINE the tofu, cocoa, sugar, and milk in a blender and process on high speed until smooth. Place in an airtight container until well chilled, at least 2 hours or overnight. (The mousse can be made 48 hours in advance and kept refrigerated.)

TO assemble the dessert, spoon the tofu mousse into a piping bag fitted with a small tip.

ARRANGE one pear on each of four dessert plates and pipe 2 tablespoons of the mousse into the center of each pear. Arrange the pear on top of the mousse. Decoratively drizzle 1 tablespoon of the coulis onto each plate and serve.

CALORIES: 330; TOTAL FAT: 2 G; CARBOHYDRATE: 73 G; DIETARY FIBER: 7 G; PROTEIN: 4 G

ZINFANDEL POACHED PEARS

MAKES 4 SERVINGS

Vegan, dairy-free, and deceptively delicious, these poached pears also make an appearance in other guises on our menus, including the salads.

It is necessary to have more liquid than you actually need in order to poach the pears. For this reason, about 1½ cups of poaching liquid will be left over from the cooking process. Don't throw this liquid away, but instead store it in an airtight container in the refrigerator and use it again to poach more pears. Or, continue to simmer the liquid until reduced by half to make a sauce. This, too, can be stored in the refrigerator for up to two days.

4 six-ounce Bosc or Anjou pears, peeled

3½ c. Zinfandel or Merlot wine

¾ c. sugar

2 tsp. ground cinnamon

2 tsp. fresh lemon juice

2 tsp. pure vanilla extract

COMBINE all the ingredients in a medium-heavy saucepan. Bring to a simmer over medium heat and cook until very tender and the blade of a knife can easily be inserted into the center, 40 to 45 minutes. (If the pears are not completely submerged in the wine, turn frequently to ensure even cooking.)

TO use the pears with the tofu mousse, transfer them to a cutting board. Using a serrated knife, carefully cut the bottom from each pear so it will stand upright. Cut the top third from each pear on an angle to make a lid. Using a melon baller, scoop the inside from the center of each pear and discard.

COVER the pears and their tops and refrigerate until ready to use.

COCONUT SORBET

MAKES 4 SERVINGS; SERVING SIZE: ¾ CUP

½ c. sugar

½ c. water

16 oz. light coconut milk

¼ c. fresh lime juice

¼ c. Malibu Caribbean Rum, or other coconut-flavored rum or light rum

COMBINE the water and sugar in a small saucepan and bring to a simmer over medium heat. Cook until the sugar is dissolved, about 3 minutes. Remove from the heat and let cool.

COMBINE the cooled syrup and the remaining ingredients in a 1-quart measuring cup, stir, cover, and refrigerate until well chilled, about 2 hours. (The mixture can be kept refrigerated in an airtight container for up to three days.)

TRANSFER the coconut mixture to an ice-cream machine and process according to the manufacturer's directions.

SERVE immediately, or place in an airtight plastic container and freeze until ready to serve. (The sorbet will keep in the freezer for up to one month.)

CALORIES: 140; TOTAL FAT: 0 G; CARBOHYDRATE: 27 G; DIETARY FIBER: 0 G; PROTEIN: 0 G

VANILLA-BEAN CHEESECAKE WITH BLUEBERRY COMPOTE

MAKES 16 SERVINGS

2 c. graham-cracker crumbs

3 Tbsp. applesauce

2 c. low-fat cottage cheese

1½ c. low-fat cream cheese

1 large egg

1 c. egg whites

2 c. raw cane sugar or granulated sugar

1½ tsp. vanilla extract

¼ tsp. salt

2 vanilla beans (scrape out the seeds and discard the outer bean)

1 recipe Blueberry Compote (recipe follows)

TO make the crust of the cheesecake, combine graham-cracker crumbs and applesauce in a bowl and mix until course crumbs have formed. Cover the bottom of a 9-inch springform pan with parchment paper and spray with nonstick cooking spray. Press the crust into the bottom of the pan with your hands. Bake the crust at 350° F for 5 minutes, and set aside. Reduce heat to 325° F.

PUREE the cottage cheese until smooth in a food processor. Transfer the cottage cheese to a standing electric mixer with a paddle attachment. Add the cream cheese, and mix on medium speed. Then add the egg, egg whites, sugar, vanilla extract, salt, and seeds from the vanilla bean. Mix until smooth, scraping down the side of the bowl as needed with a rubber spatula.

POUR the mixture into the springform cake pan with crust. Cover the bottom and sides of the cake pan with one piece of aluminum foil (make sure that the foil comes at least ¾ of the way up the side of the cake pan). Place the cake pan in a large shallow baking dish and fill halfway with water.

BAKE at 325° F for about 55 minutes to an hour, or until set on top and the cake springs back when you press lightly on the top. Remove and cool in the refrigerator for 4 hours before serving.

CALORIES: 250; TOTAL FAT: 5 G; CARBOHYDRATE: 45 G; DIETARY FIBER: 1 G; PROTEIN: 8 G

BLUEBERRY COMPOTE

2½ c. fresh blueberries

1 tsp. lemon juice

⅓ c. water

¼ c. granulated sugar

COMBINE all ingredients into a saucepot and simmer over low heat for 8 minutes or until the sauce is slightly reduced and a syrup-like consistency. Serve warm over a slice of cheesecake.

MINDFULNESS, BALANCE, AND CHOICE

Miraval believes that every day is an opportunity to embrace what it feels like to be *mindful*. Being "in the moment" takes practice, yet it is exhilarating and produces new experiences at every turn. We sincerely hope that our cookbook has given you the inspiration and tools to bring mindfulness to your table.

We also designed this book to share our belief in *balance*. From nutrient-packed dishes to decadent desserts, we hope you will confidently create utterly delicious and satisfying meals.

Lastly, Miraval holds the highest regard for the *choices* that we all make in our path toward a healthier lifestyle.

With such an abundance of recipes in these pages, we wish every reader to become passionate about his or her own wellness and practice making mindful choices about nourishment and diet, without compromising quality and taste.

We thank you for enjoying our cookbook and encourage you to refer to it for years to come on your journey to a better, more fulfilling life. At Miraval, we open eyes, minds, and hearts. We sincerely hope that you embrace our culinary expertise and find the knowledge in these pages empowering so that you can live a life in balance.

Sincerely,
THE MIRAVAL LIFE IN BALANCE TEAM

The Miraval Culinary Team

287

INDEX OF RECIPES

ACKNOWLEDGMENTS

The process of creating *Mindful Eating* was a collective and collaborative initiative at the request of our owners, Miraval Villa owners, and the thousands of Miraval guests over the past 16 years who have realized that healthy food can taste great. A cookbook has been the number one request from Miraval guests for years running, a testament to the hard-working, dedicated culinary team. The compilation of recipes in this book is often referred to as our guest favorites, the most requested by our loyal spa goers.

Miraval wishes to expressly thank Executive Chef Chad Luethje, Executive Sous Chef Justin Cline Macy, Pastry Chef Kim Macy, and the entire culinary team whose creative abilities in transforming healthy food into gourmet cuisine is often described as miraculous.

Additionally, Miraval extends thanks to staff members who share our Mindfulness philosophy every day with our guests in assisting others to live in the moment and be mindful of what we put in our bodies for fuel and enjoyment, and to savor both as gifts in life—especially our owners Steve and Jean Case; Philippe Bourguignon, CEO/Chairman of Miraval Resorts; Michael Tompkins, President/General Manager; Registered Dietician Junelle Lupiani; Kris Wright; JD Martin; Leeann Ray; and the entire Food and Beverage team.

Throughout the years, Miraval has maintained a relationship with one of the brightest Tucson companies, Many Hats Advertising. The assistance of Cyndy Neighbors and her professional team has been a gift that Miraval is grateful for every day.

Having had a long-standing partnership with Hay House, Miraval would be remiss not to mention Louise Hay and Reid Tracy for their loyal support and encouragement of our brand.

Finally, Miraval wishes to acknowledge the writing talents of Trevor Wisdom. Ms. Wisdom's knowledge, experience, and kitchen fortitude assisted in everyone sitting down and bringing this book, and our food, to you.

Mindfully yours . . .

Mind Your Body,
Mend Your Spirit

Hay House is the ultimate resource for inspirational and health-conscious books, audio programs, movies, events, e-newsletters, member communities, and much more.

Visit **www.hayhouse.com®** today and nourish your soul.

UPLIFTING EVENTS

Join your favorite authors at live events in a city near you or log on to **www.hayhouse.com** to visit with Hay House authors online during live, interactive Web events.

INSPIRATIONAL RADIO

Daily inspiration while you're at work or at home. Enjoy radio programs featuring your favorite authors, streaming live on the Internet 24/7 at **HayHouseRadio.com®**. Tune in and tune up your spirit!

VIP STATUS

Join the Hay House VIP membership program today and enjoy exclusive discounts on books, CDs, calendars, card decks, and more. You'll also receive 10% off all event reservations (excluding cruises). Visit **www.hayhouse.com/wisdom** to join the Hay House Wisdom Community™.

Visit **www.hayhouse.com** and enter priority code 2723
during checkout for special savings!
(One coupon per customer.)

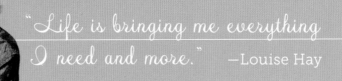